It's a Stupid Game

It'll Never Amount to Anything

It's a Stupid Game
It'll Never Amount to Anything

THE GOLF CARTOONS OF
JOSEPH FARRIS

Skyhorse Publishing

Skyhorse Publishing books may be purchased in bulk at special discounts for sales promotion, corporate gifts, fund-raising, or educational purposes. Special editions can also be created to specifications. For details, contact the Special Sales Department, Skyhorse Publishing, 307 West 36th Street, 11th Floor, New York, NY 10018 or info@skyhorsepublishing.com.

Skyhorse® and Skyhorse Publishing® are registered trademarks of Skyhorse Publishing, Inc.®, a Delaware corporation.

Visit our website at www.skyhorsepublishing.com.

10 9 8 7 6 5 4 3 2 1

Library of Congress Cataloging-in-Publication Data is available on file.

Cover illustration credit: Joseph Farris

ISBN: 978-1-63220-697-8
Ebook ISBN: 978-1-63220-999-3

Printed in China

INTRODUCTION

Throughout my career as a cartoonist for *The New Yorker, Barron's, Golf magazine, Playboy* and scores of other publications, I've found the game of golf a foil for my humor. Many of my cartoons deal with the frustrations of the game spent in the rough and bunkers—something like the waste of time of many office meetings. I'm amused by the fanaticism/addiction of many golfers. I graphically show this in one cartoon where a golfer's last wish is to be buried with his golf clubs. In another, I shift my focus and show a newly married couple with a *"Just Married"* sign on their golf cart spending their honeymoon on a golf course. Sex, a driving force in most of us, has to compete with golf when there is a choice of one or the other.

Many golfers seek the wisdom of great golfers for a cutting edge in their game even when the wisdom can be contradictory. One of the golfers in my gallery even resorts to a guru high atop a mountain perch for advice. Perhaps the one cartoon that pretty much summarizes the goal of the serious golfer and his struggle to reach the top is my depiction of a golfer as Sisyphus, pushing a huge golf ball up a steep hill only to have it fail to reach the top and roll back down over and over in an endless cycle.

My first introduction to the game began when I discovered an old set of golf clubs in an abandoned outhouse on a property my wife and I purchased many years ago. I suspect the location was an omen for my golfing career. They weren't the finest set of golf clubs in the world—in fact they were probably the *worst* set in the world.

Many cartoonists lived in Fairfield County in Connecticut to be near New York City where most of their client magazines were located. The majority of my colleagues seemed to be golf addicts. It's possible that hitting a golf ball might have been a fantasy for clobbering some of the editors who seemed to take a delight in rejecting our work (or perhaps us).

The cartoonists held an annual golf tournament and a foursome of three of my friends and I decided to enter. We were the last foursome out. We were the first foursome back. We were the only foursome to quit after nine holes. We were terrible.

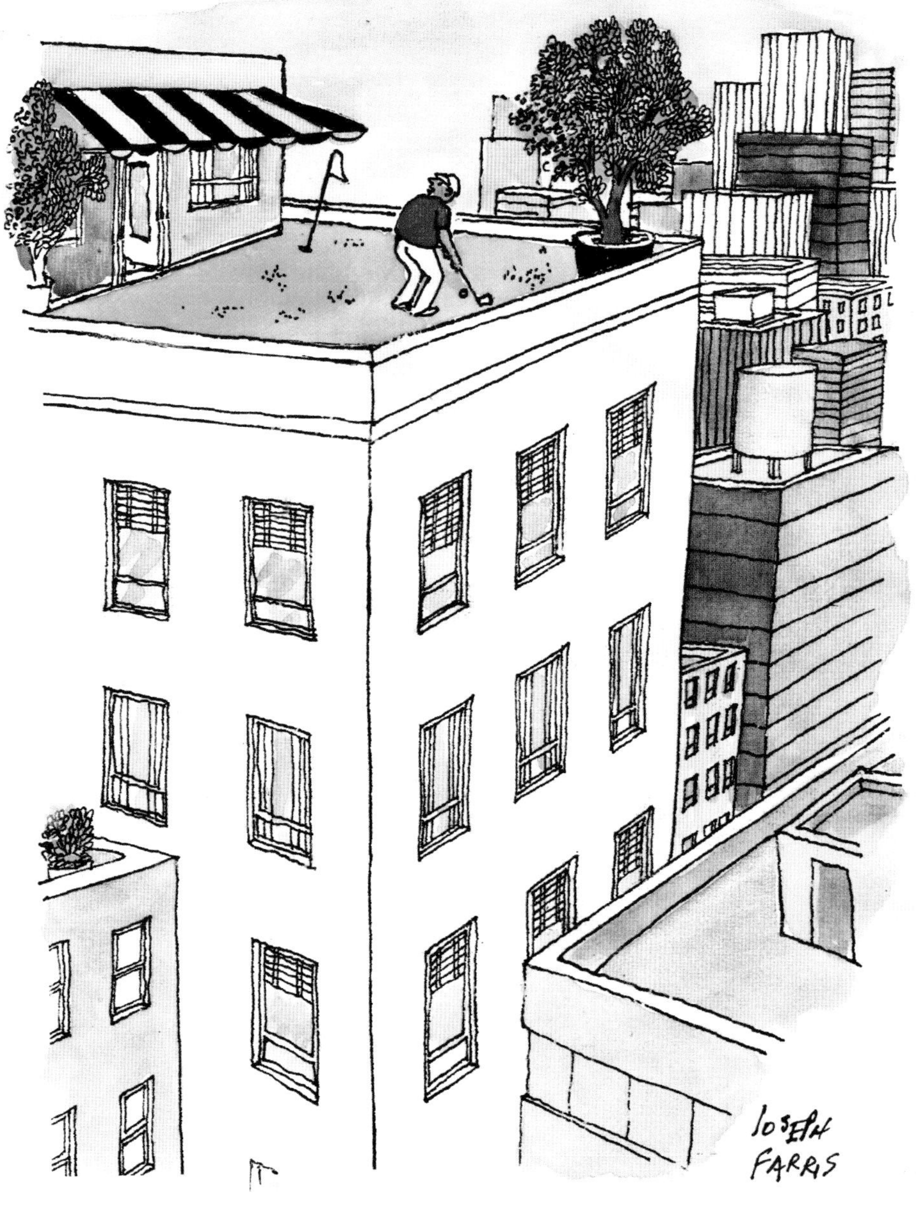
JOSEPH FARRIS

"I'm out here on the golf course."

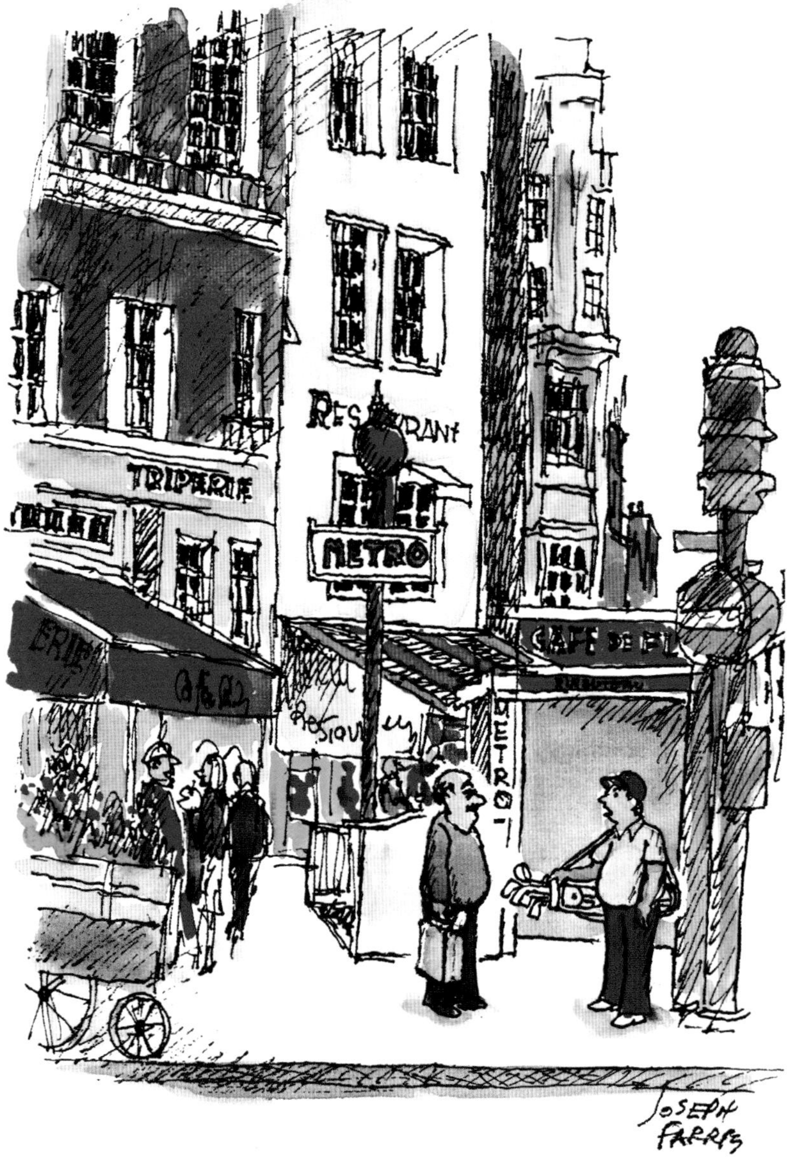
TRIPERIE
METRO
METRO
JOSEPH FARRIS

"I think I'm lost. This isn't the
Le Golf National L'Albatros course, is it?"

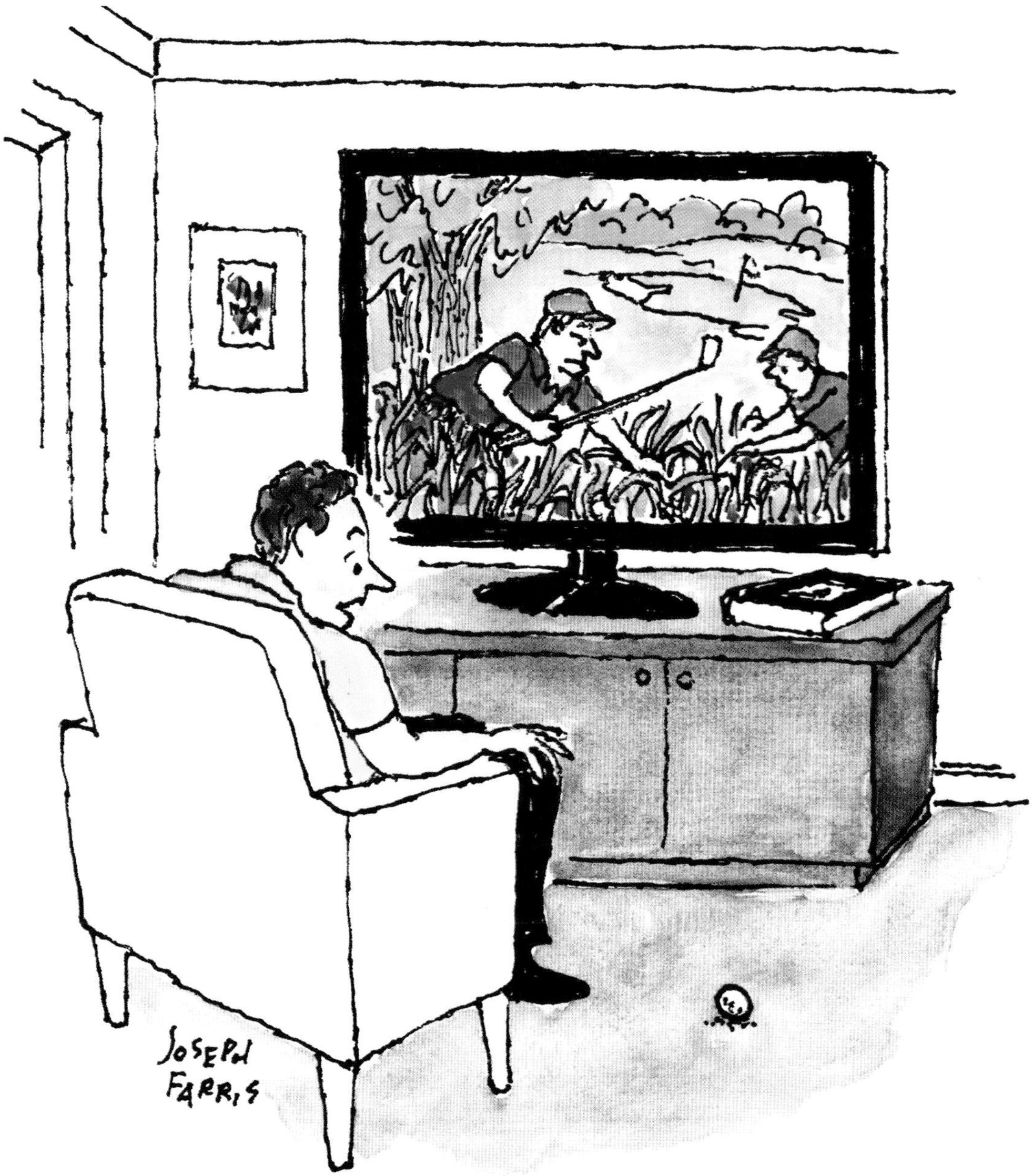
JOSEPH
FARRIS

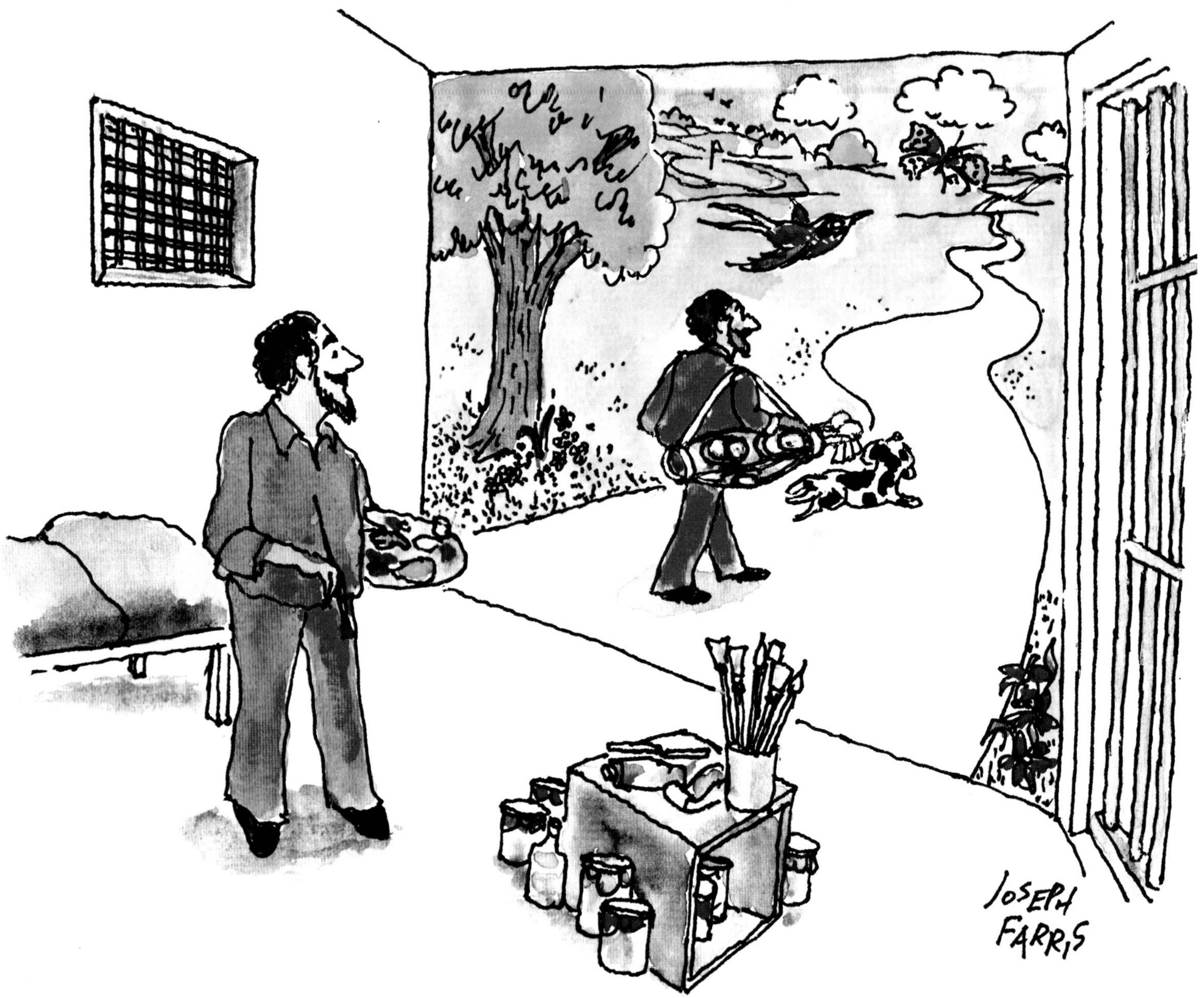
JOSEPH
FARRIS

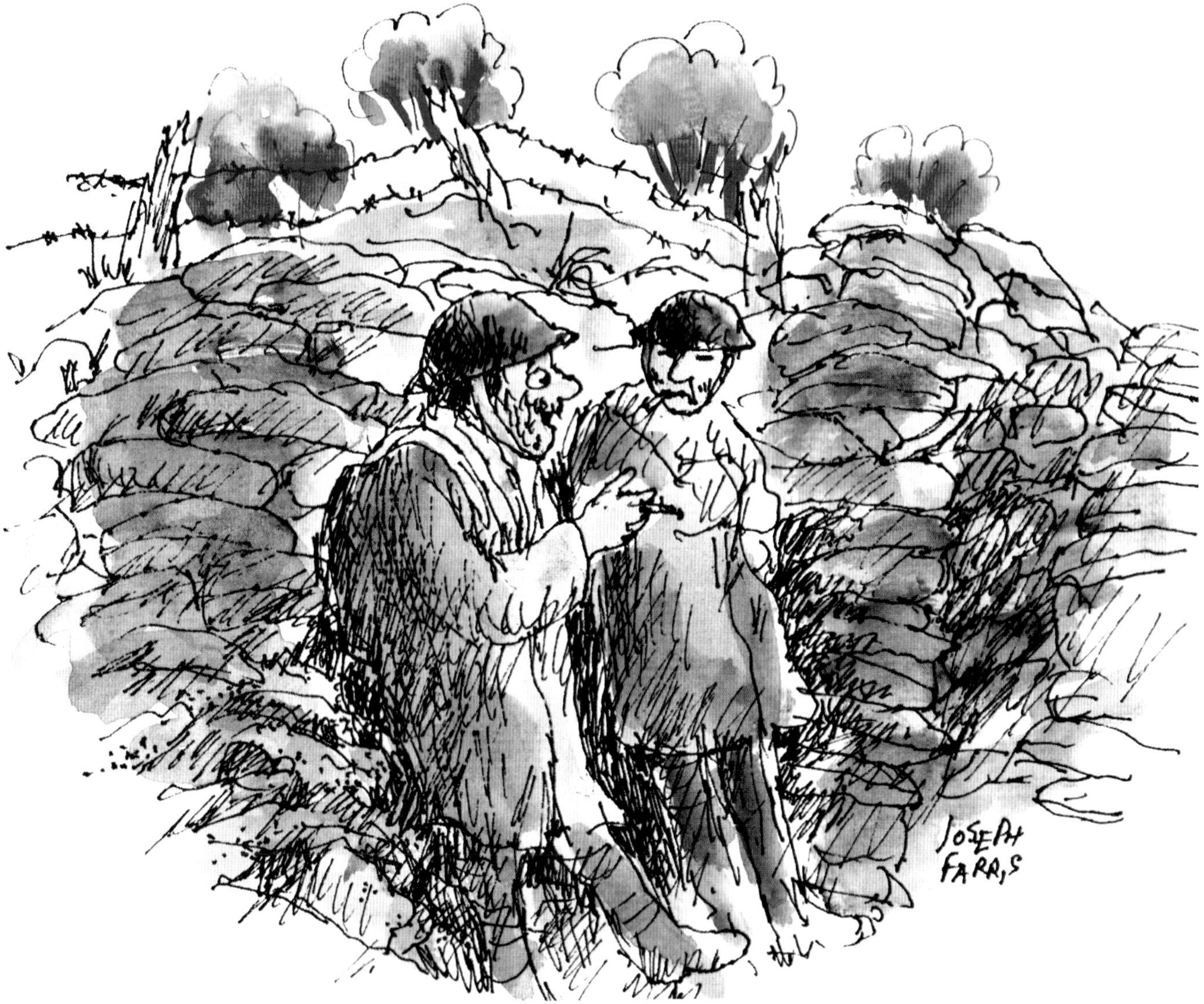
JOSEPH FARRIS

“I'll sure be glad when this war to end all wars is over and I can get back to playing golf for the rest of my life.

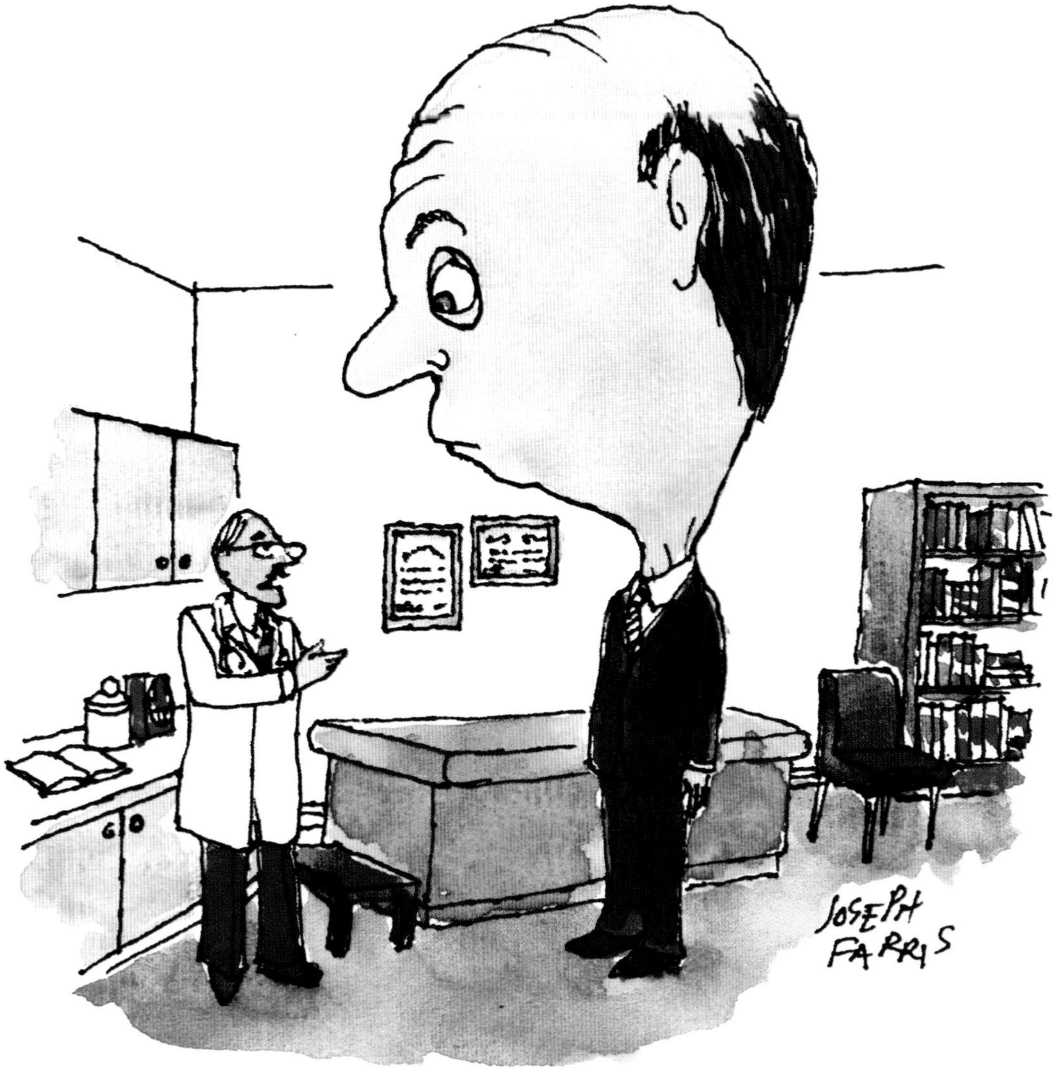
JOSEPH FARRIS

"Let me get this straight. You first noticed your big head right after you scored a hole-in-one?"

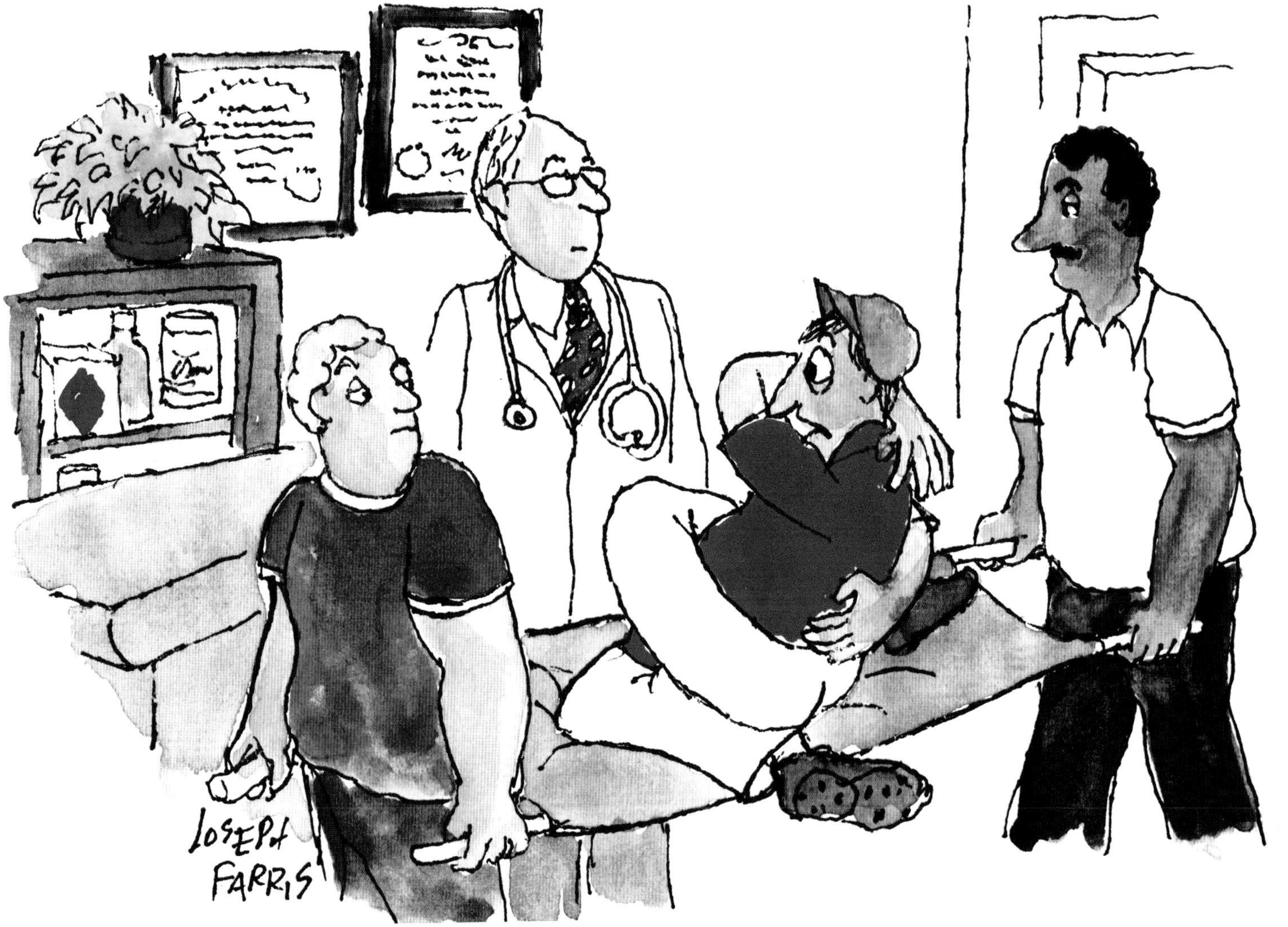
JOSEPH FARRIS

"It happened when I was trying to hit my ball out of a tricky bunker on the 8th hole."

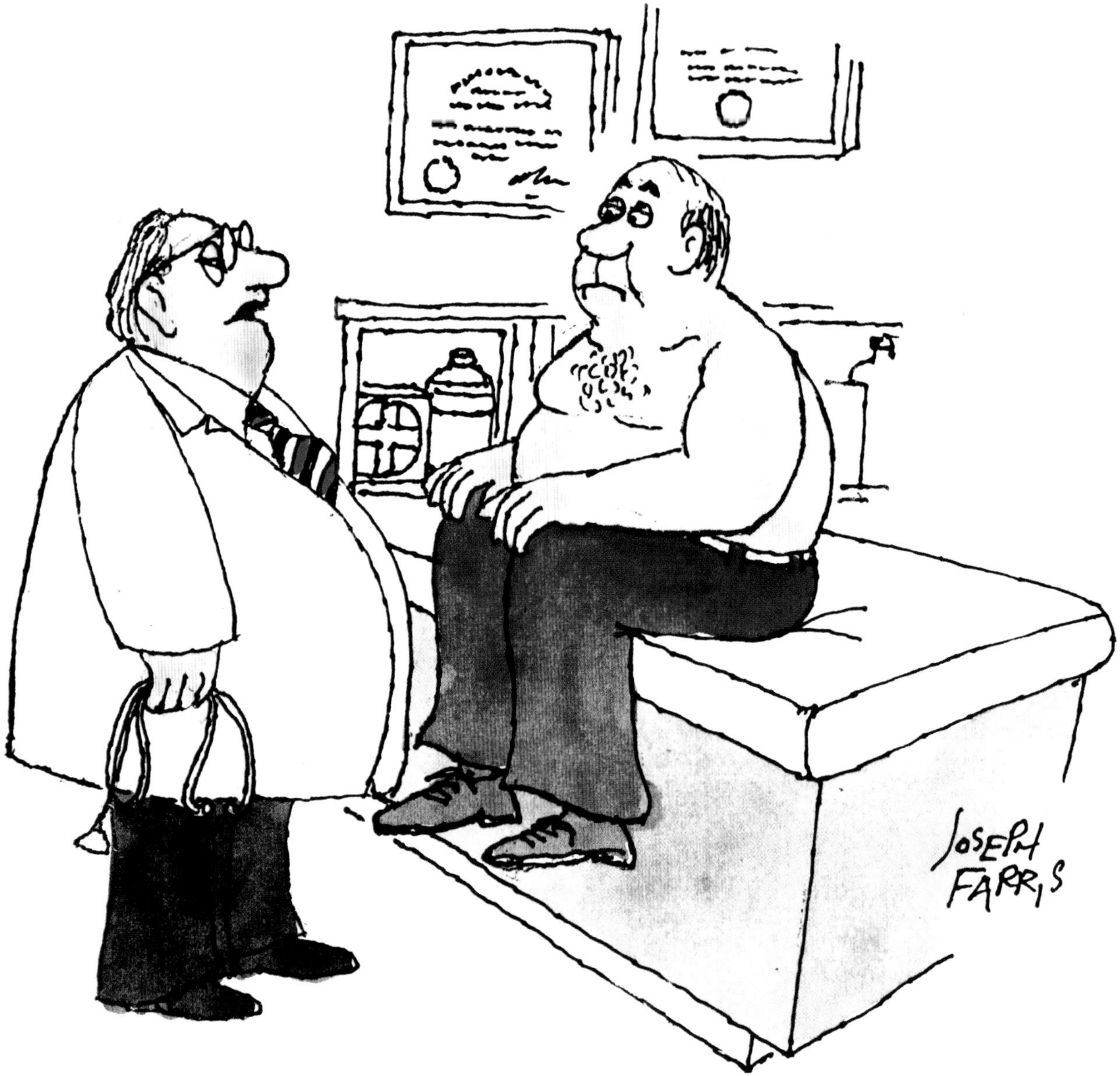
JOSEPH FARRIS

“You’re obese. Get some exercise. Take up golf.”

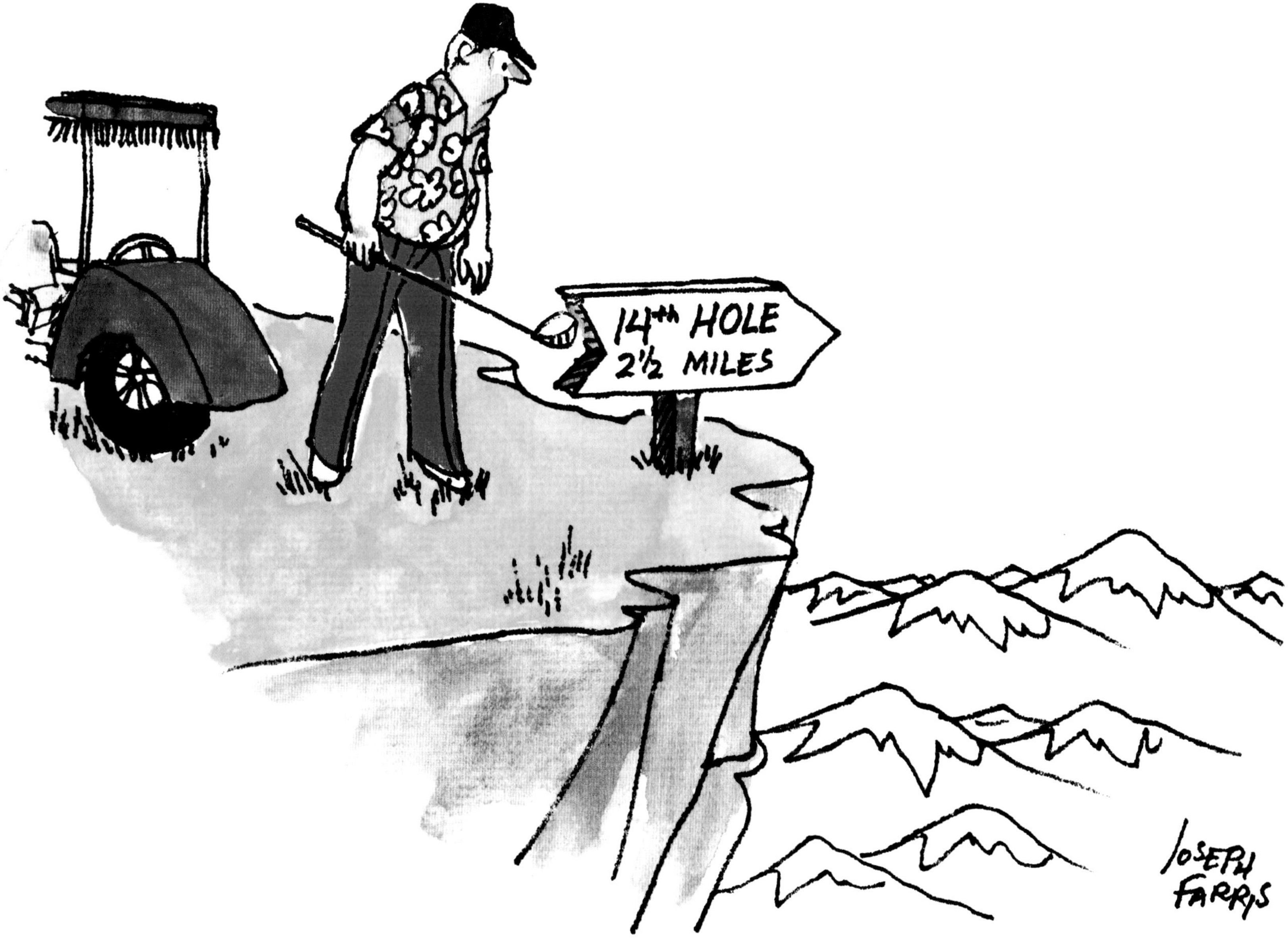
14th HOLE
2½ MILES
JOSEPH FARRIS

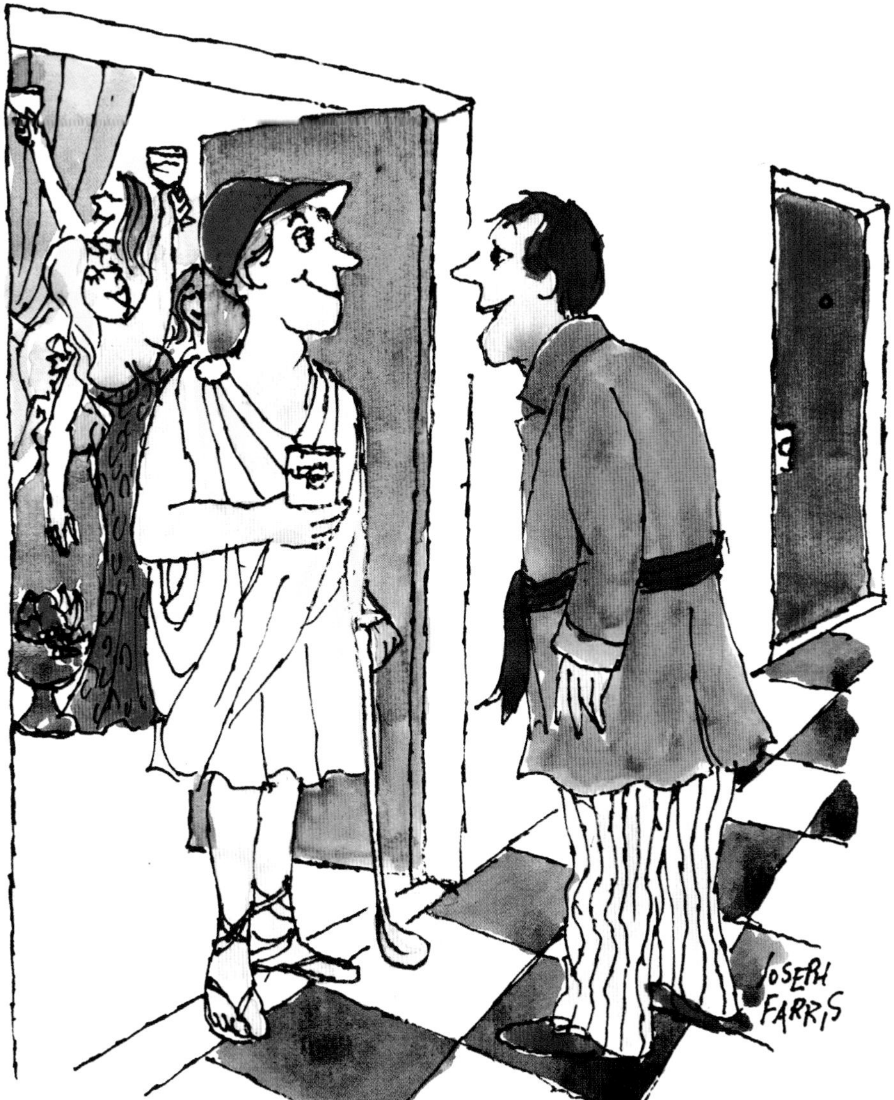
JOSEPH FARRIS

"This isn't meant to be a complaint but how can you afford this when as a professional golfer you've never even made the cut?"

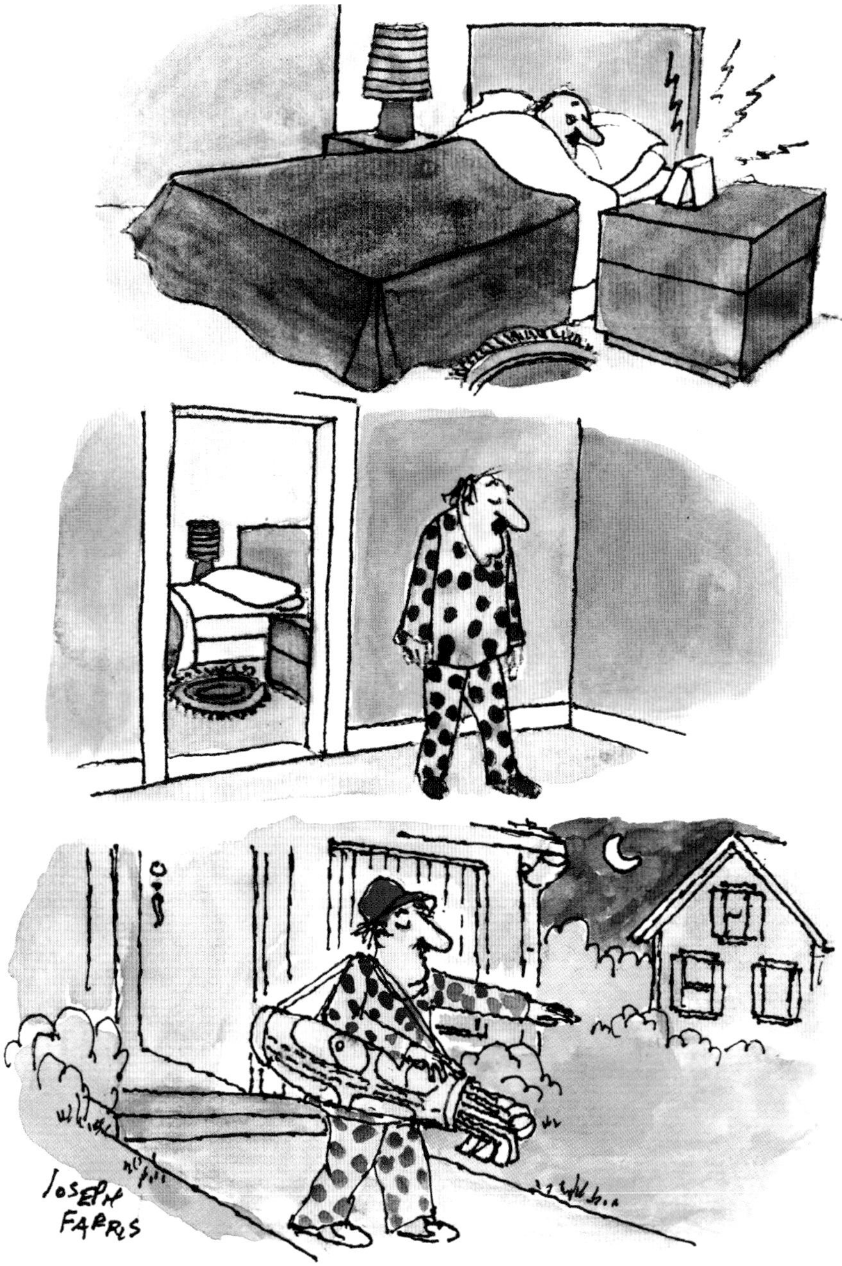
JOSEPH FARRIS

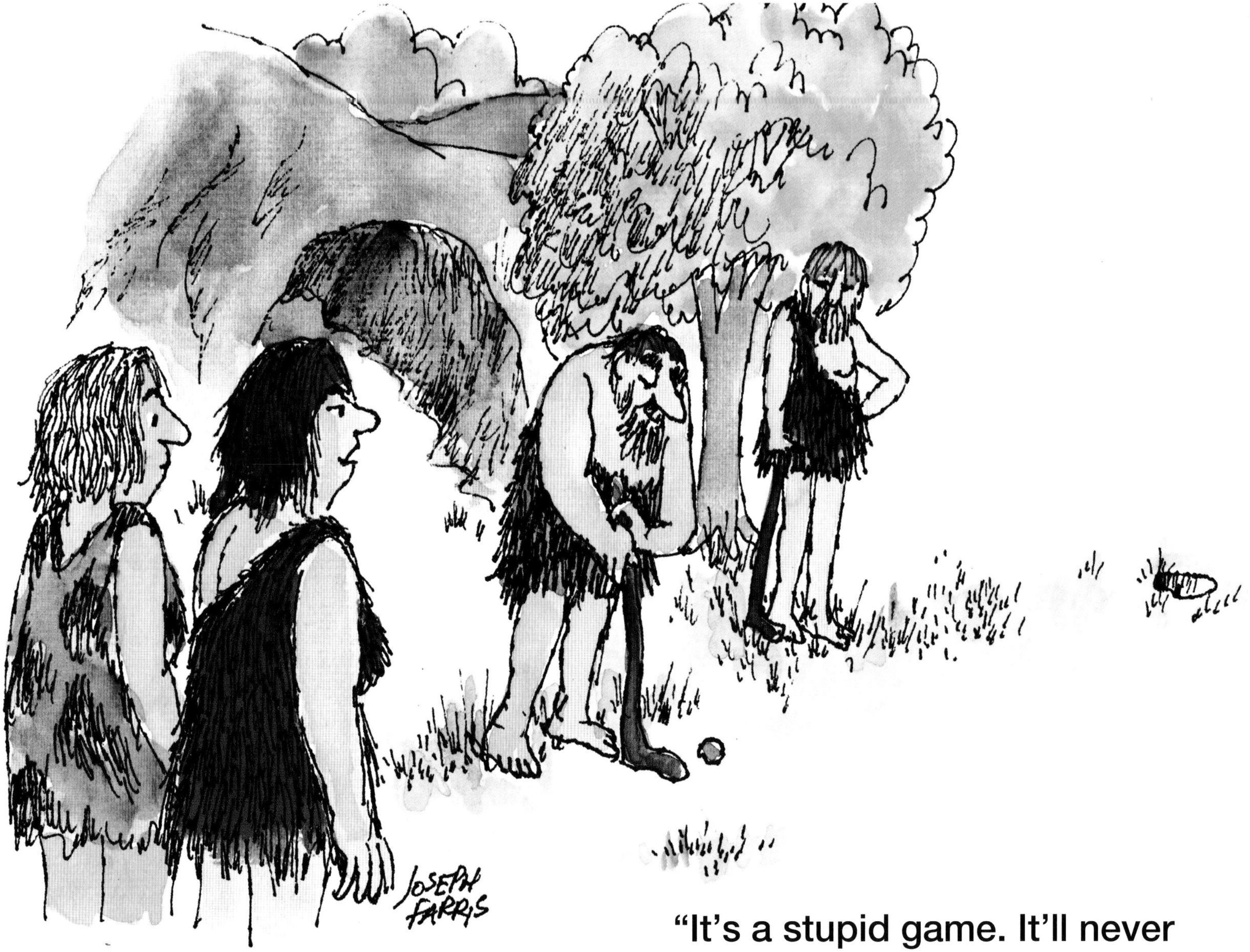
JOSEPH FARRIS

"It's a stupid game. It'll never amount to anything."

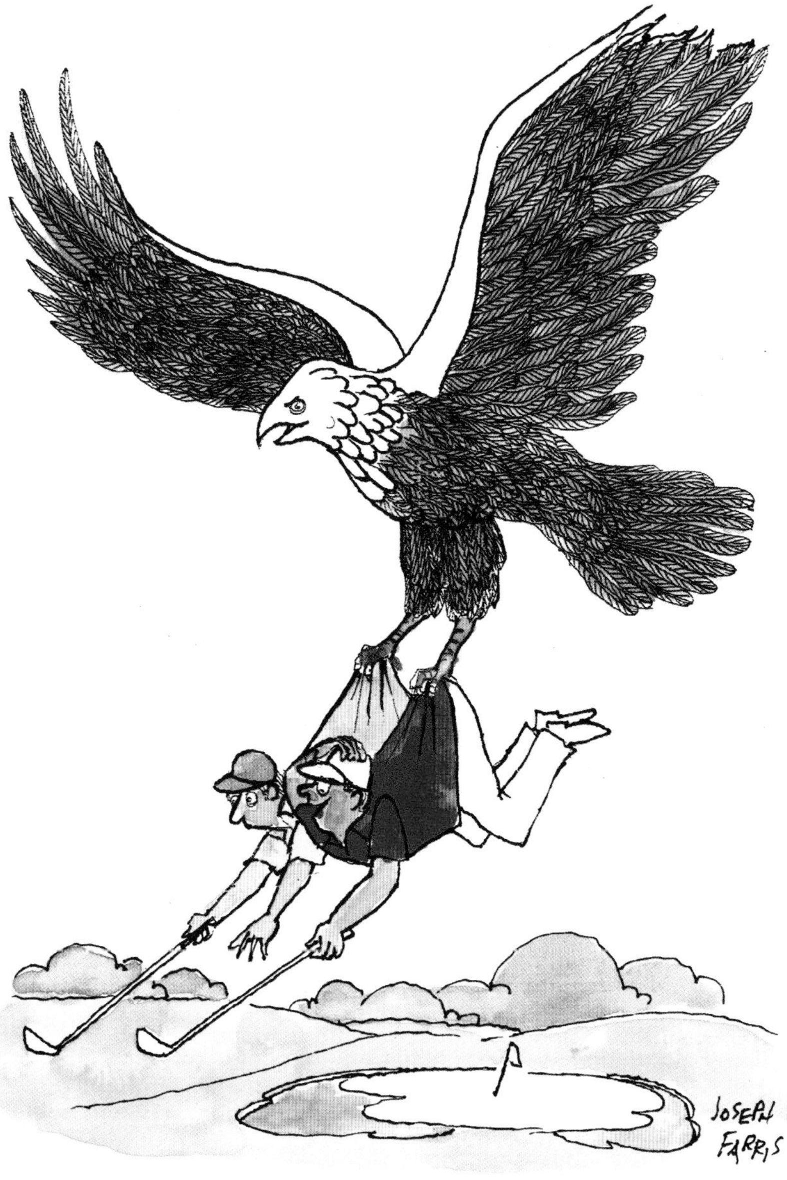
JOSEPH FARRIS

"What a coincidence! I just shot an eagle!"

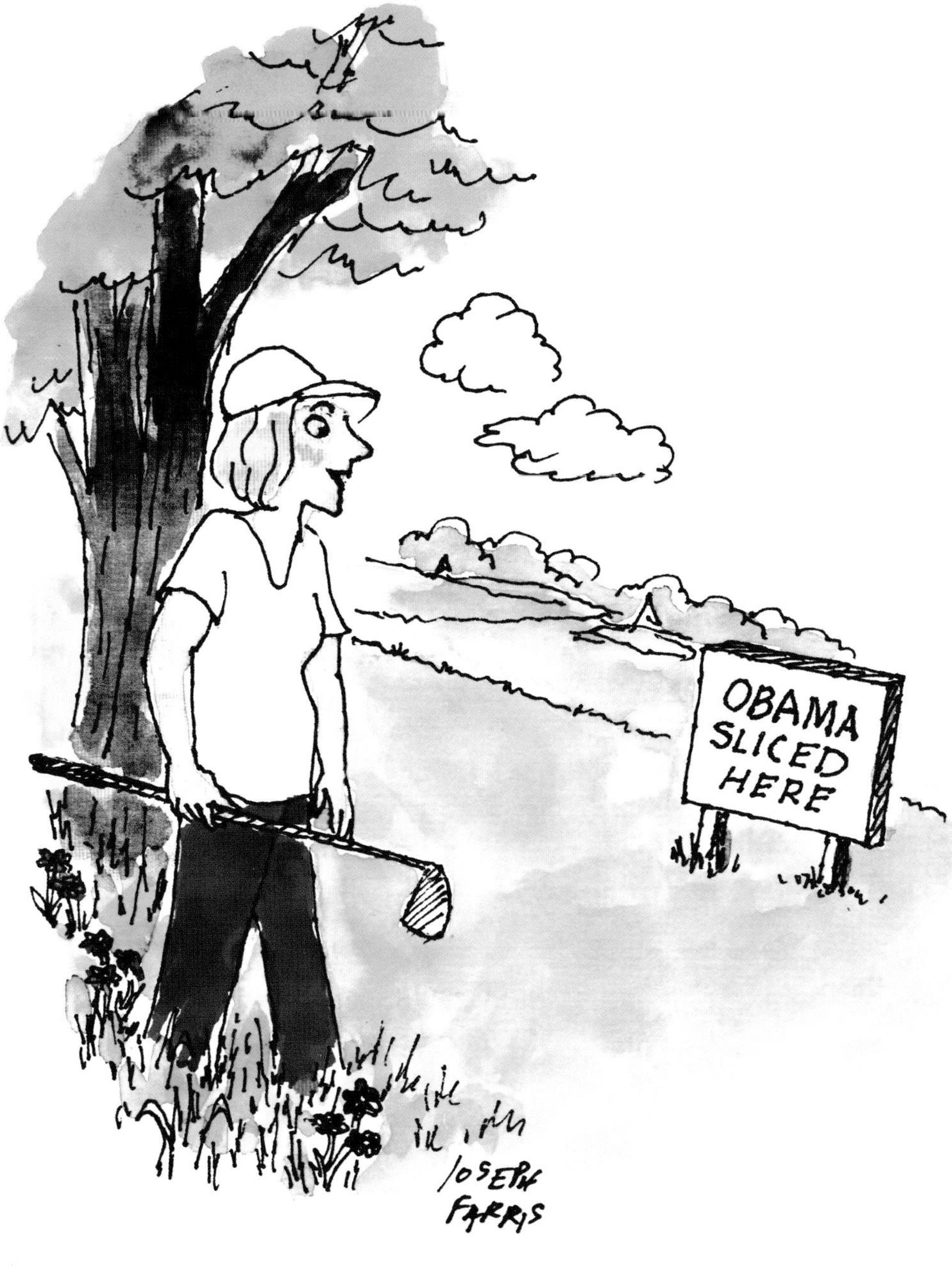
OBAMA
SLICED
HERE
JOSEPH
FARRIS

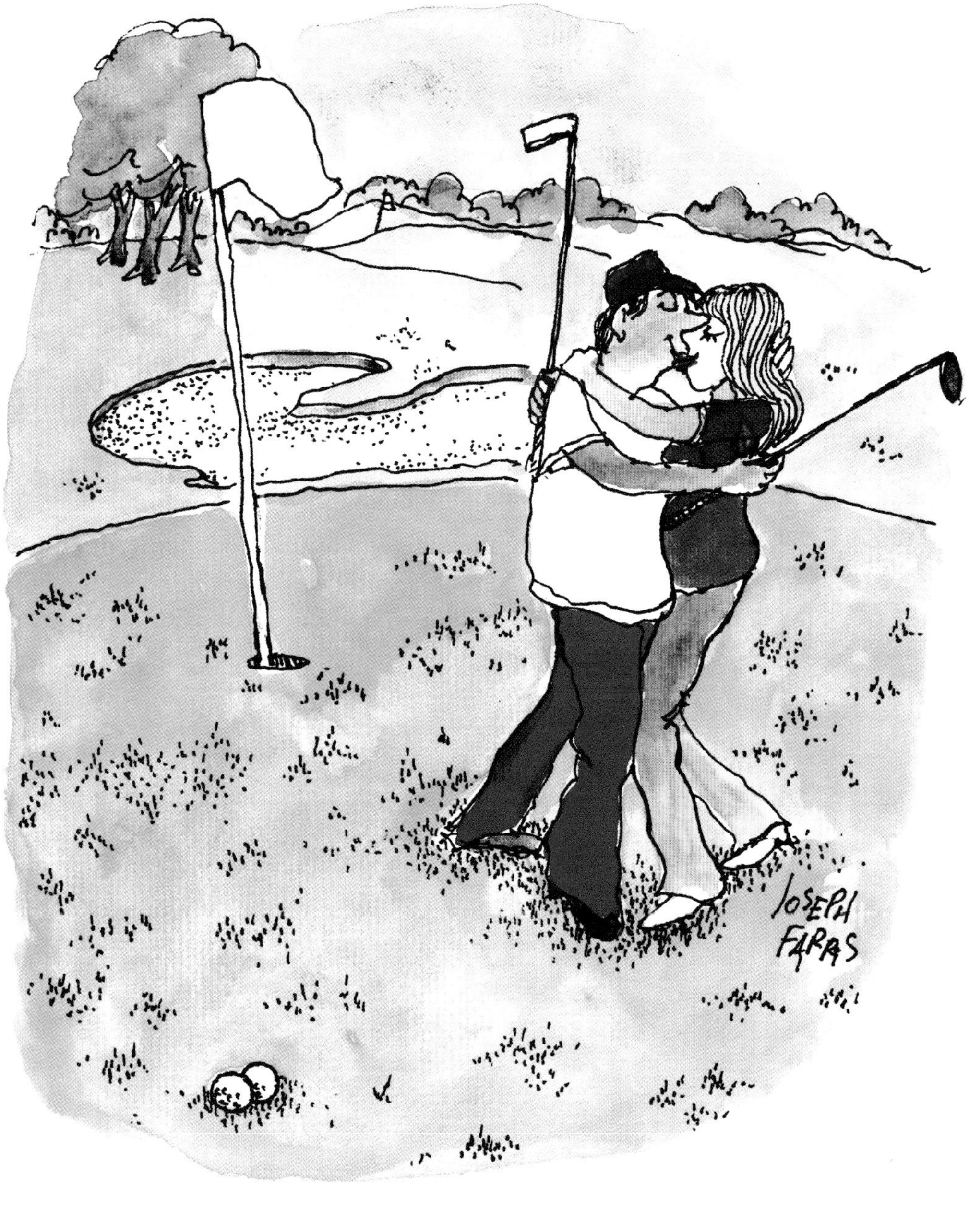
JOSEPH FARRIS

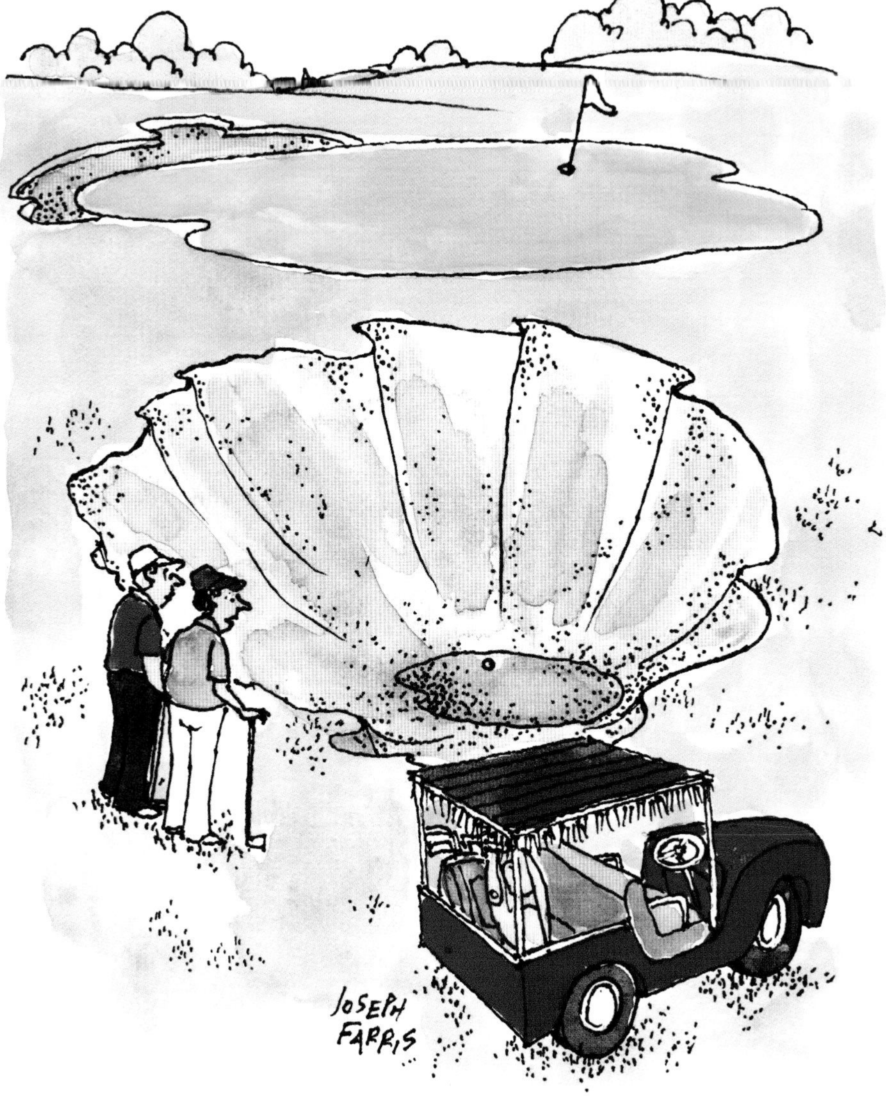
JOSEPH FARRIS

“They wanted to make this hole tougher. Personally, I think they went overboard!”

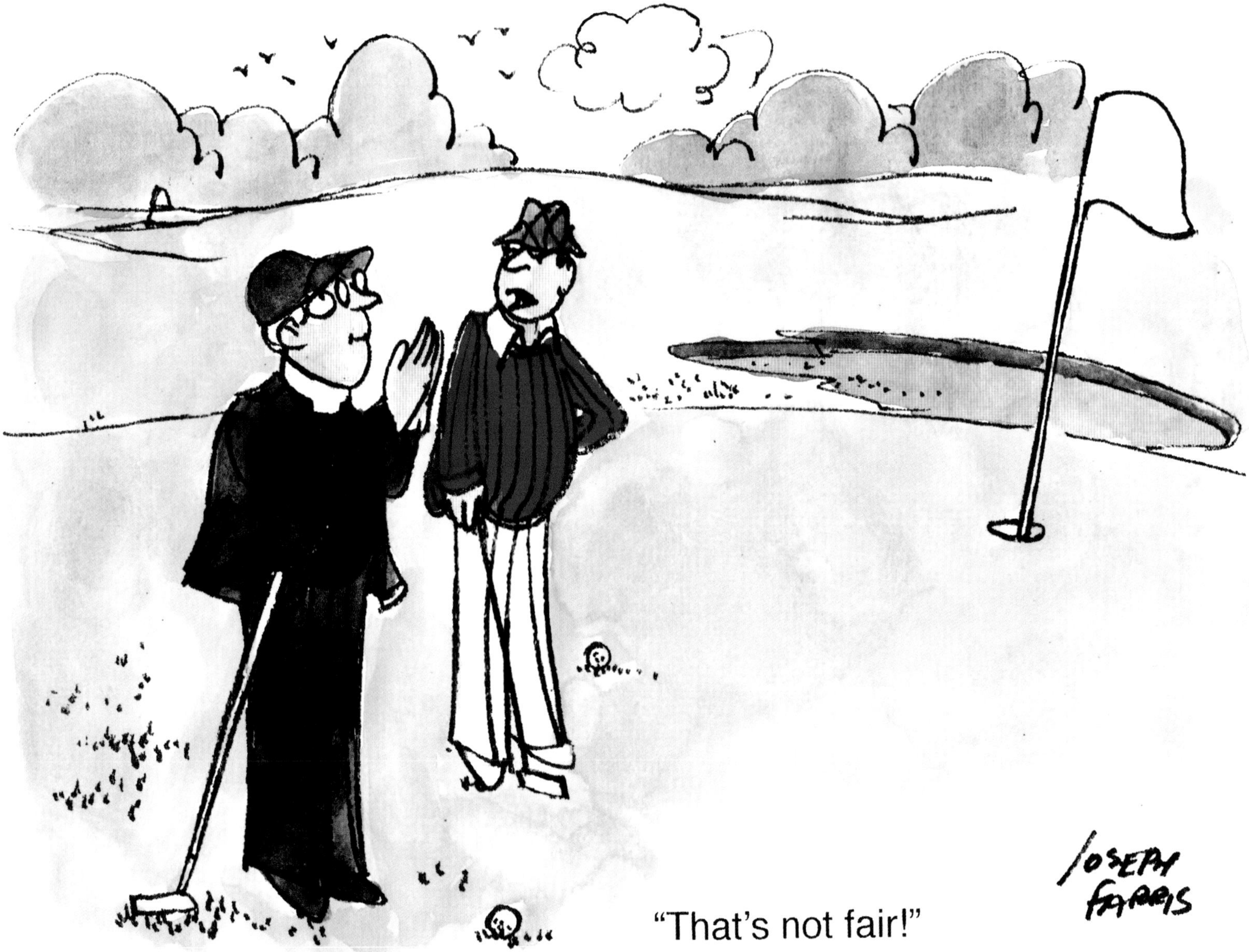
JOSEPH FARRIS

"That's not fair!"

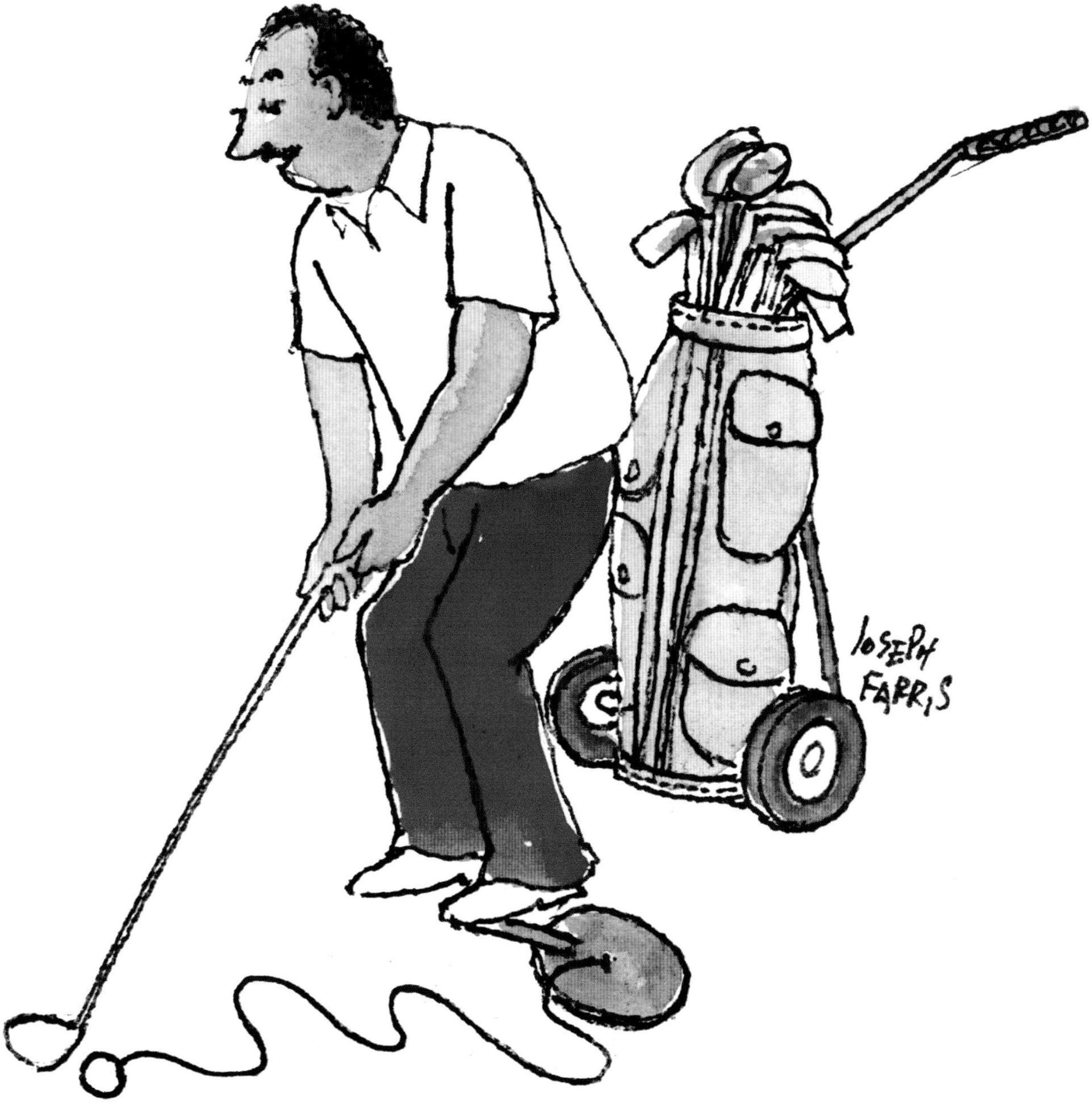
JOSEPH
FARRIS

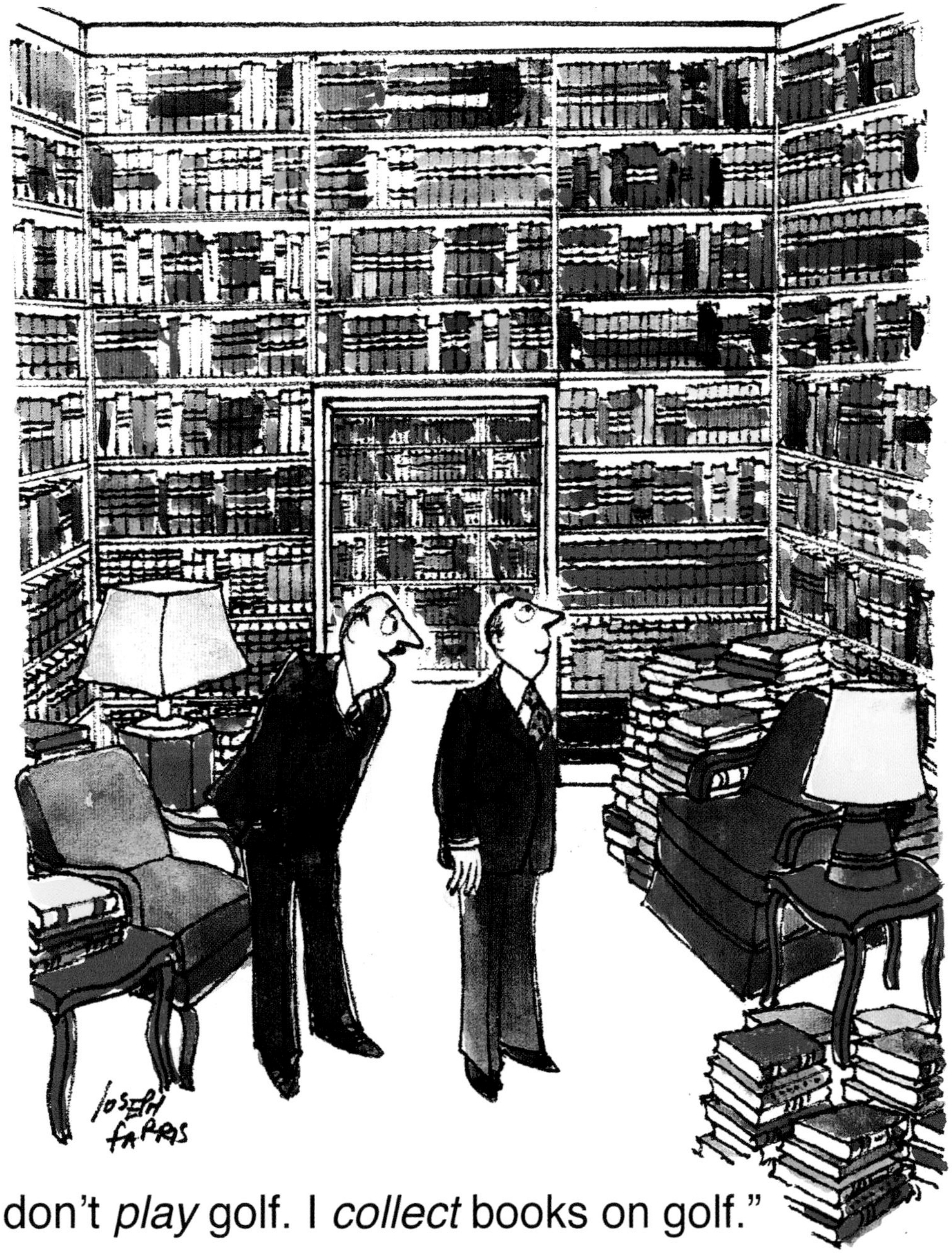
JOSEPH
FARRIS

“I don’t *play* golf. I *collect* books on golf.”

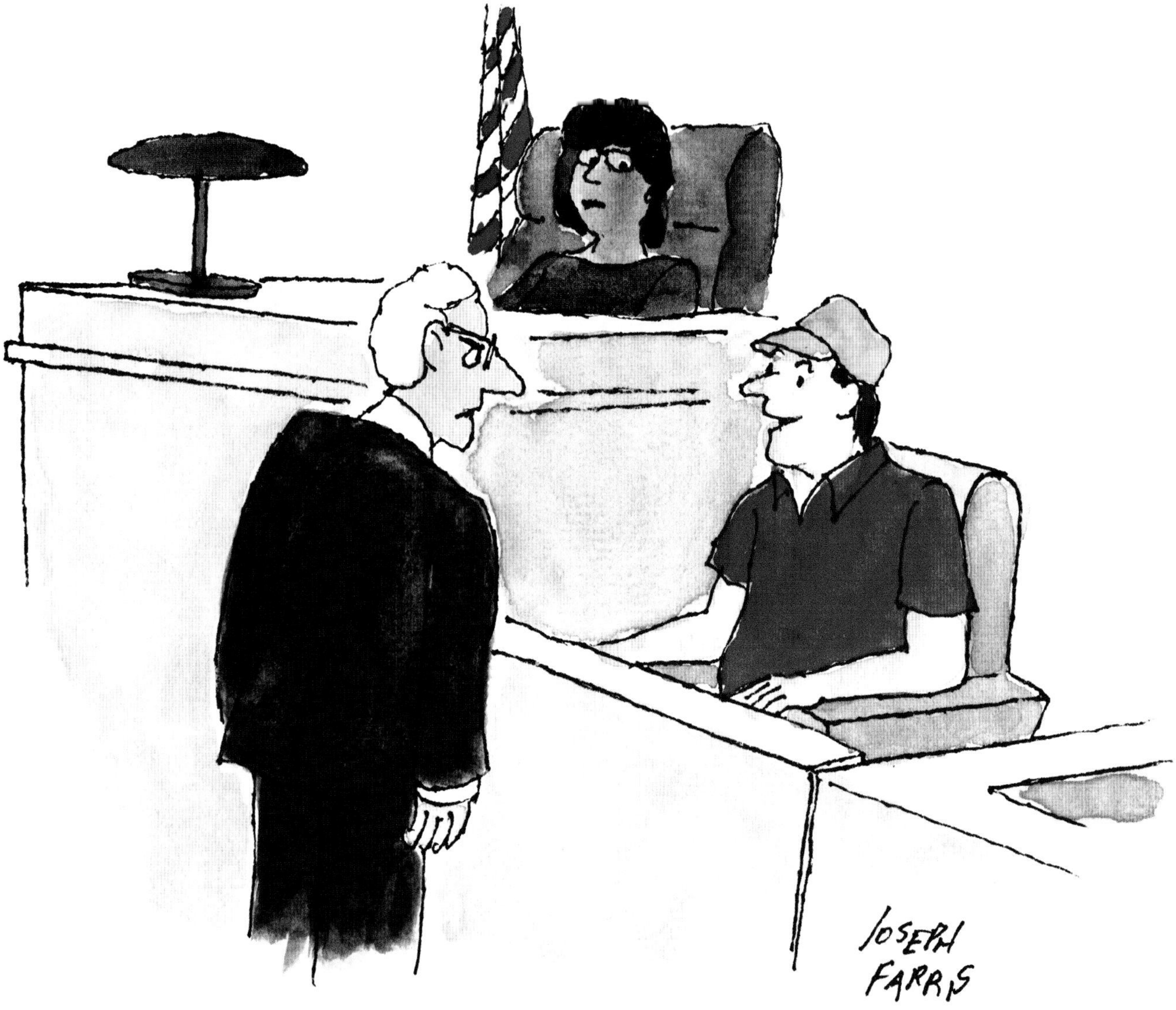
JOSEPH FARRIS

"At the time mentioned, I was stuck in a 6th hole bunker at Pebble Beach."

JOSEPH FARRIS

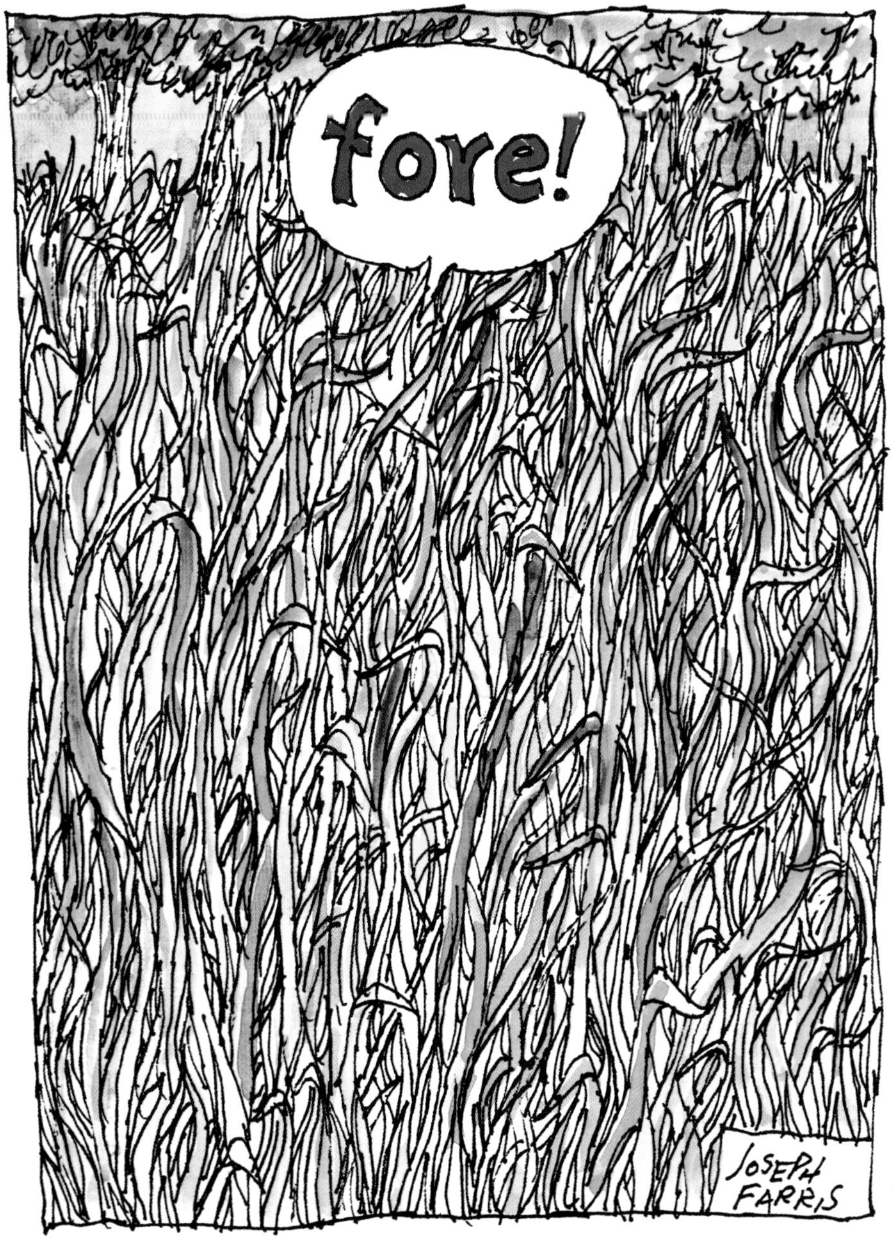
fore!
JOSEPH FARRIS

"Thank you, thank you, thank you...."

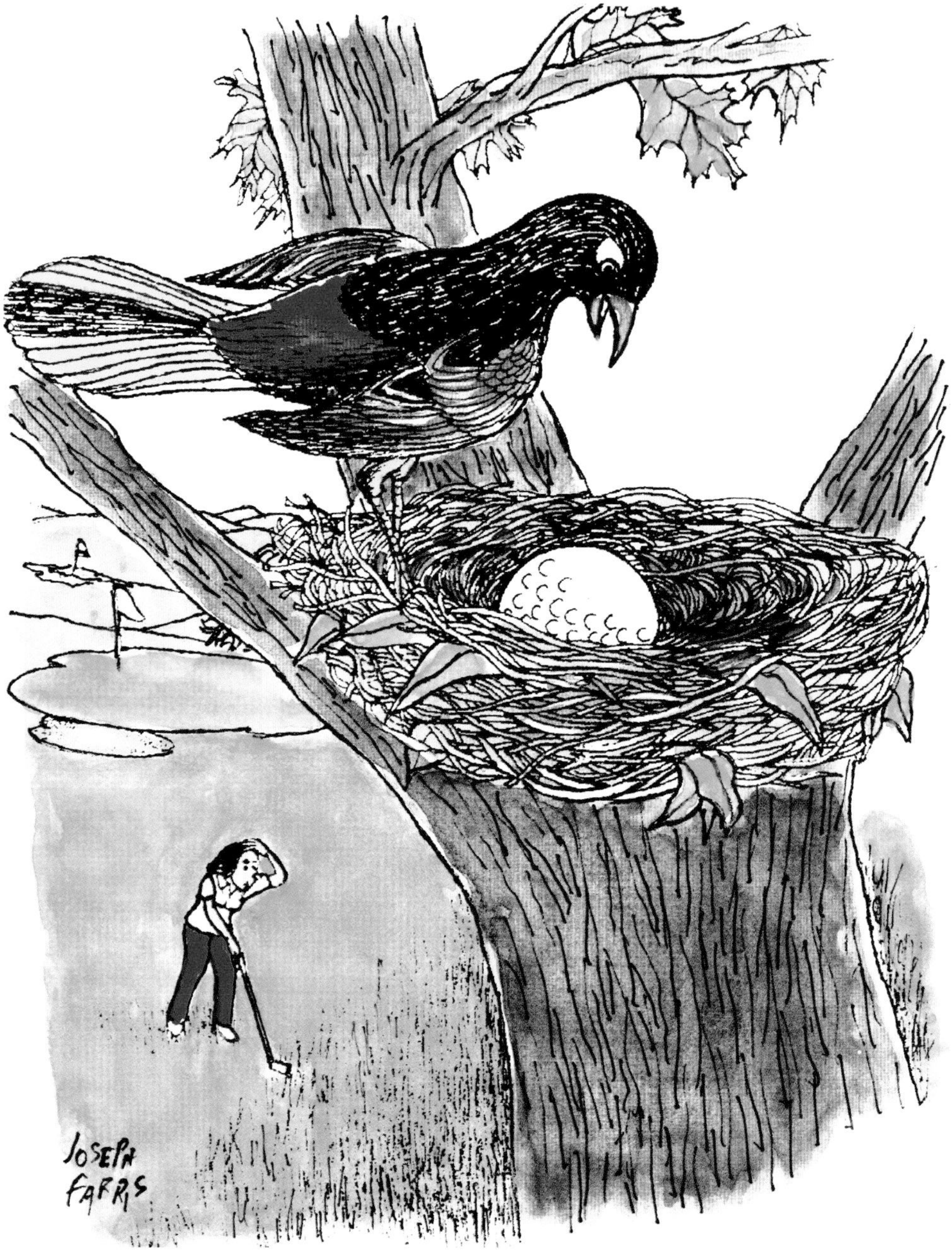
JOSEPH
FARRIS

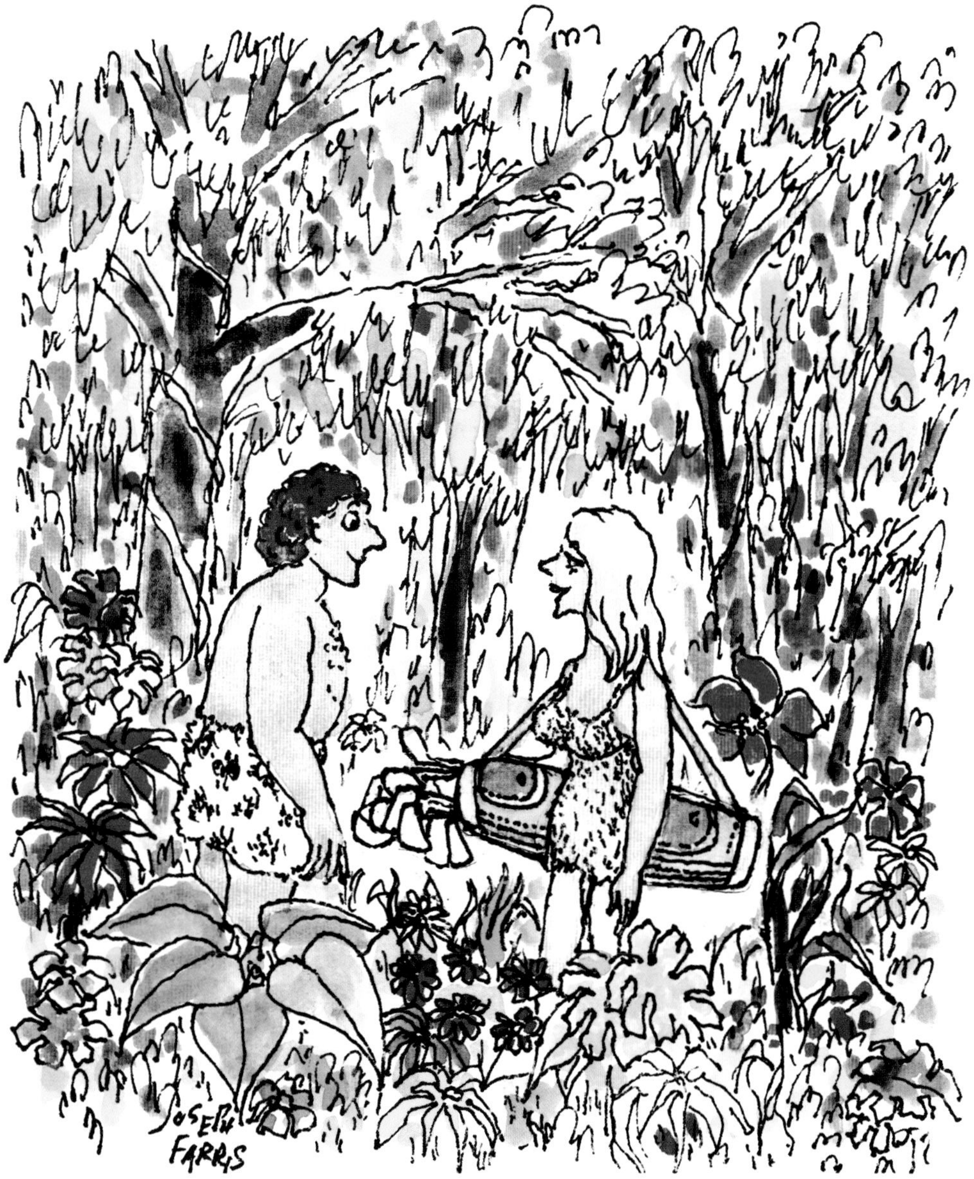
JOSEPH
FARRIS

"No Tarzan, me not Jane. Me woman golfer."

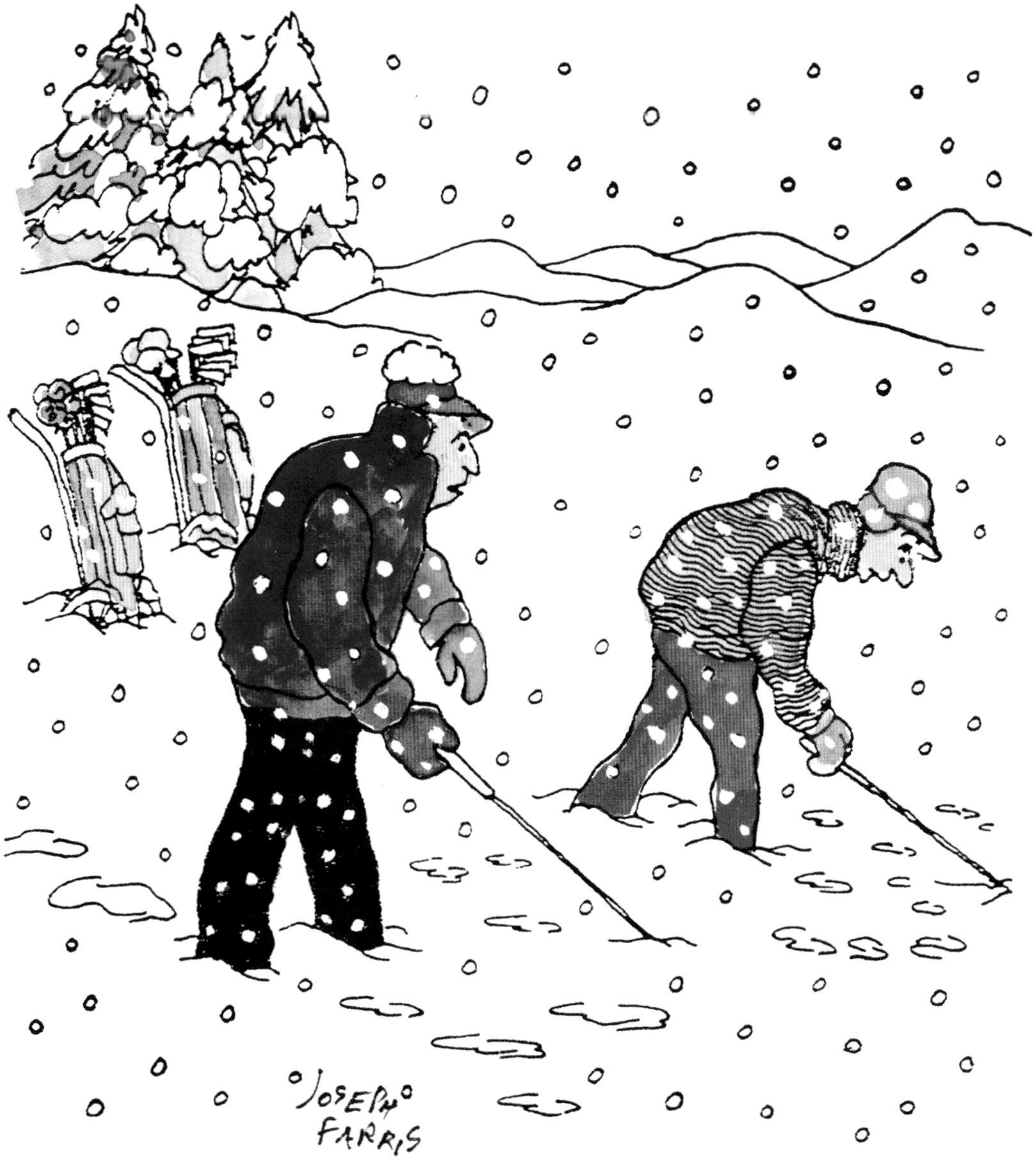
JOSEPH FARRIS

“Maybe we ought to call it quits for the season.”

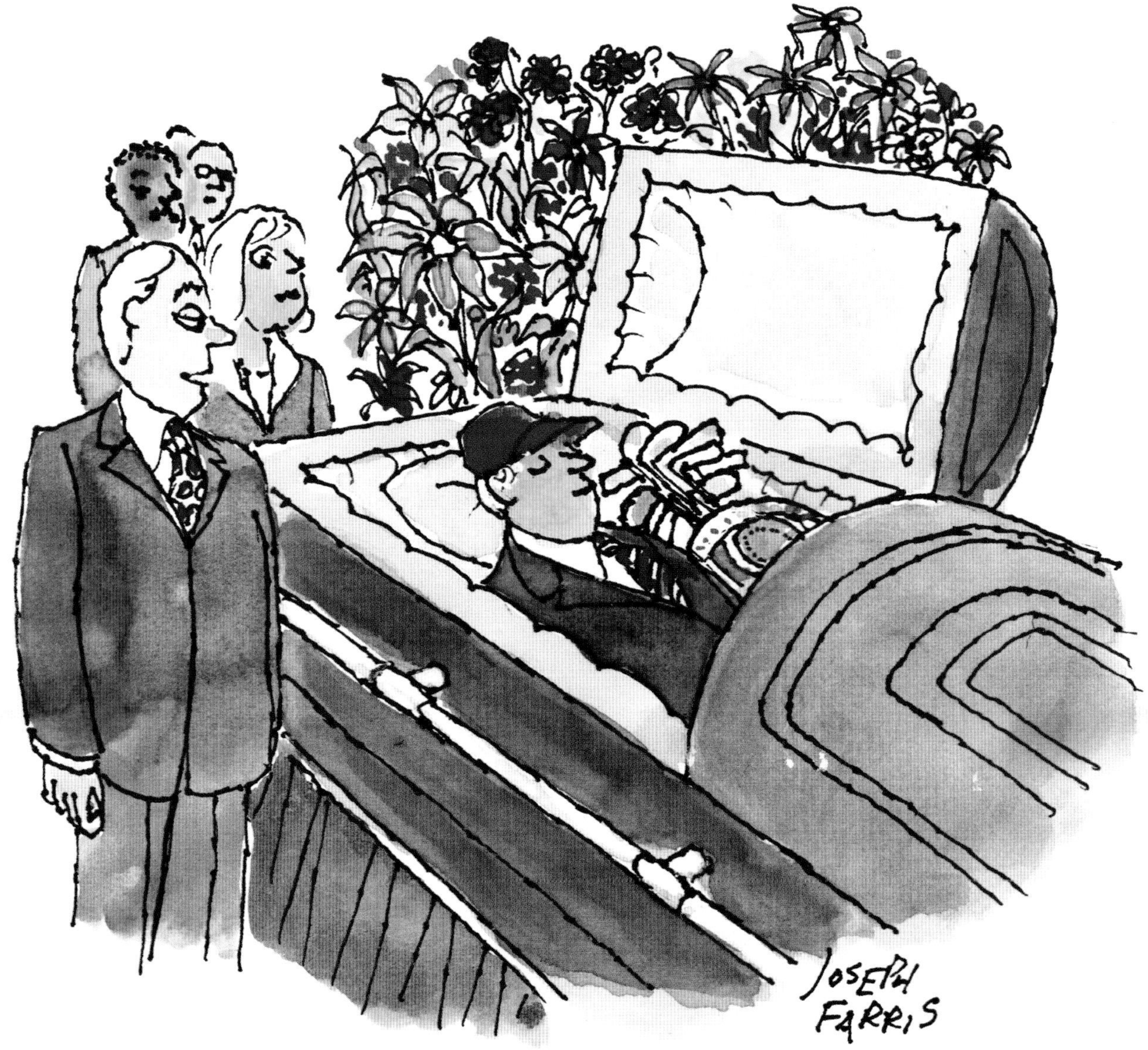
JOSEPH FARRIS

"It was his last wish."

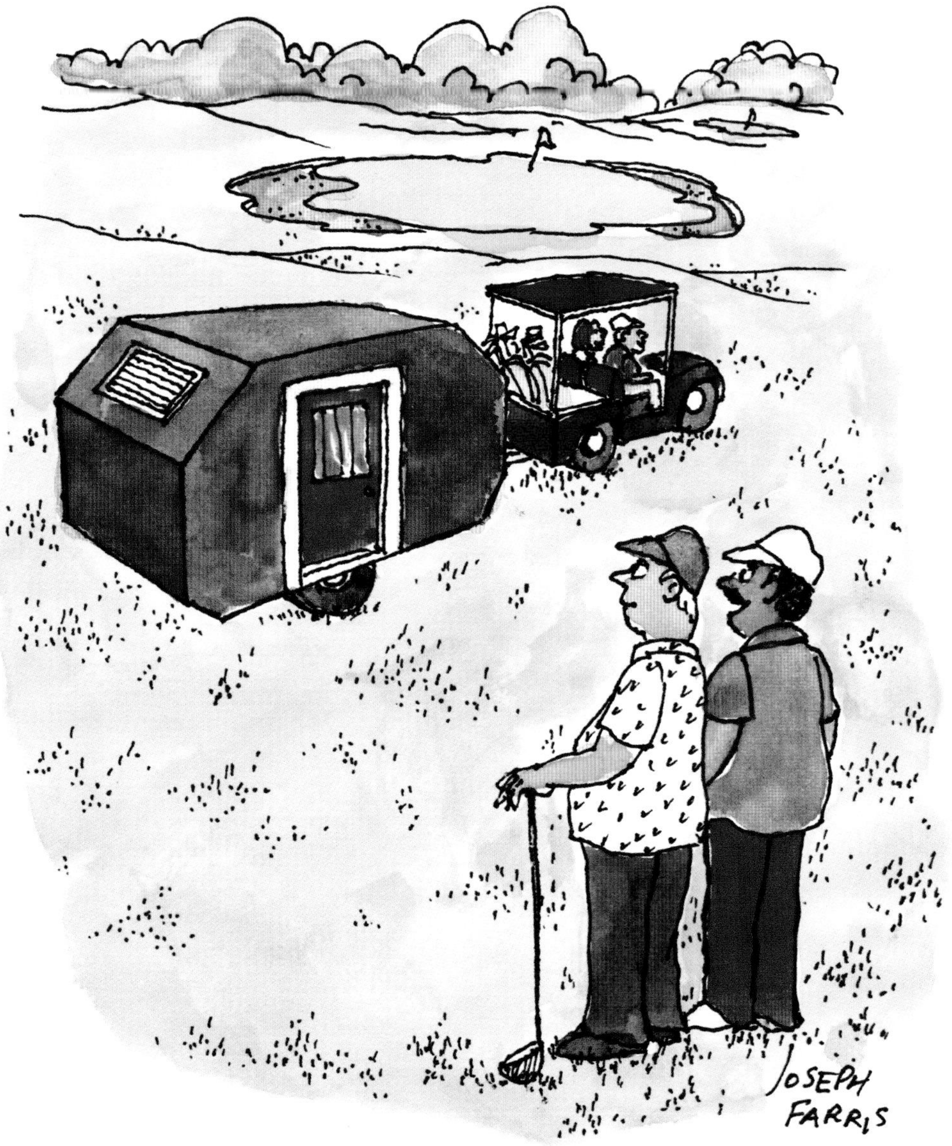
JOSEPH FARRIS

"They're spending their vacation on the golf course."

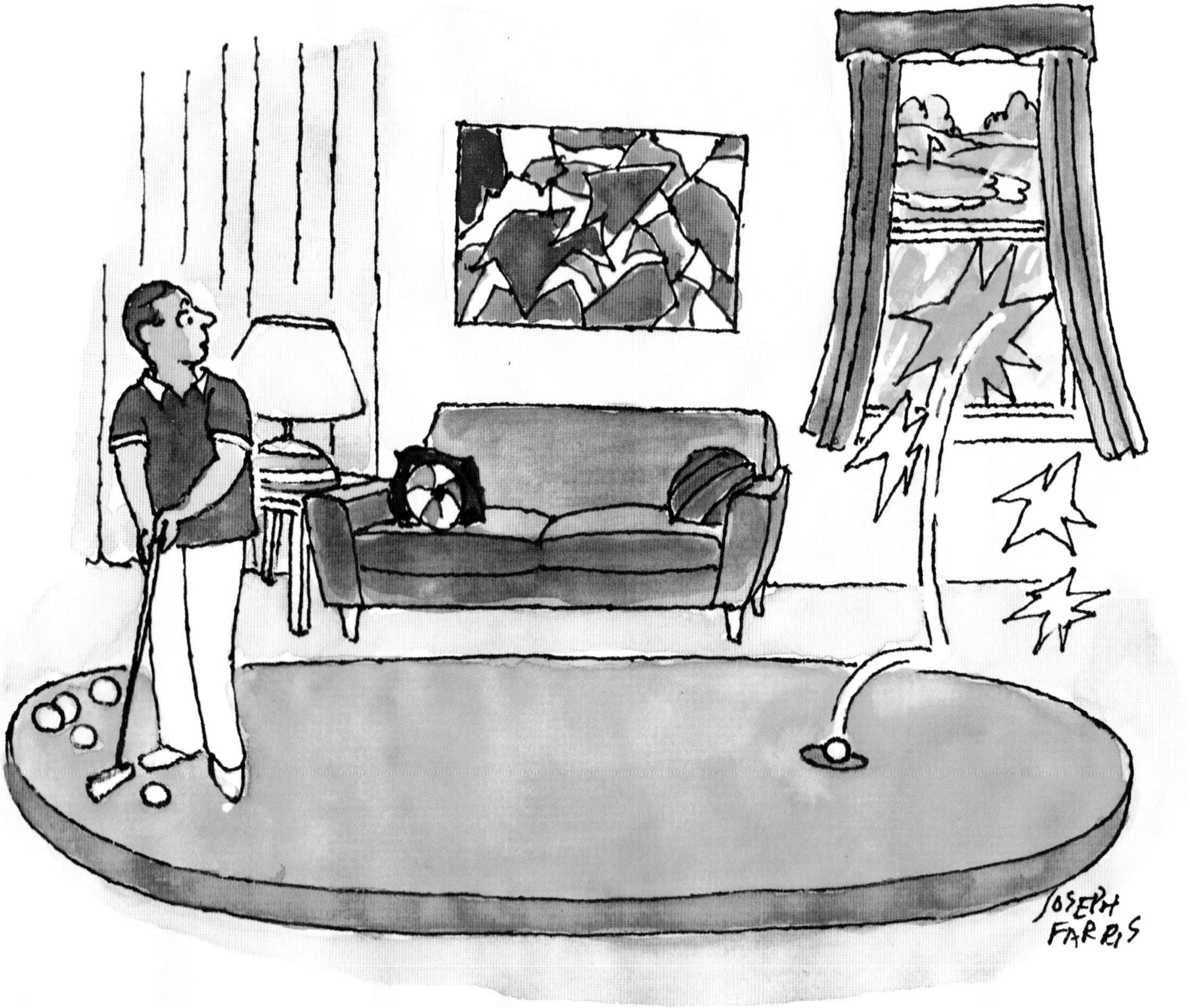
JOSEPH
FARRIS

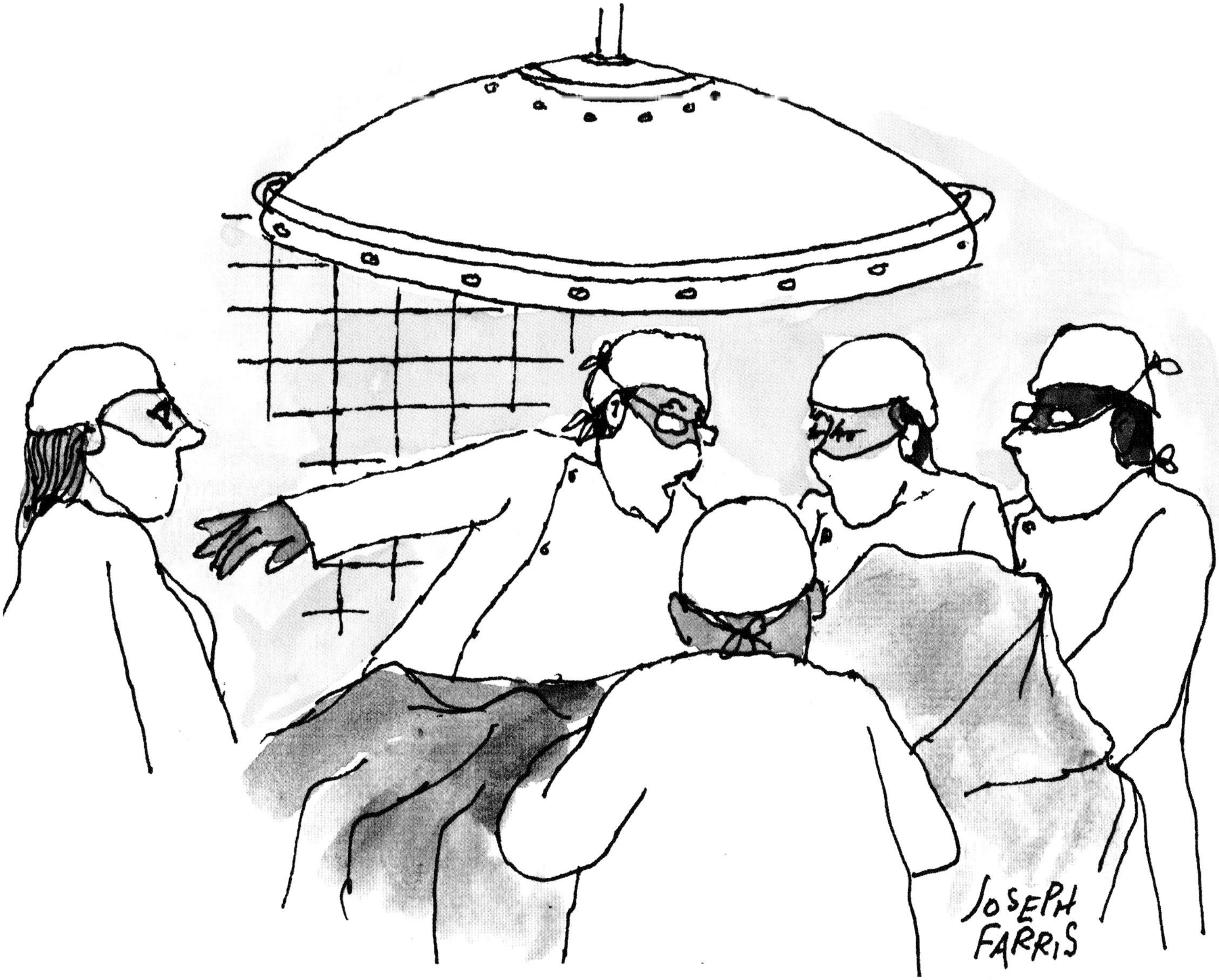
JOSEPH FARRIS

"Putter...I mean *scalpel* !"

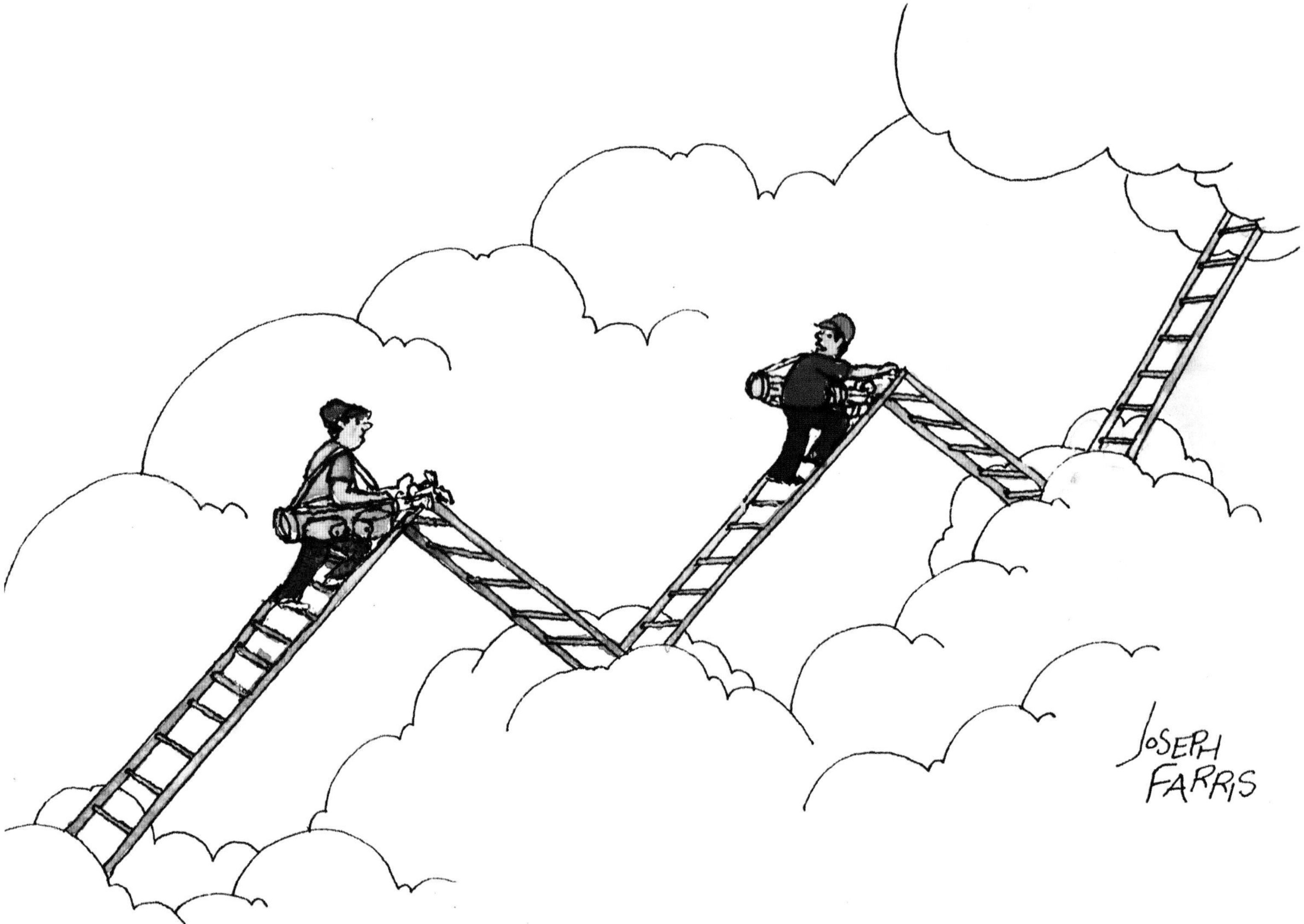
JOSEPH FARRIS

"Did you think the ladder to success to the top of the leadership board would be straight up?"

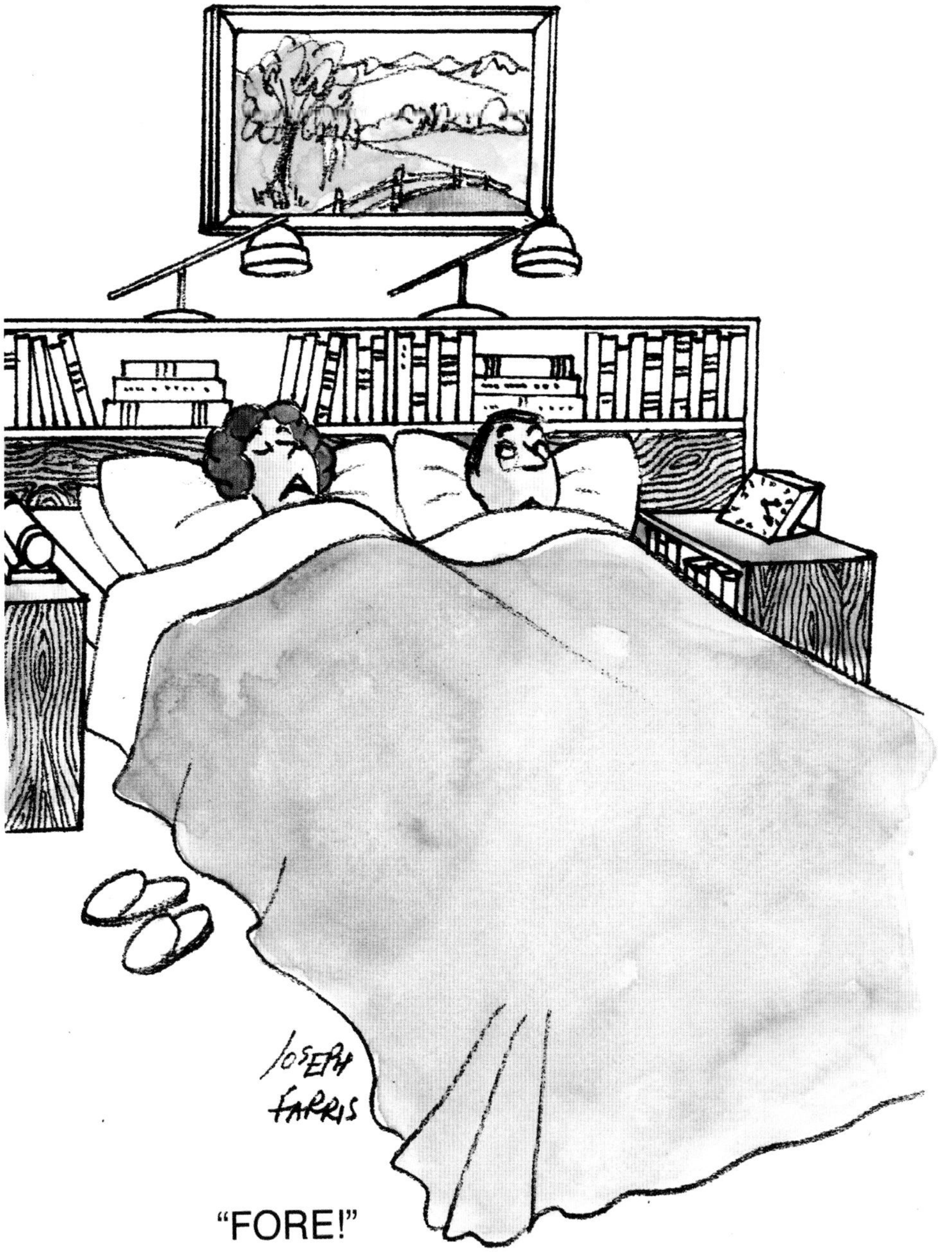
JOSEPH FARRIS

“FORE!”

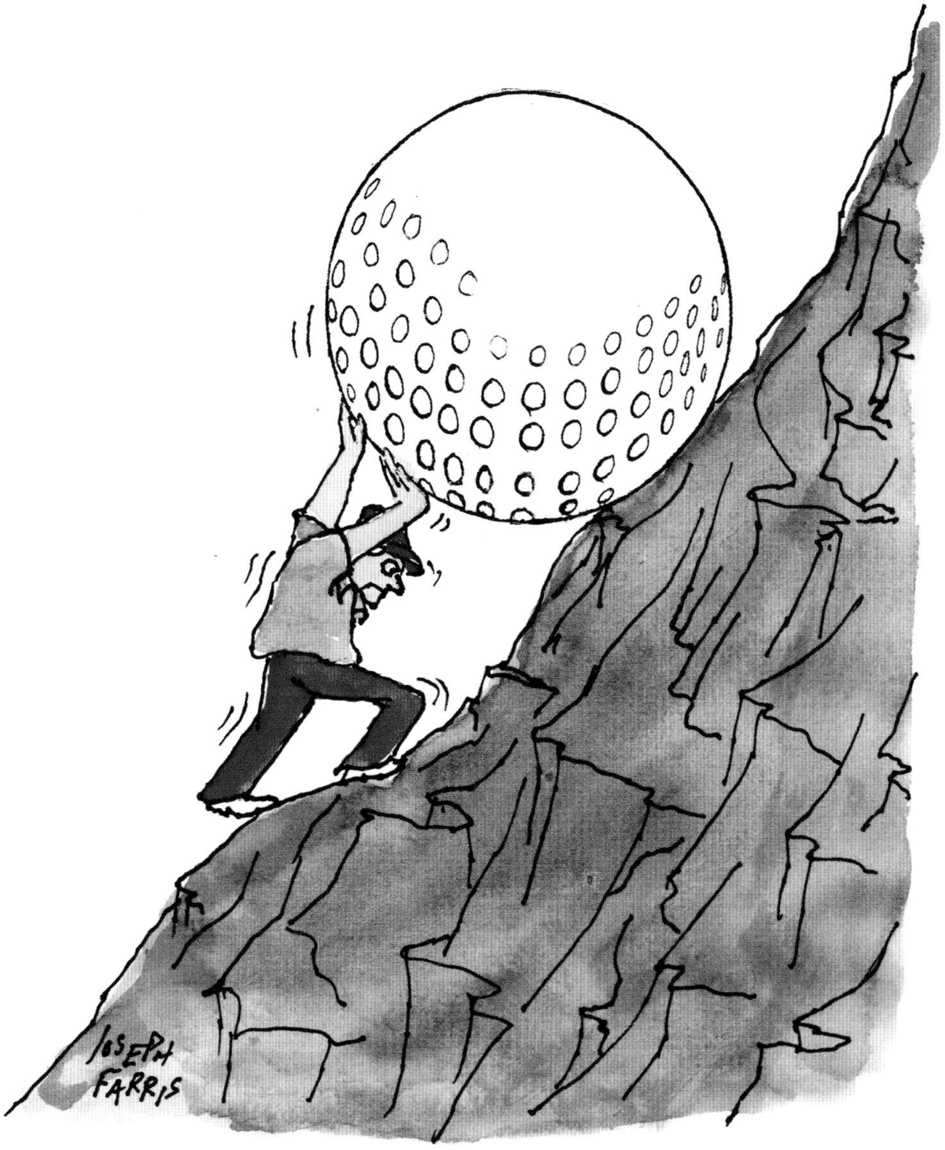
JOSEPH FARRIS

SISYPHUS, THE GOLFER

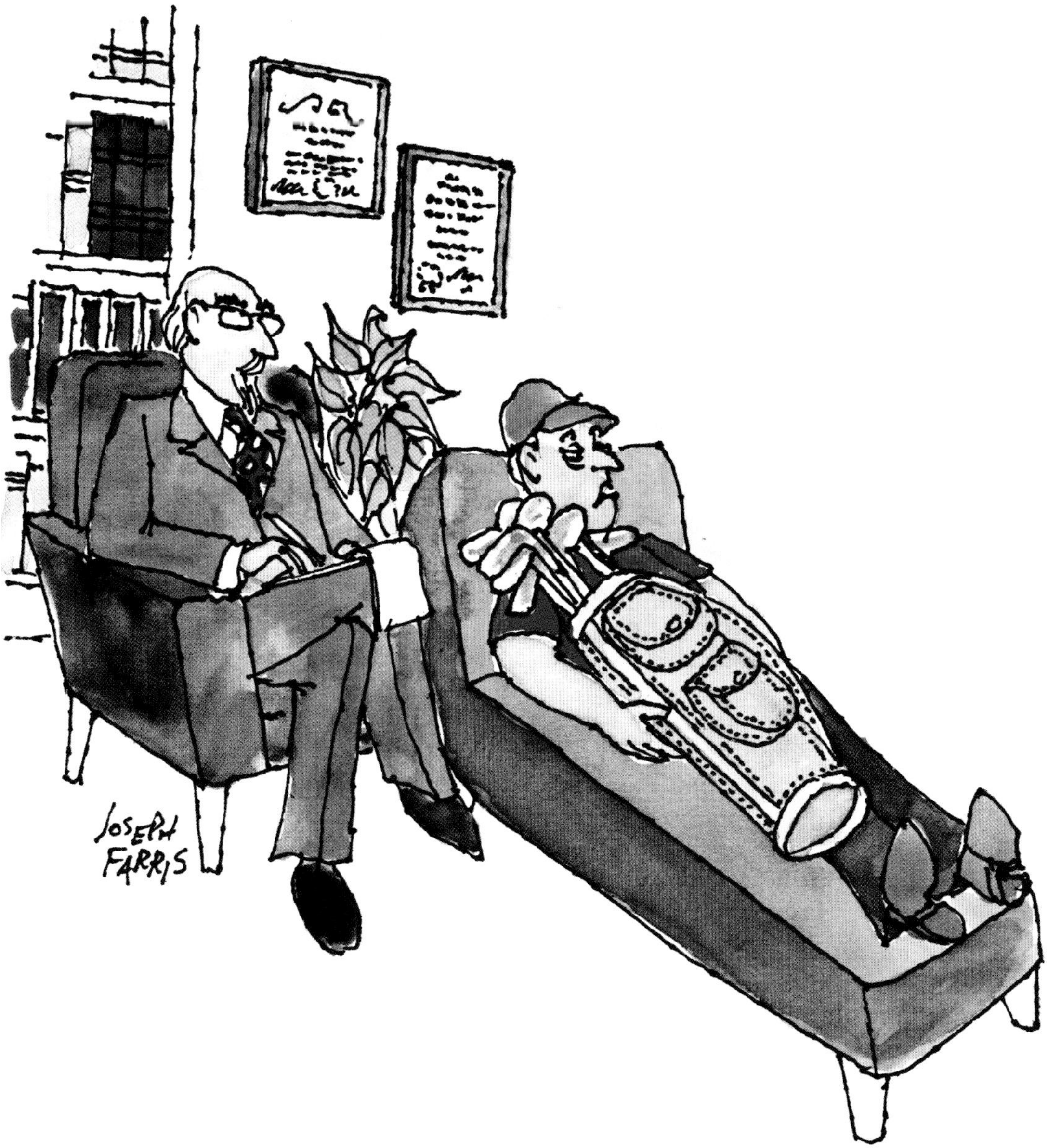
JOSEPH FARRIS

"My wife accuses me of being obsessed with golf."

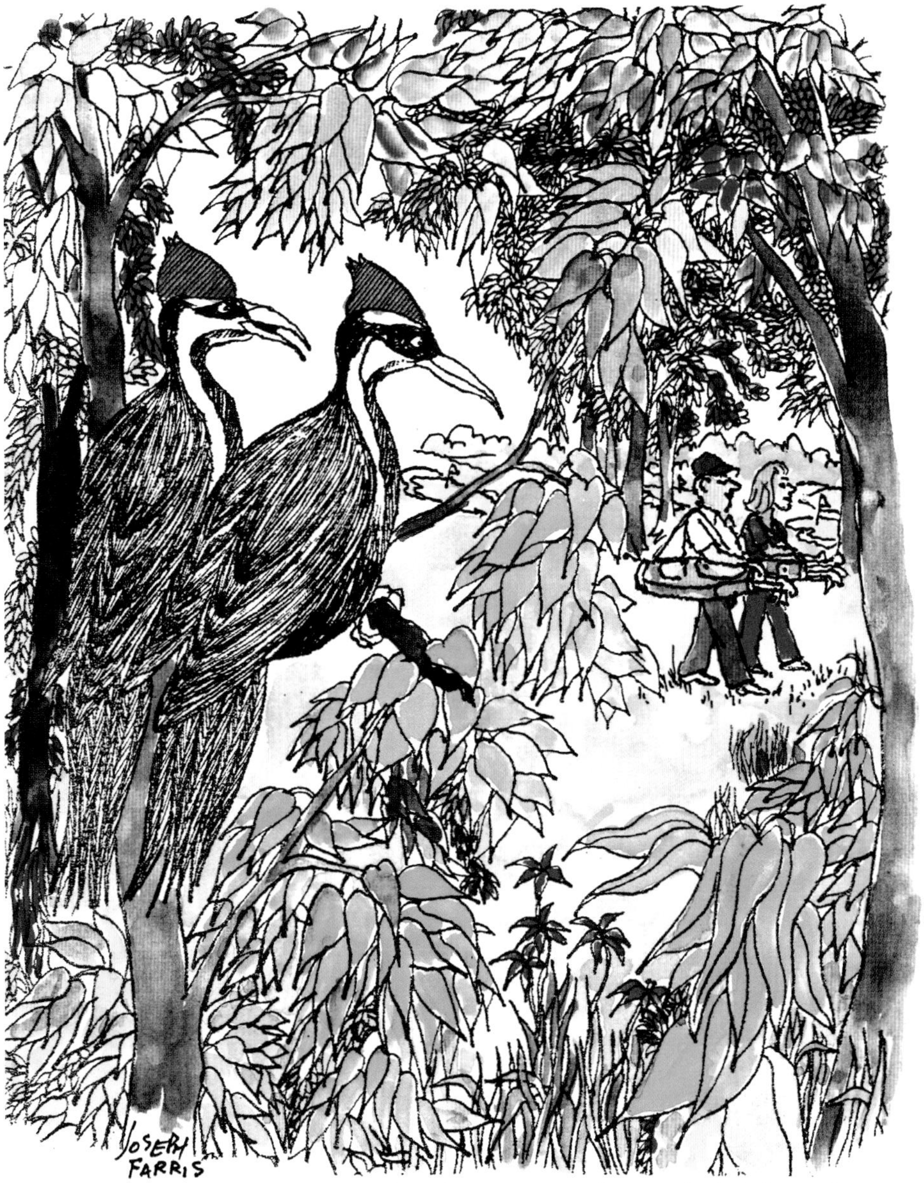
JOSEPH FARRIS

"I checked them out in the *Complete Field Guide to Humans*. They're called '*Golfers*'."

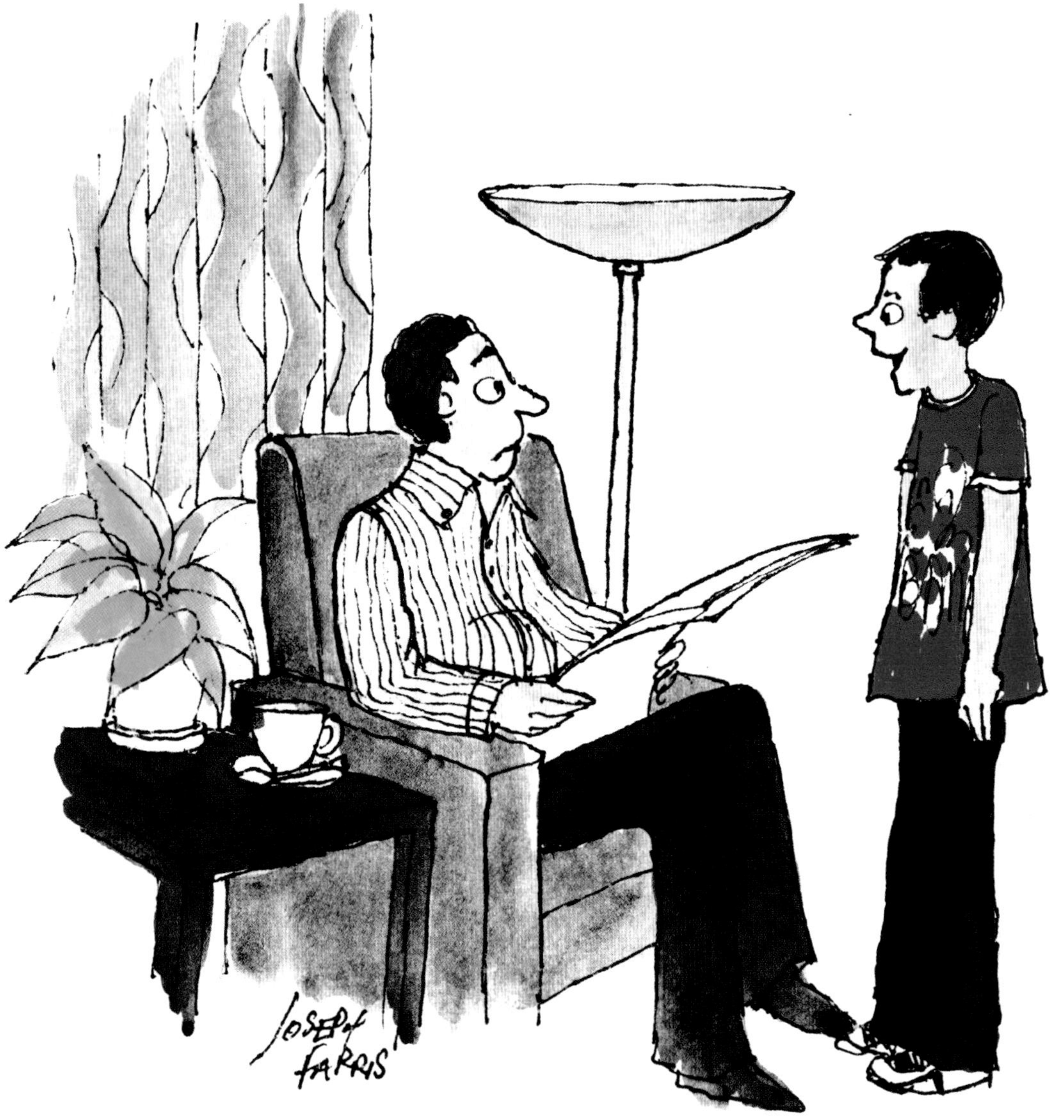
JOSEPH FARRIS

"Say, Dad, may I borrow your car, your golf clubs, your golf cart and fifty dollars?"

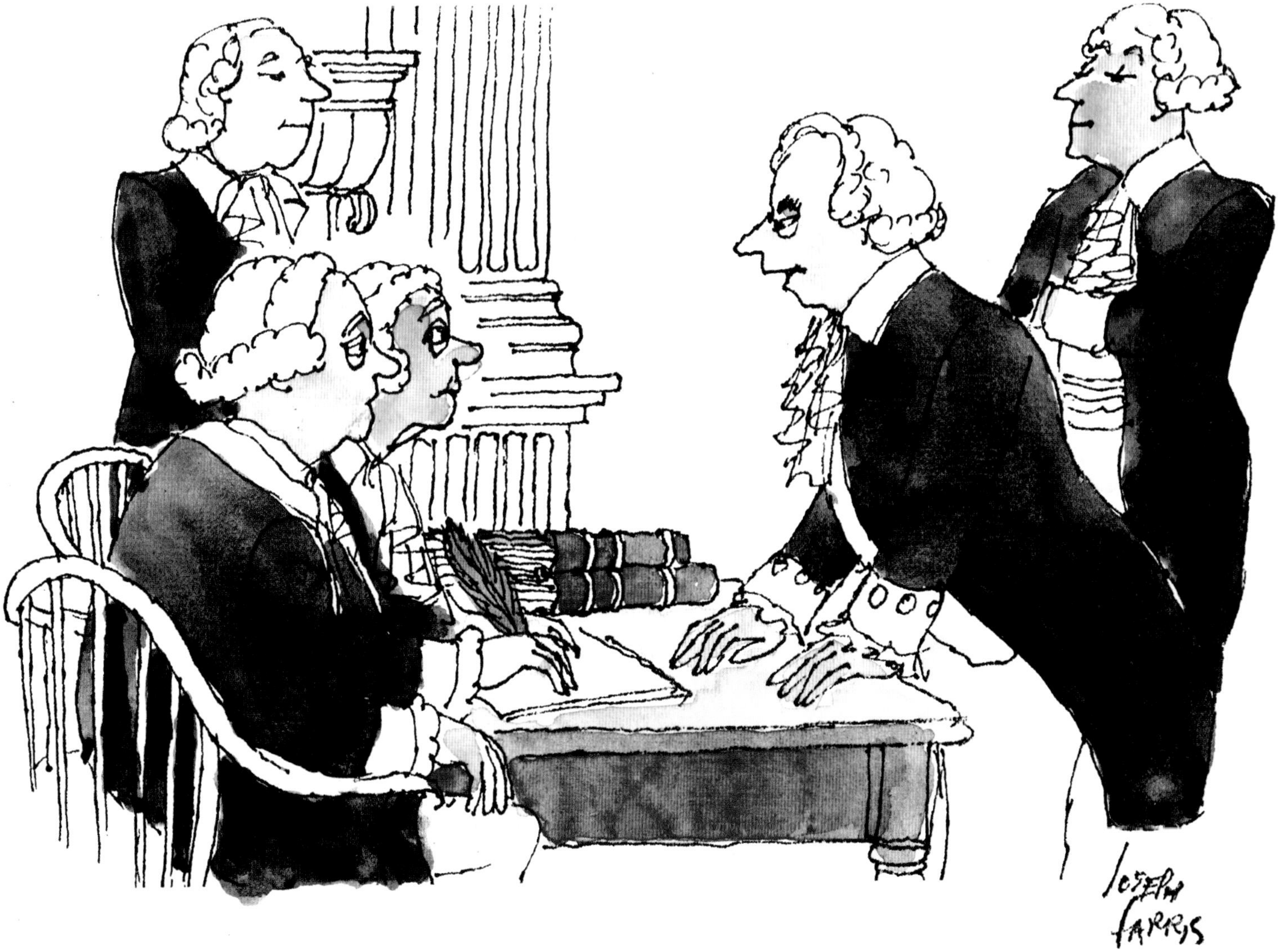

"Let's include on the new Capitol grounds room for a little game from the old country called 'golf'."

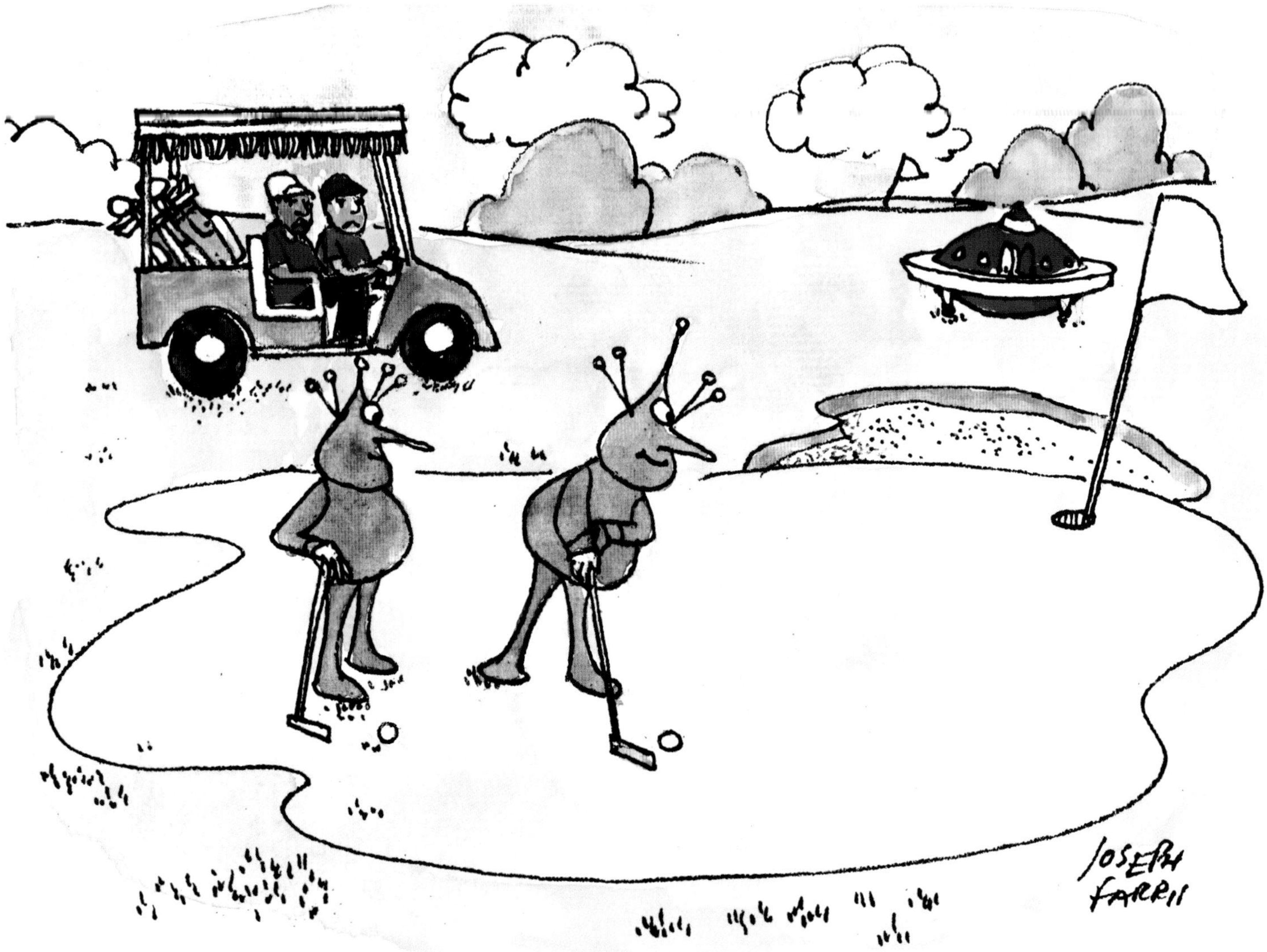
JOSEPH FARRIS

"Wait a minute! They don't look like Pebble Beach members!"

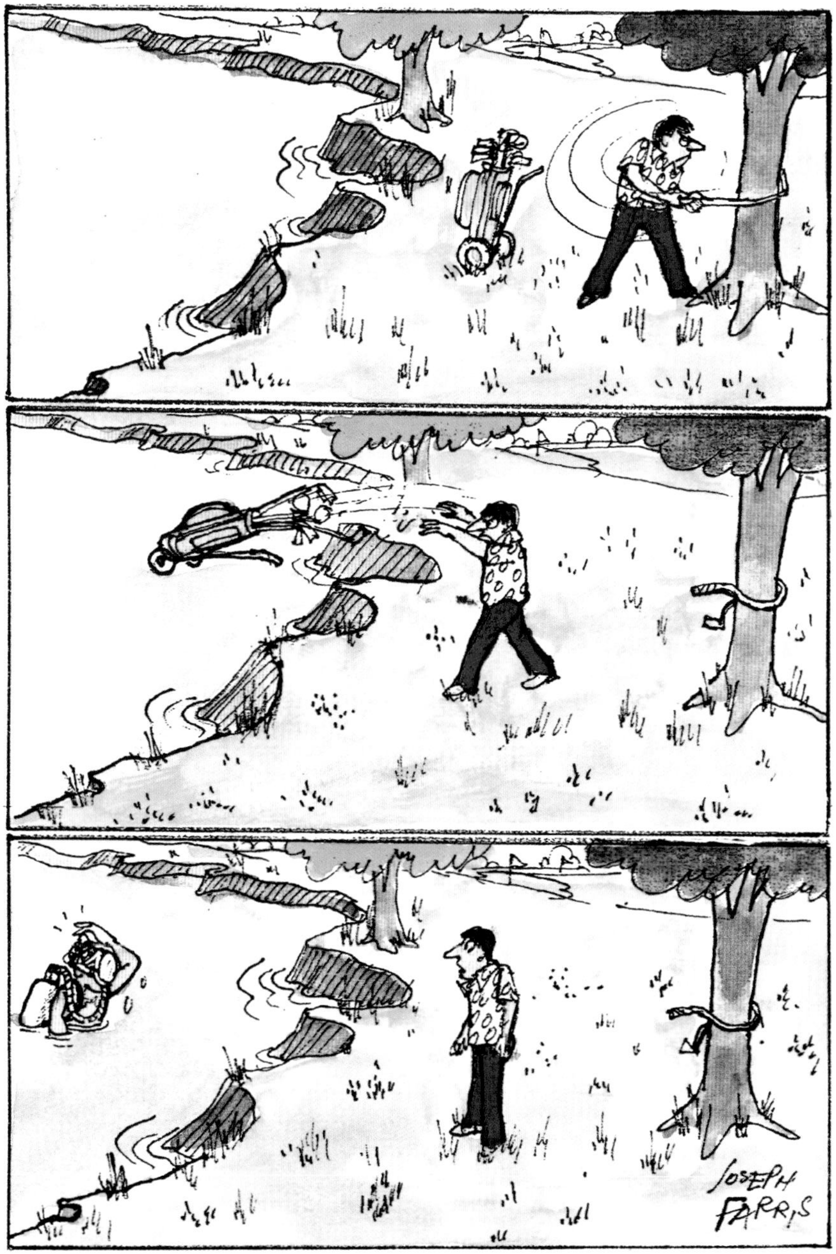
JOSEPH
FARRIS

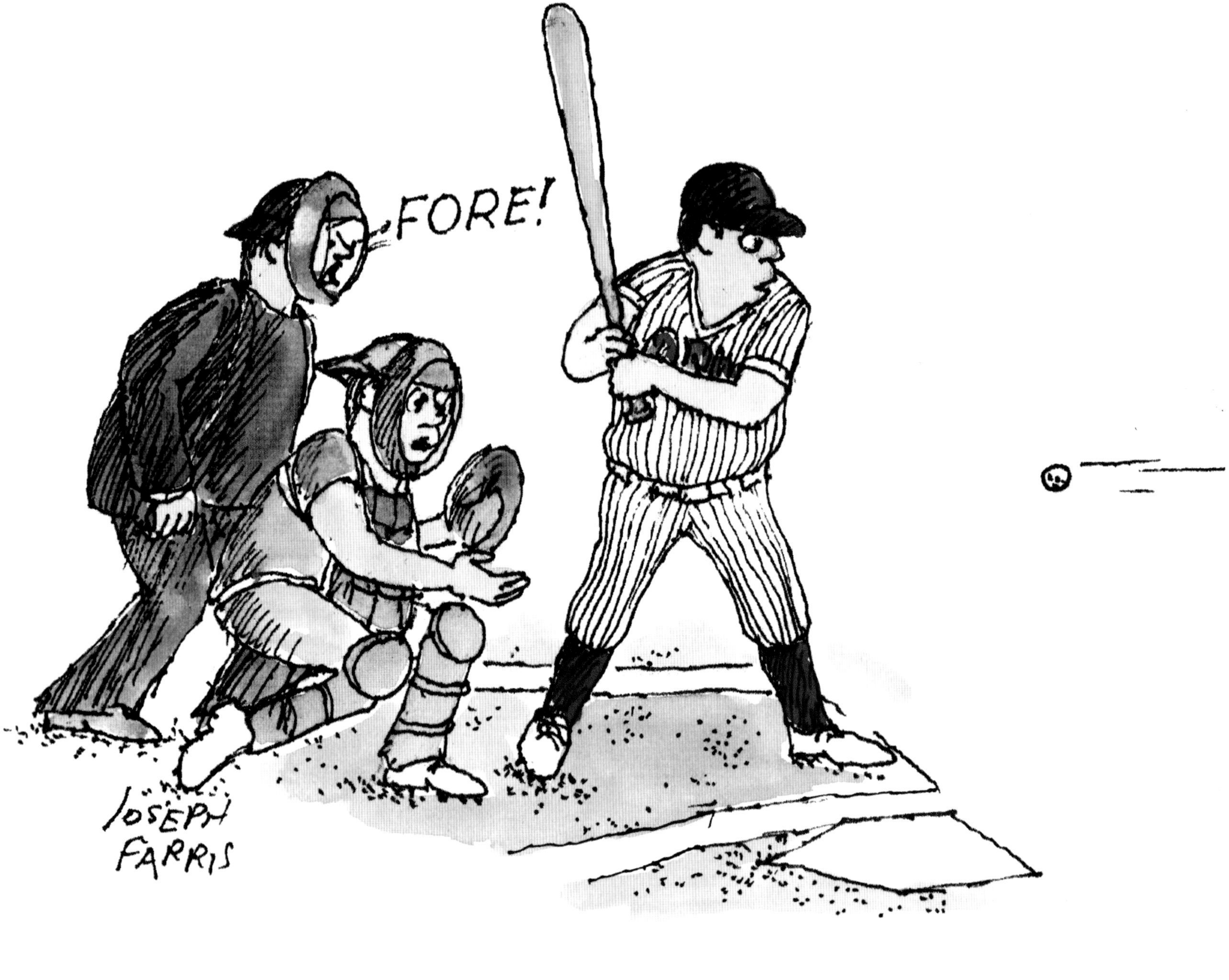
FORE!
JOSEPH FARRIS

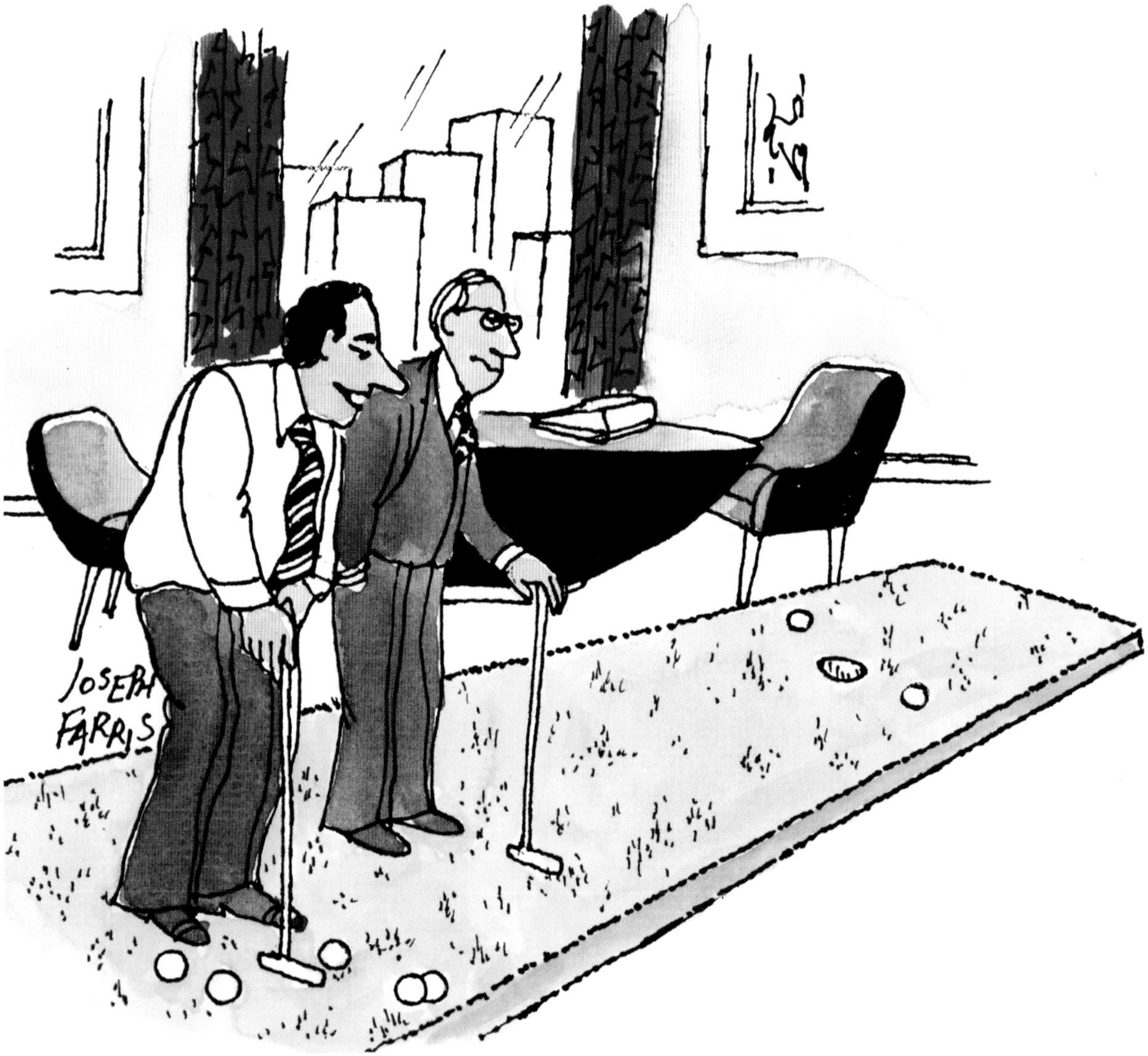
JOSEPH FARRIS

"I'm thinking of replacing this artificial turf with real grass."

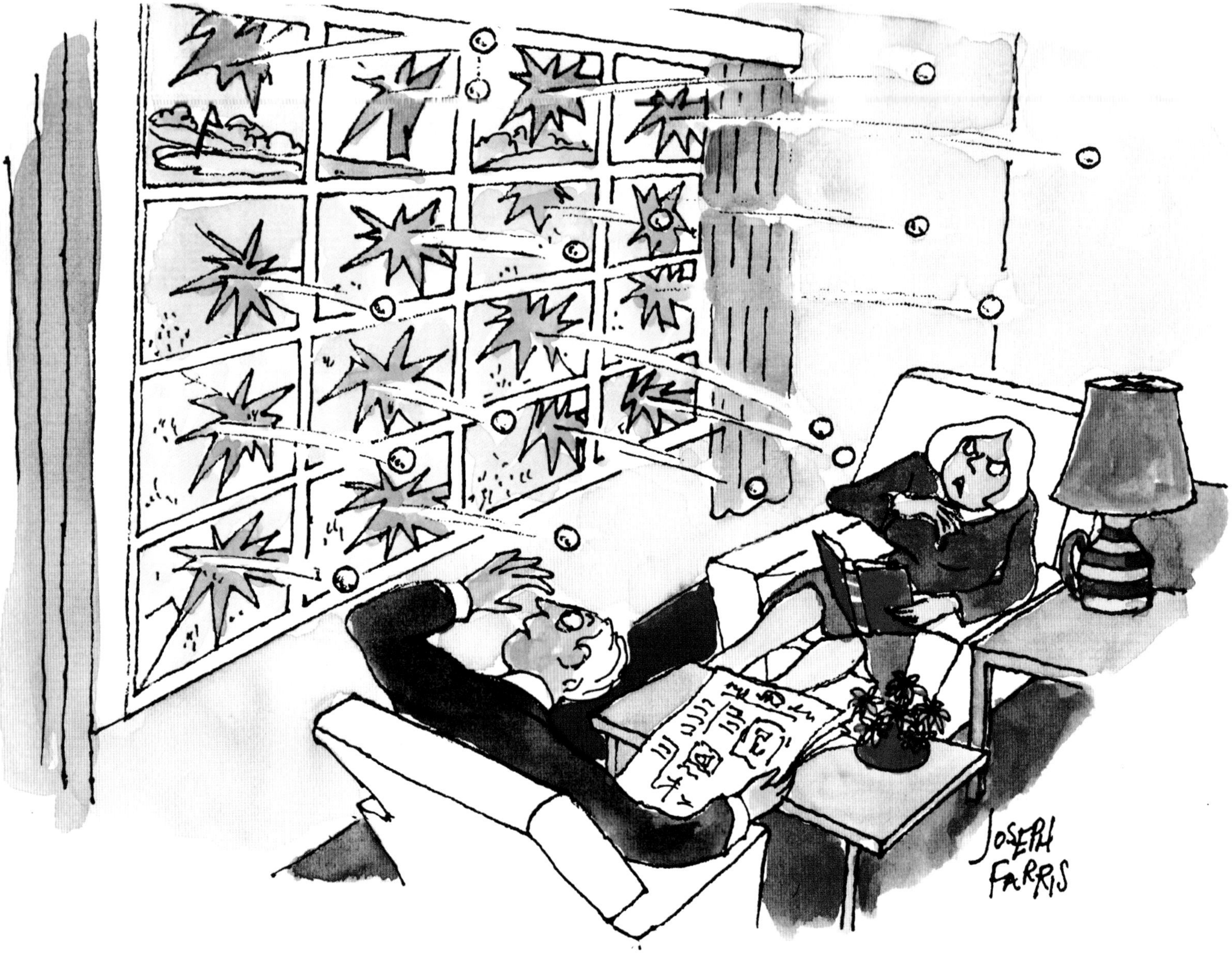
JOSEPH FARRIS

"That does it—we're moving!"

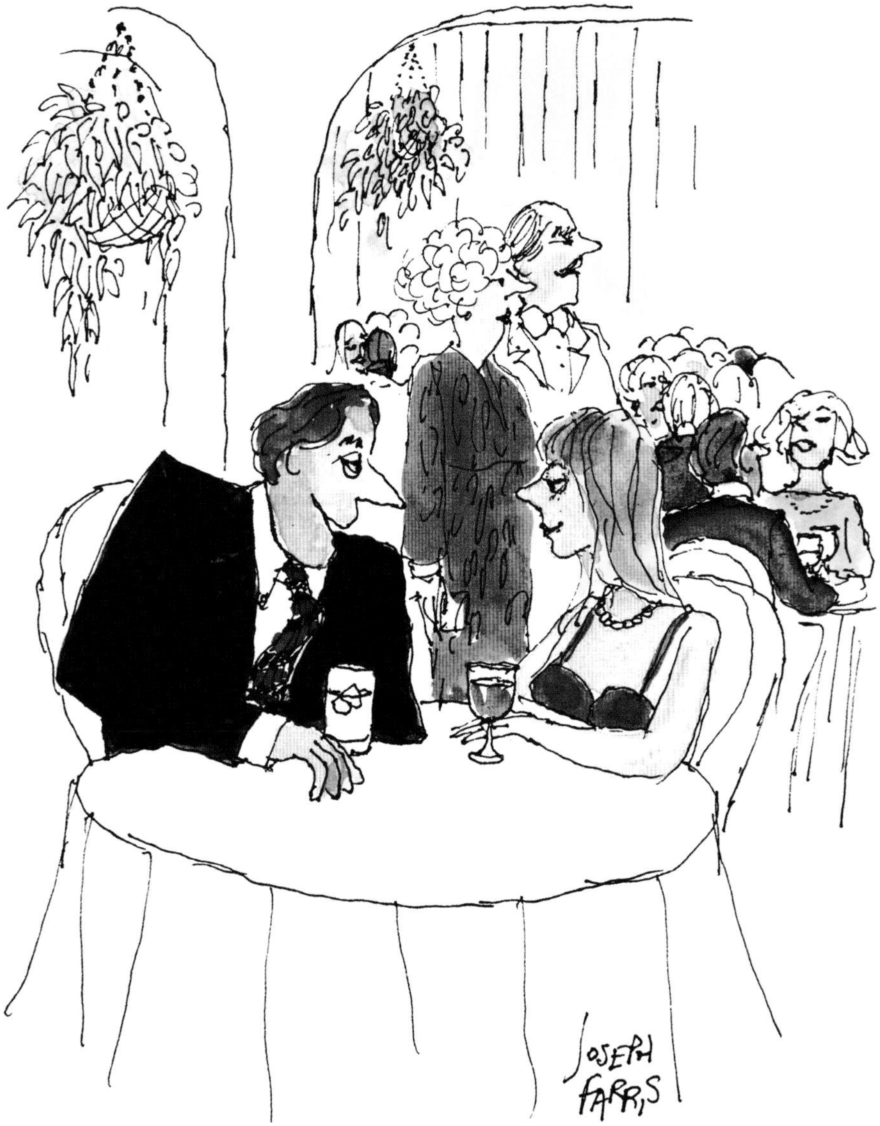
JOSEPH FARRIS

"I was awarded this green jacket for winning the Masters tournament—in a dream."

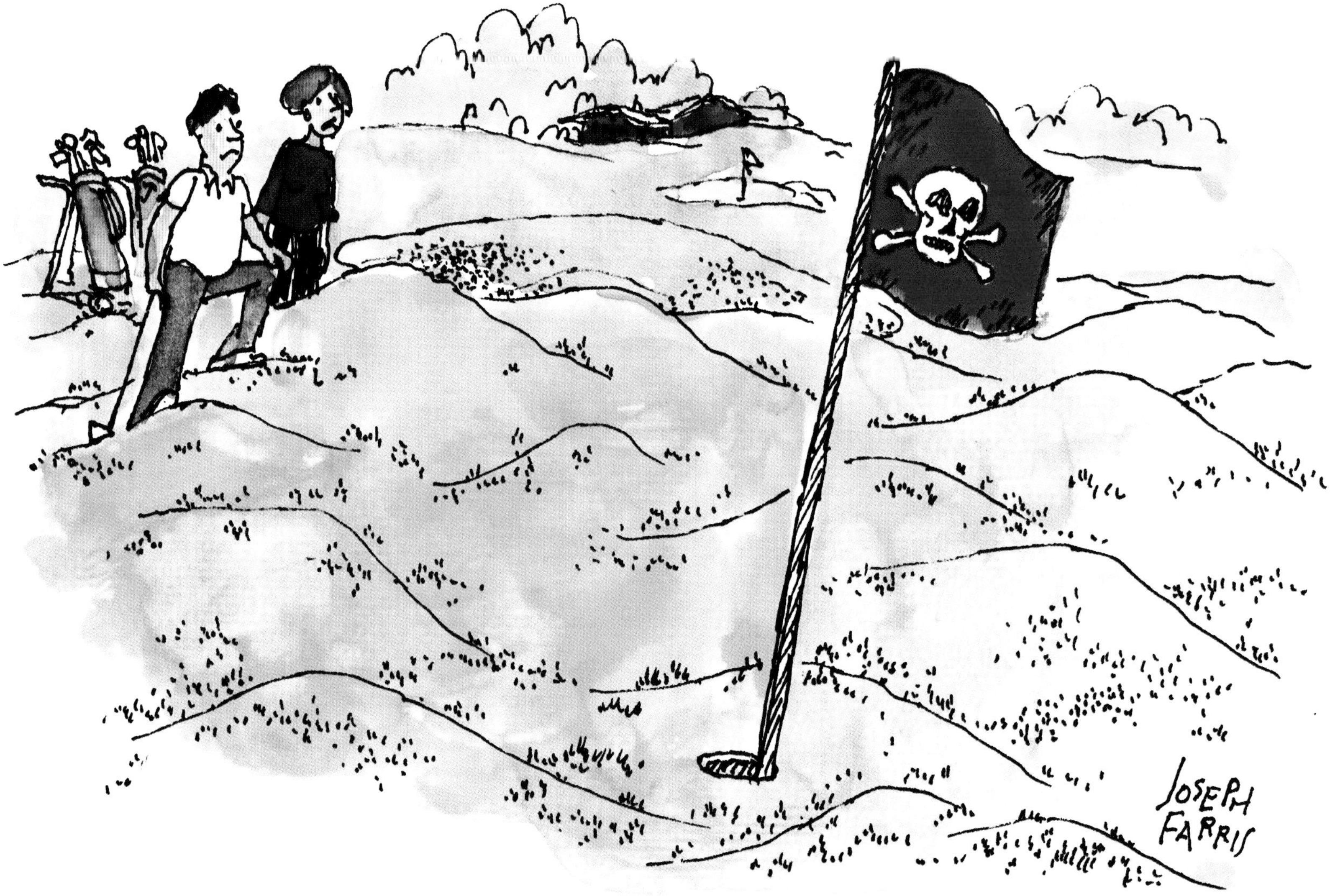
JOSEPH FARRIS

"This is a killer hole!"

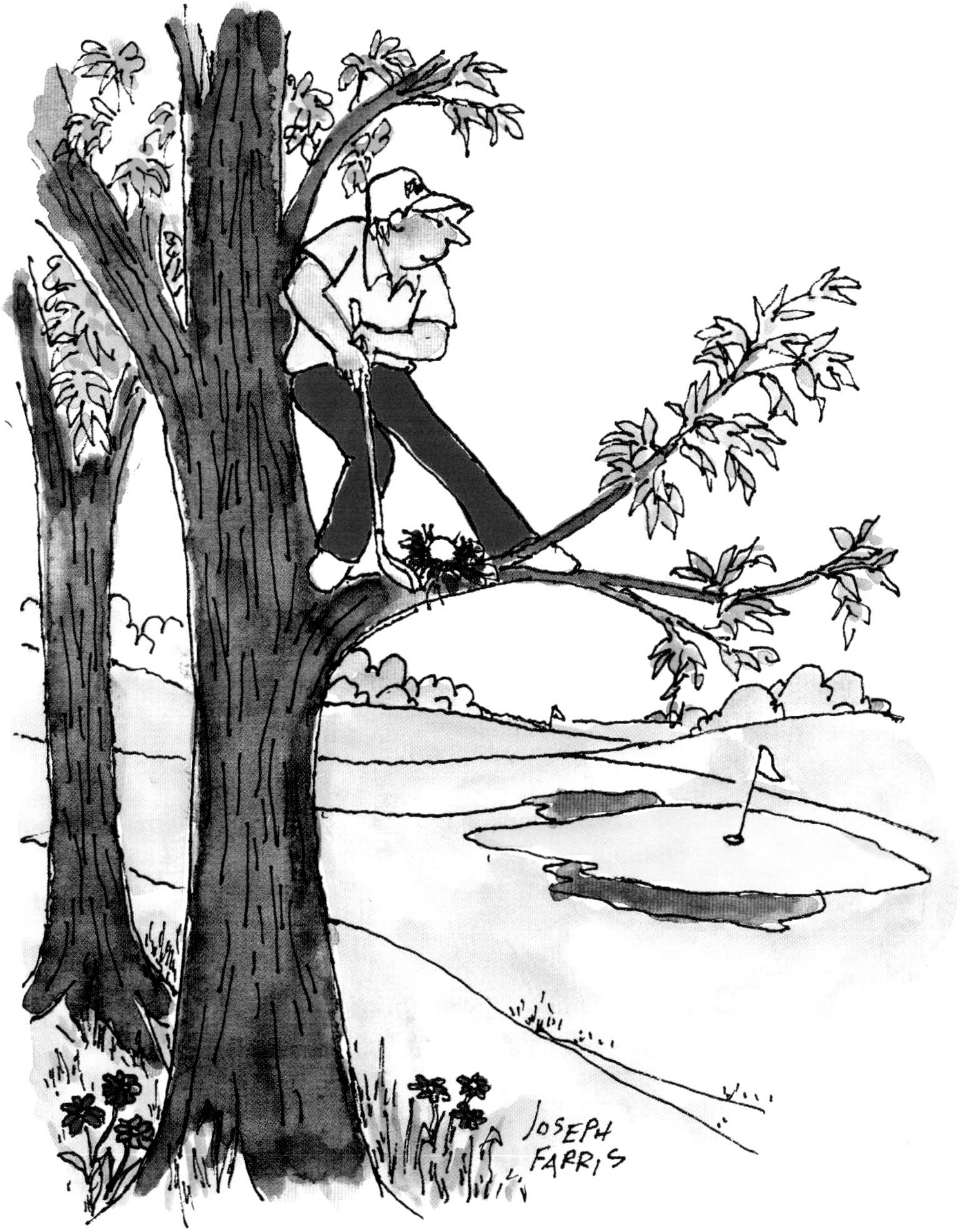
JOSEPH
FARRIS

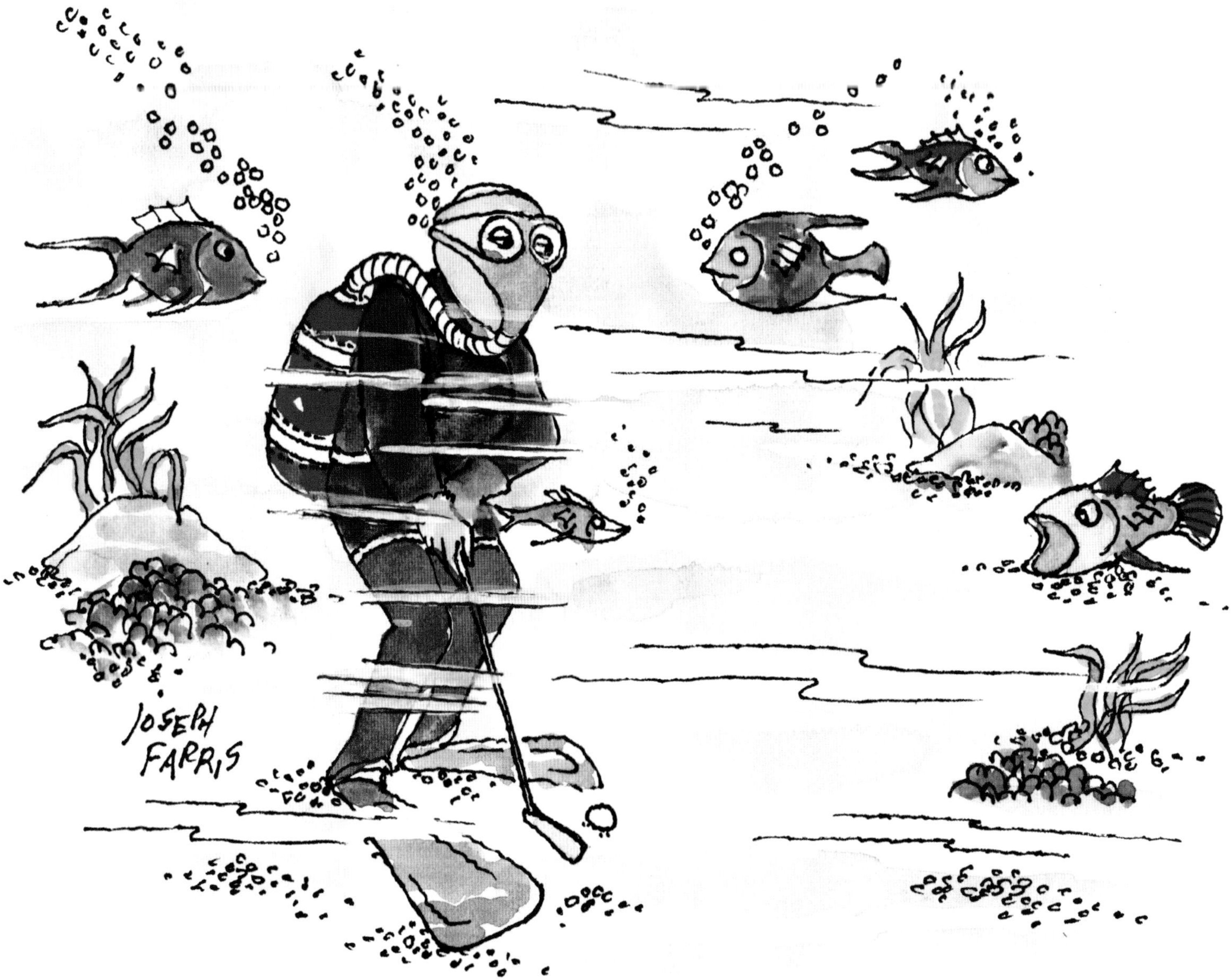
JOSEPH FARRIS

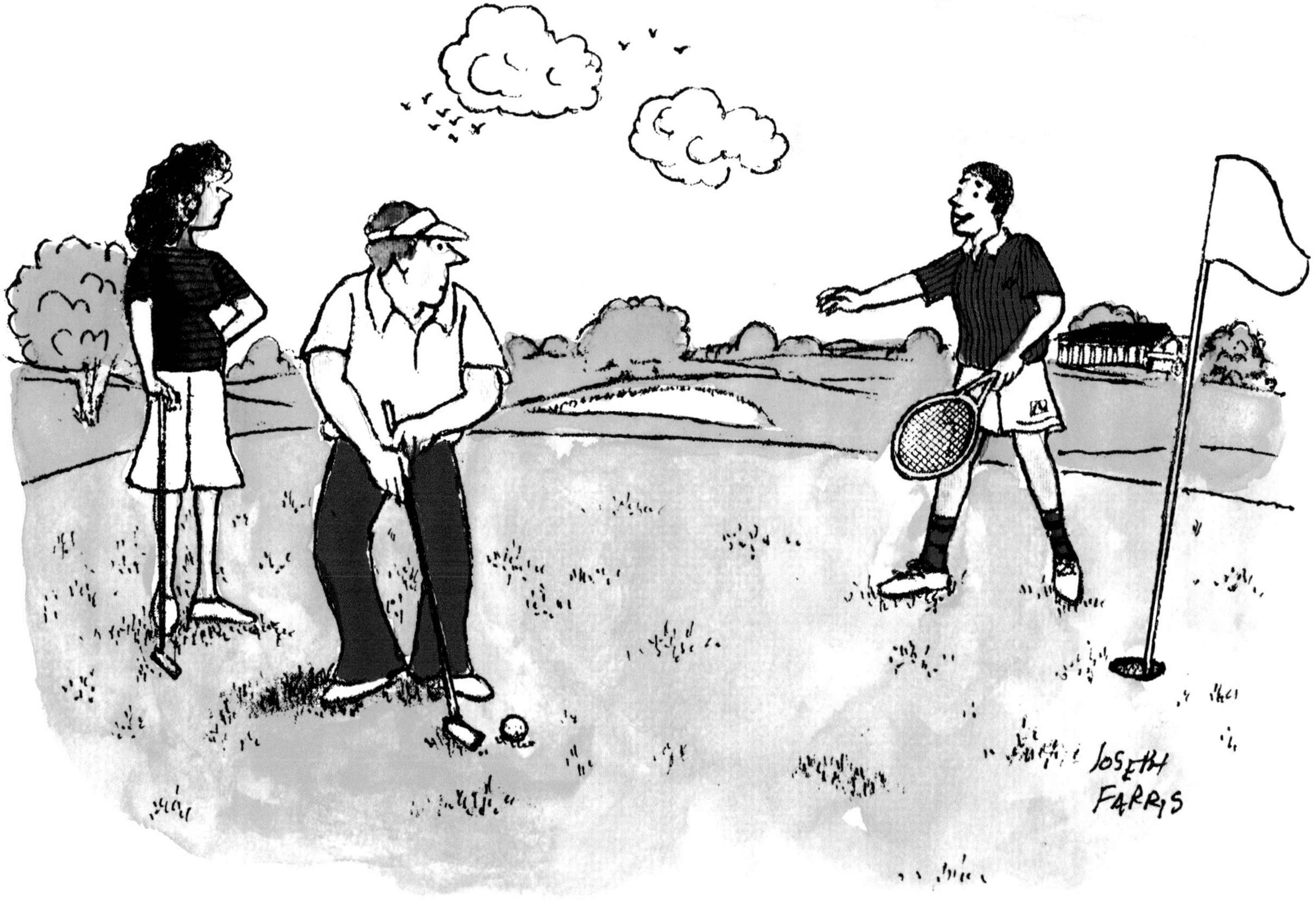
JOSEPH
FARRIS

"Tennis, anyone?"

"I'm playing 18 floors."

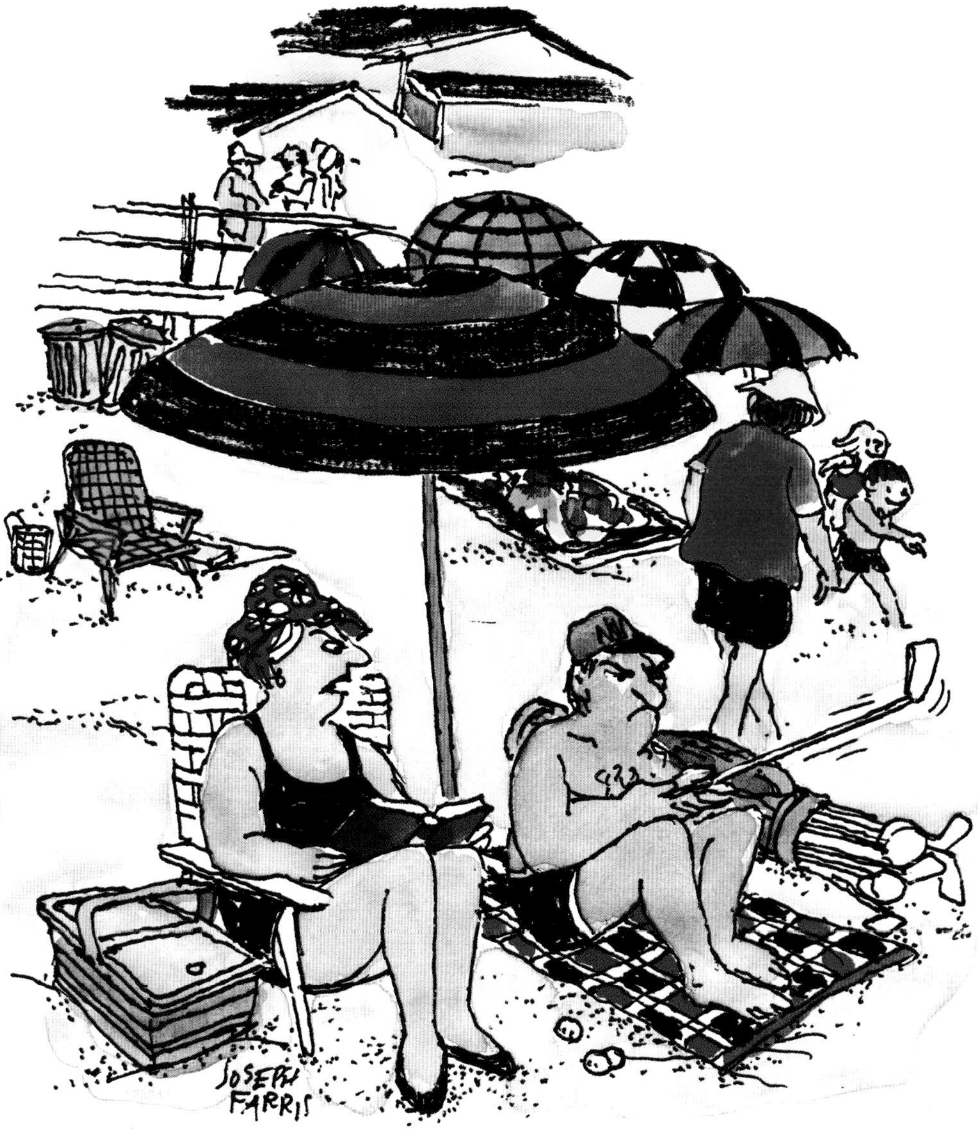
JOSEPH FARRIS

“For God’s sake—go play your golf!”

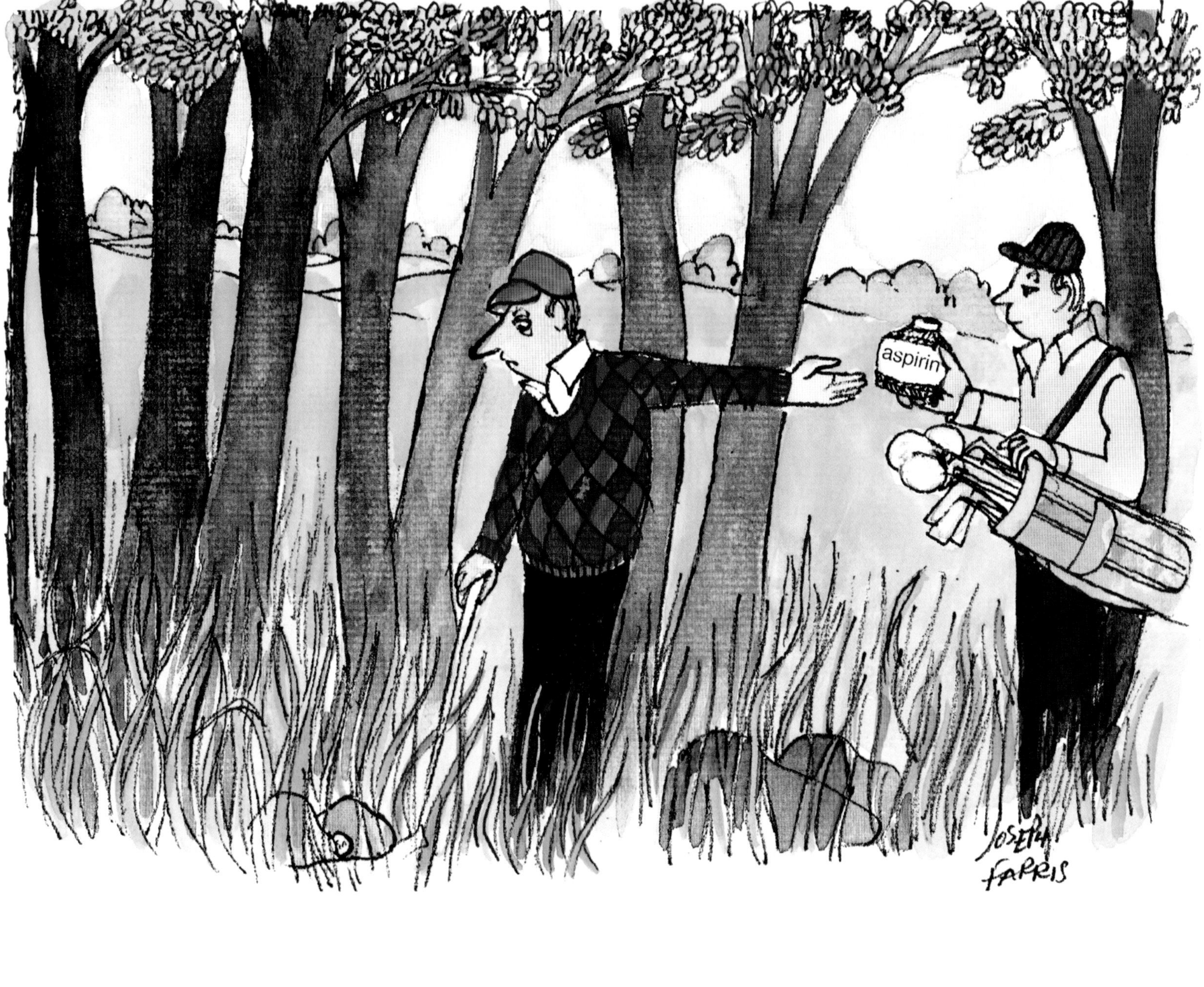
aspirin
JOSEPH FARRIS

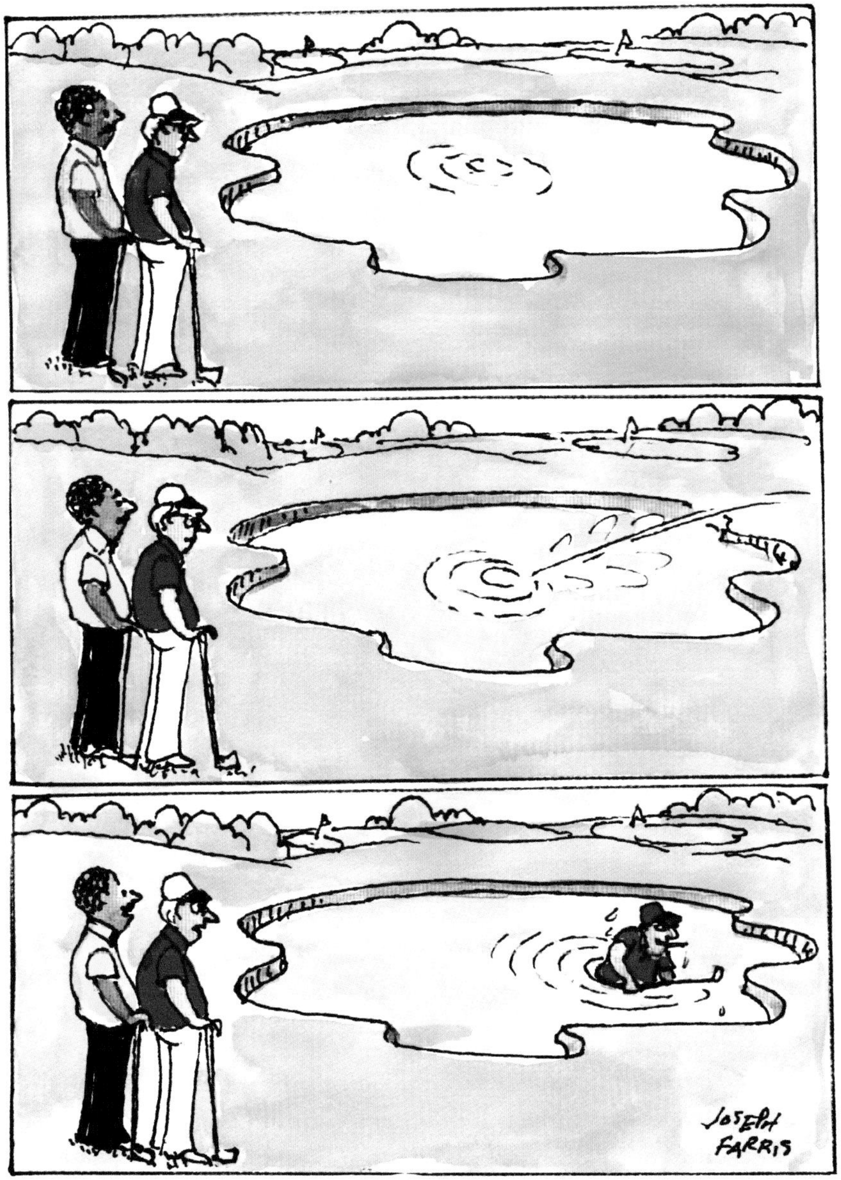
JOSEPH FARRIS

"That's why he's the boss and we're employees."

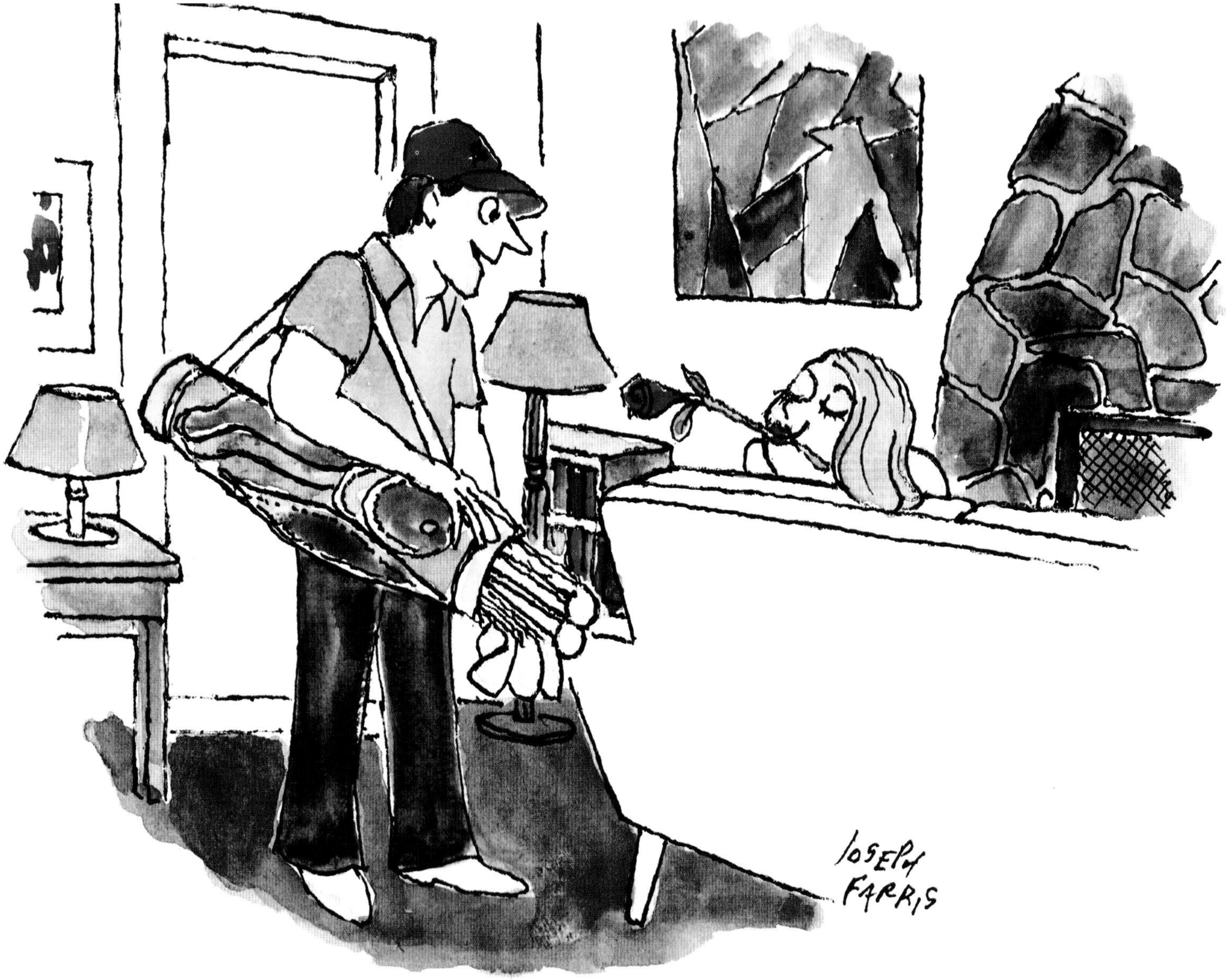
JOSEPH FARRIS

"What a choice—golf or sex!"

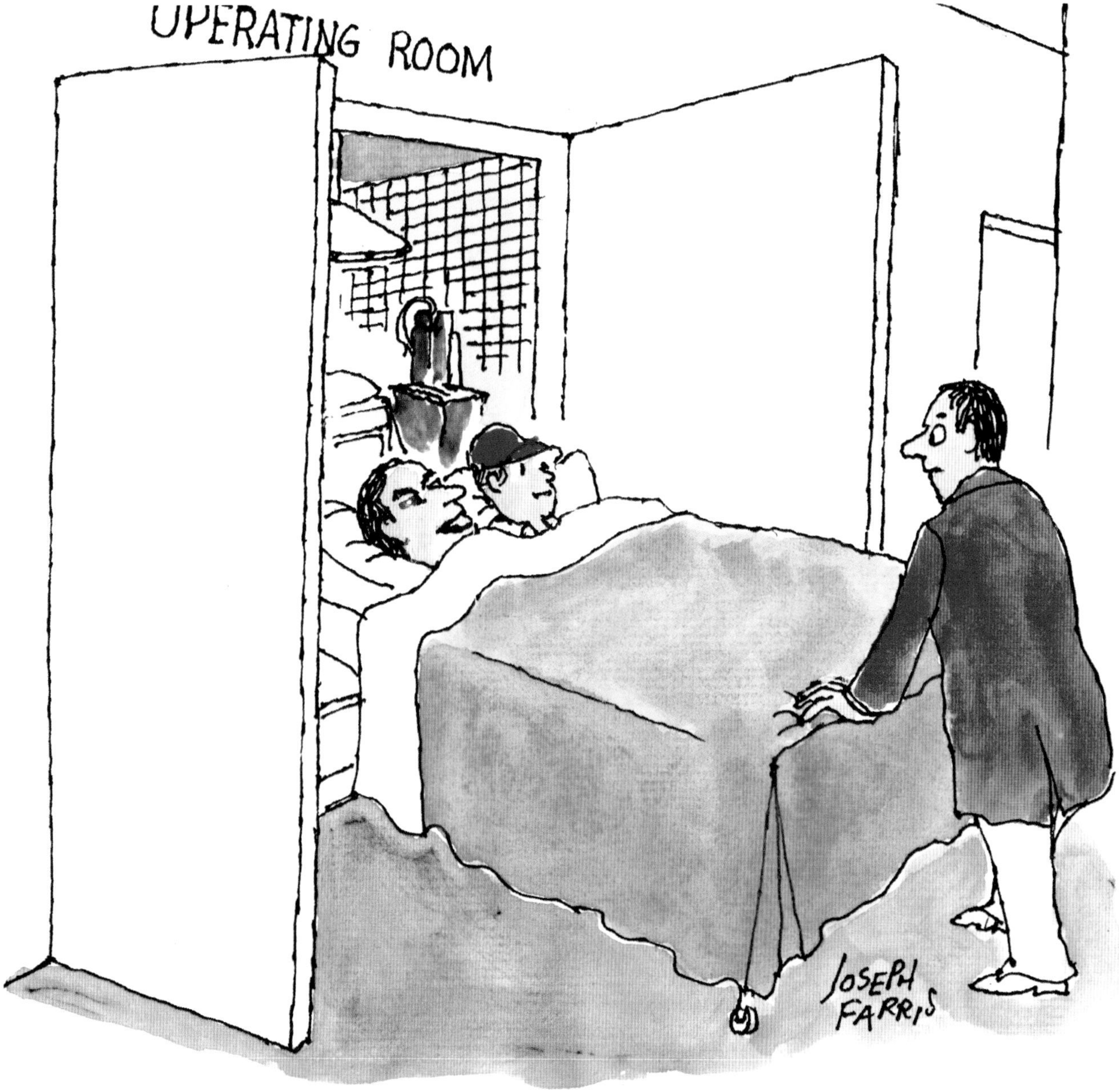
OPERATING ROOM
JOSEPH FARRIS

"My caddie."

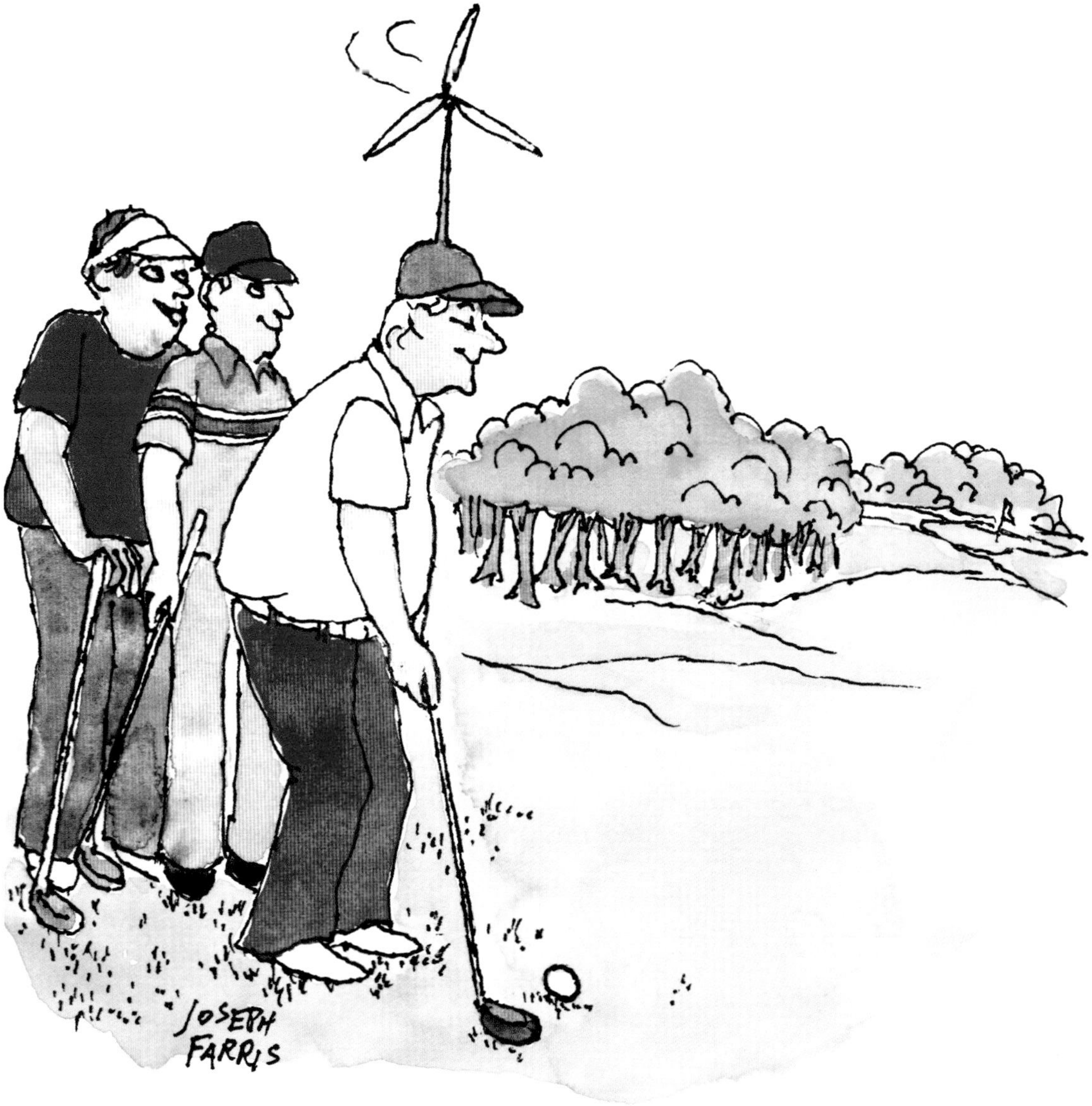
JOSEPH FARRIS

"He claims it gives him more energy in his drives."

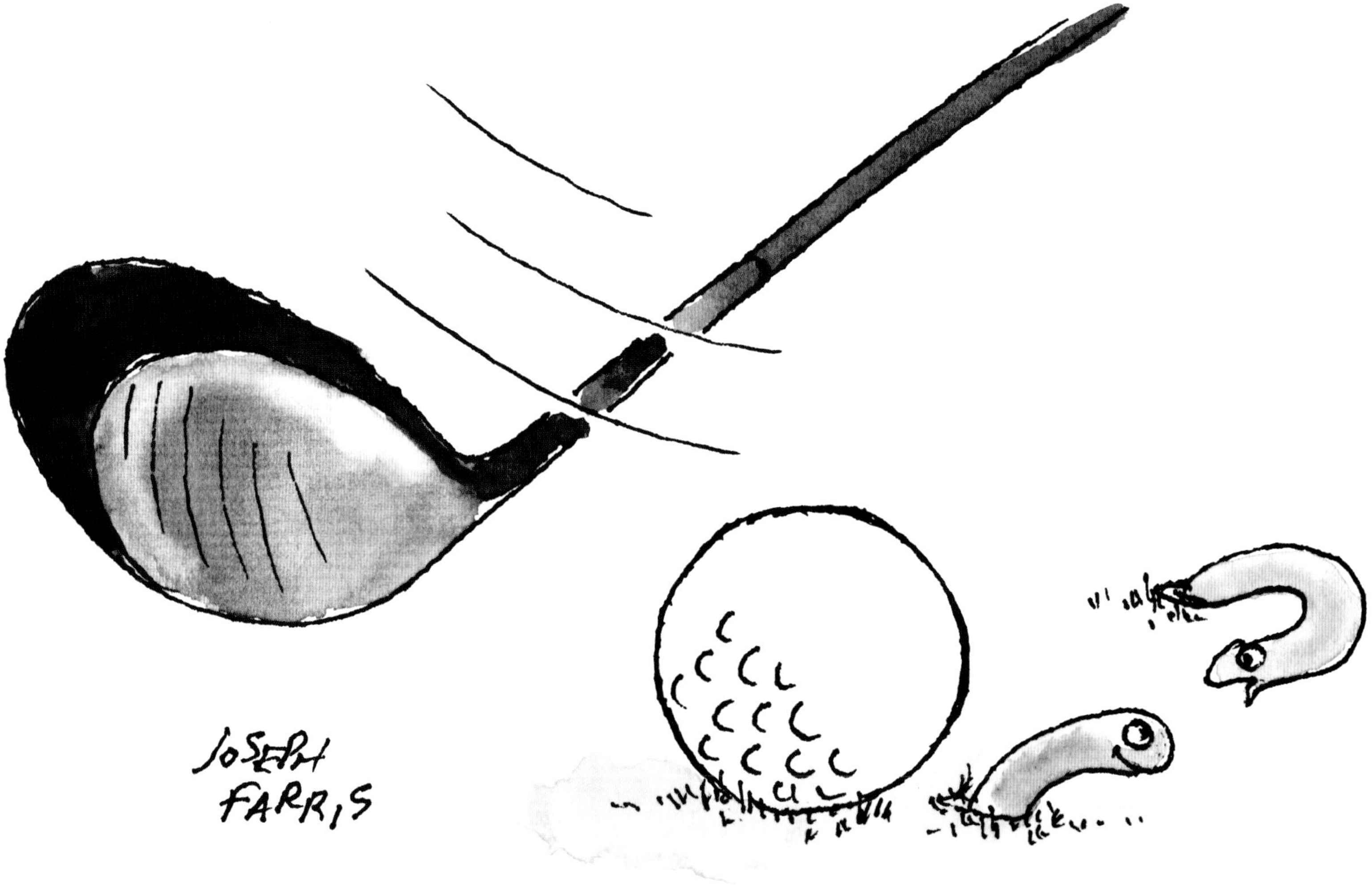
JOSEPH
FARRIS

"Duck!"

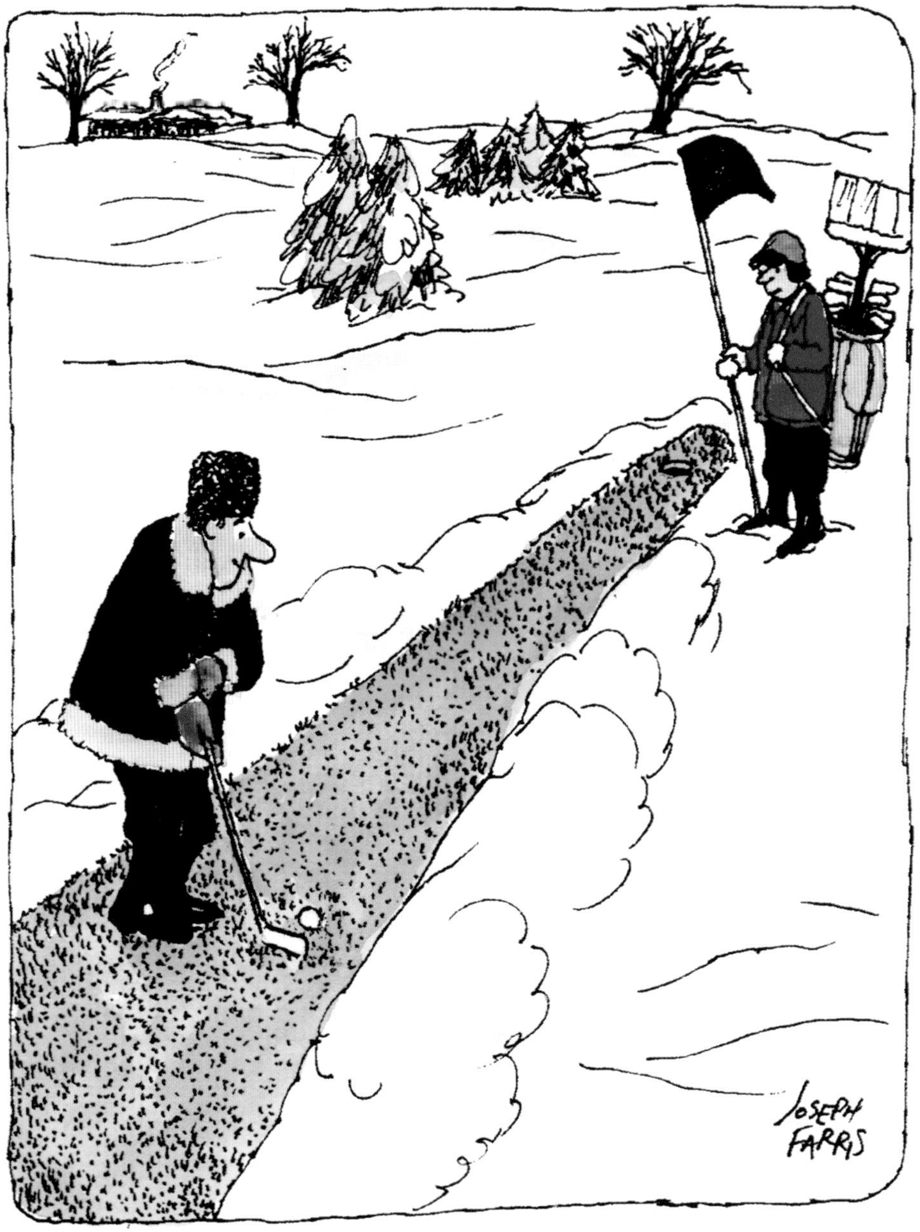
JOSEPH FARRIS

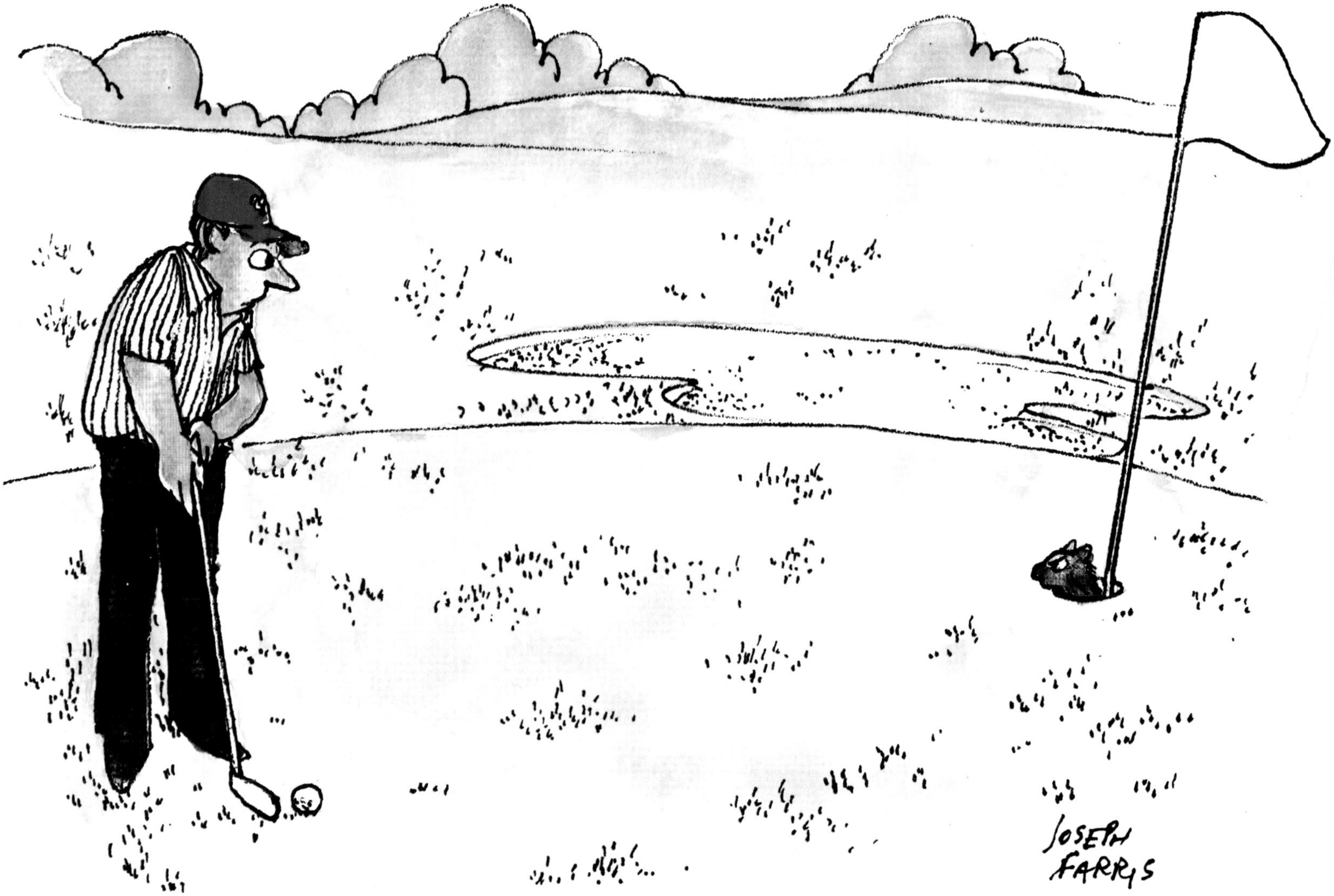
JOSEPH FARRIS

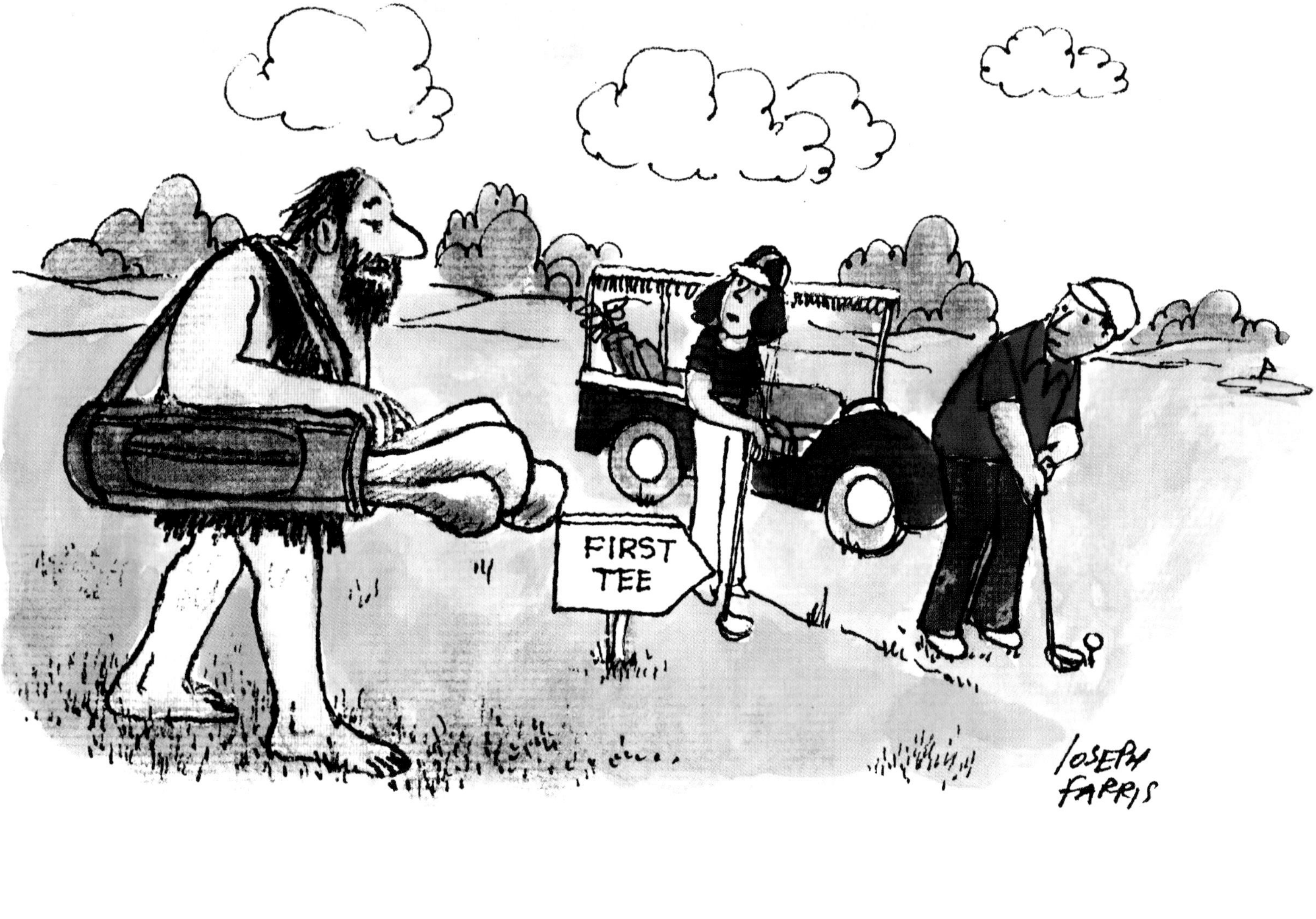
FIRST
TEE
JOSEPH
FARRIS

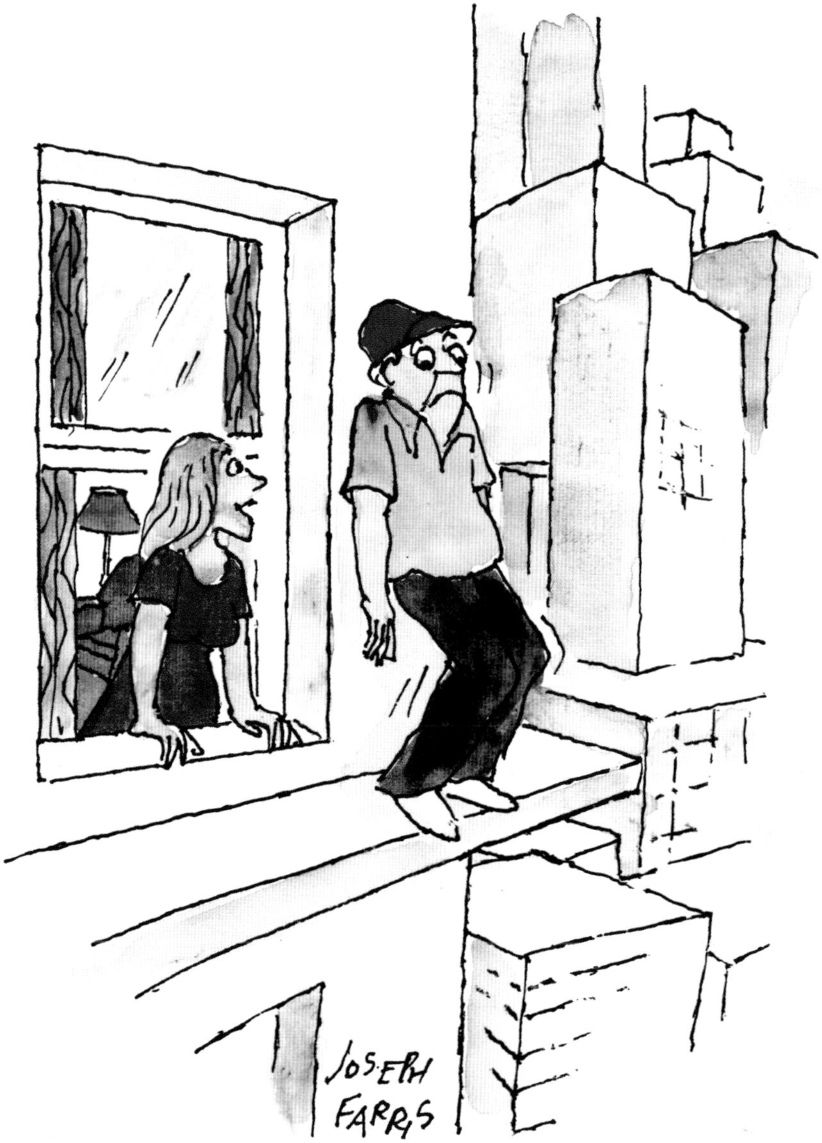
JOSEPH
FARRIS

"Don't jump! Official World Golf Ranking
has put you in the top 10,000!"

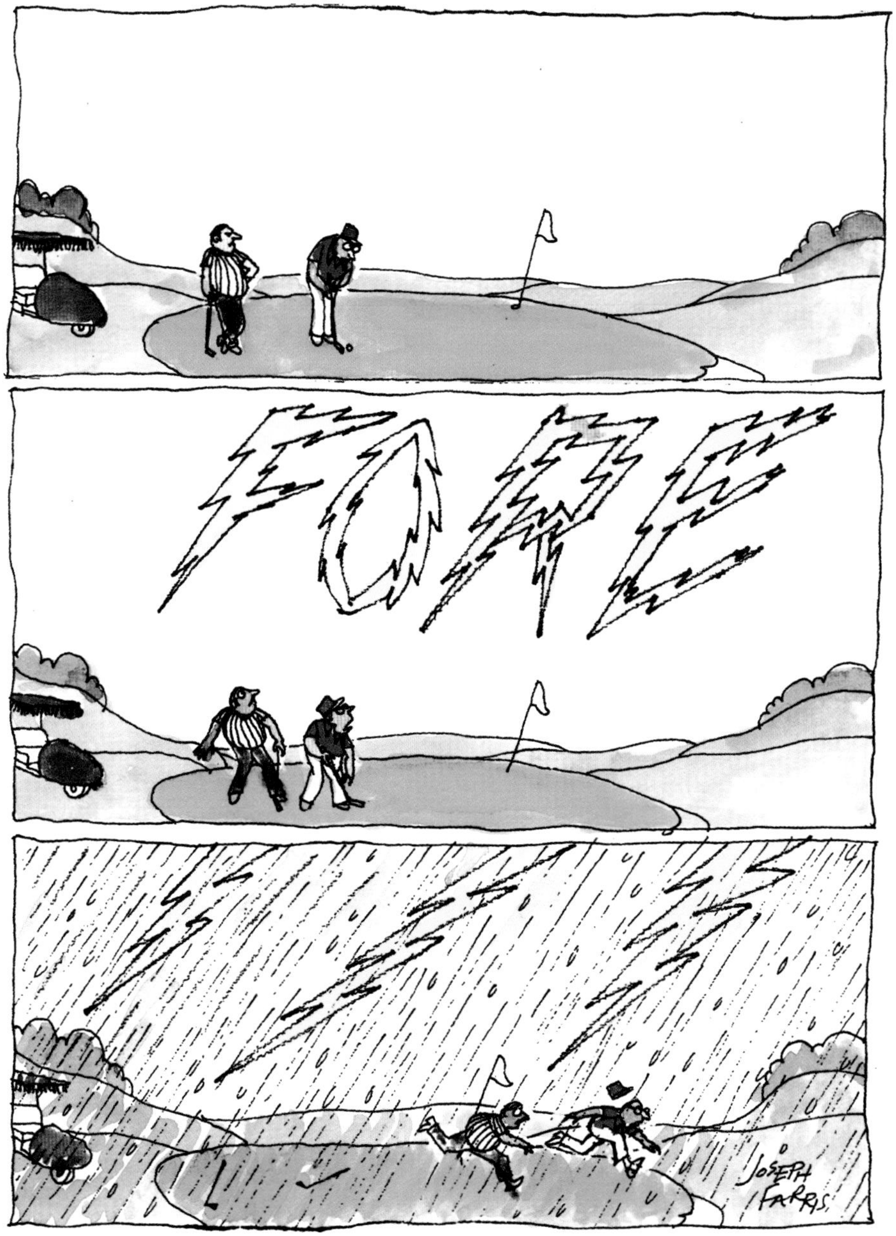
FORE
JOSEPH FARRIS

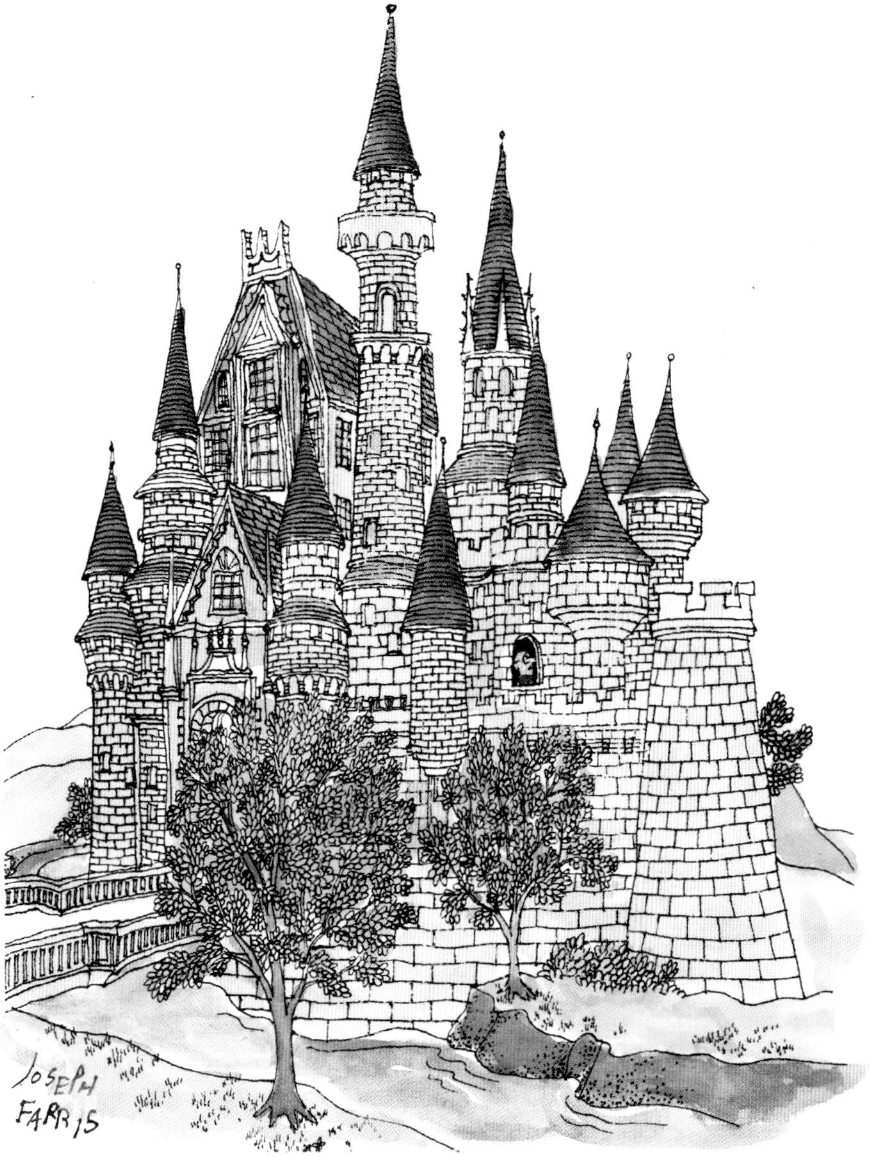
JOSEPH FARRIS

"Gwen, do you know where in hell my golf clubs are?"

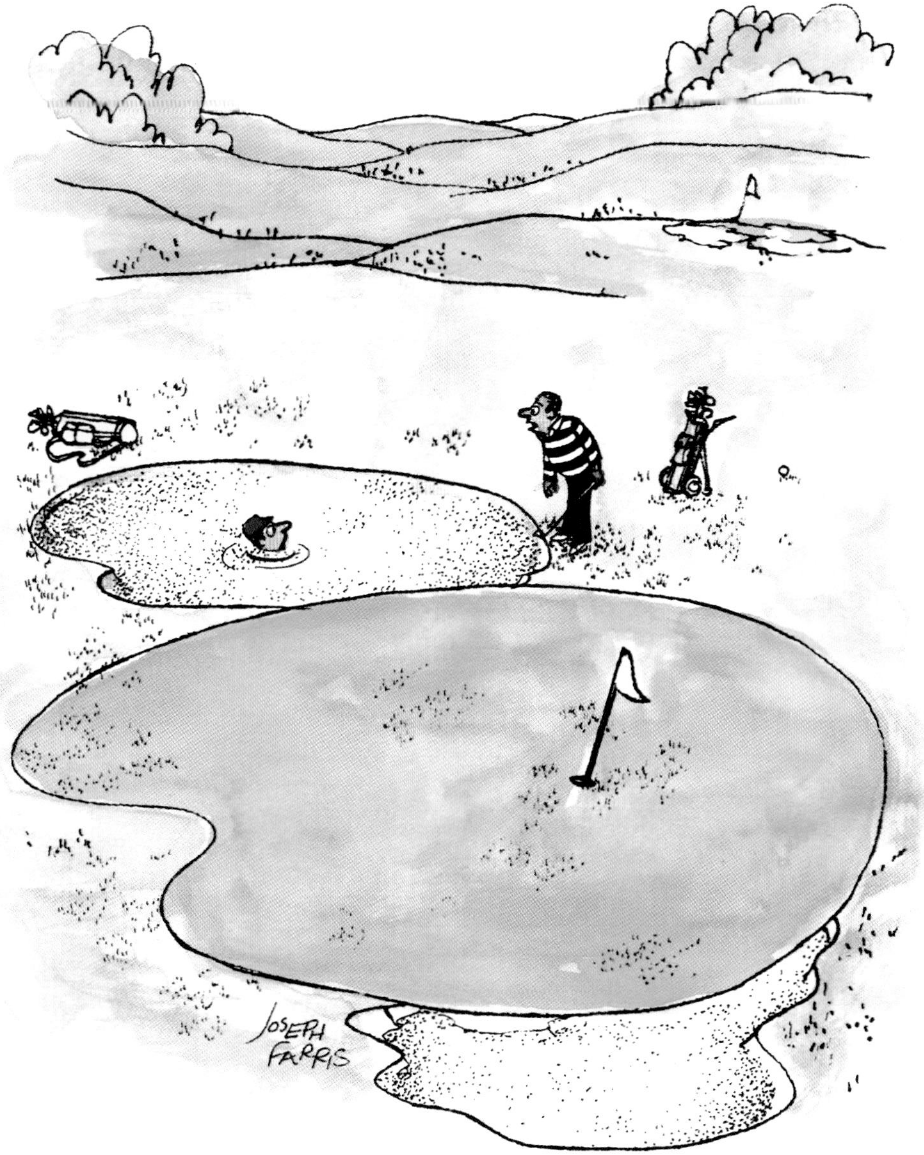
JOSEPH FARRIS

"I told you this was a tough hole."

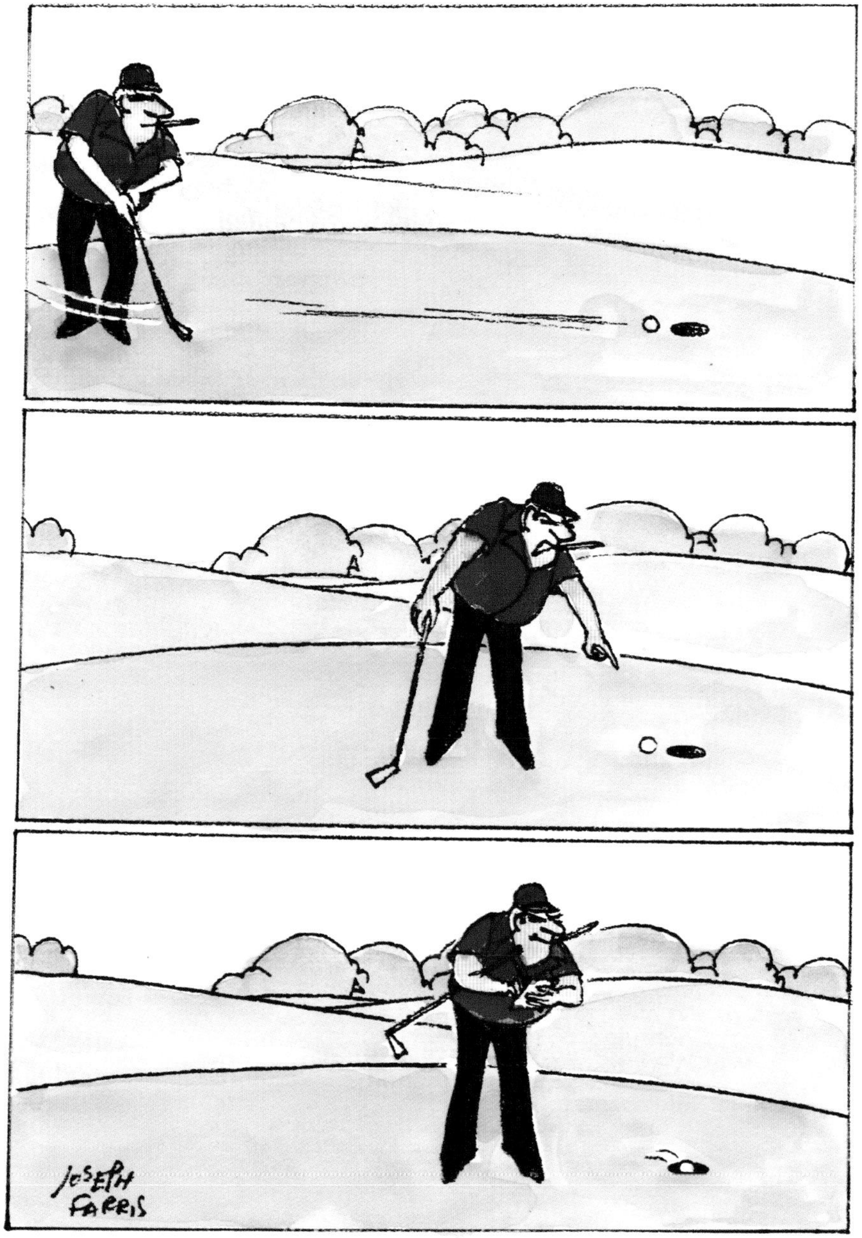
JOSEPH
FARRIS

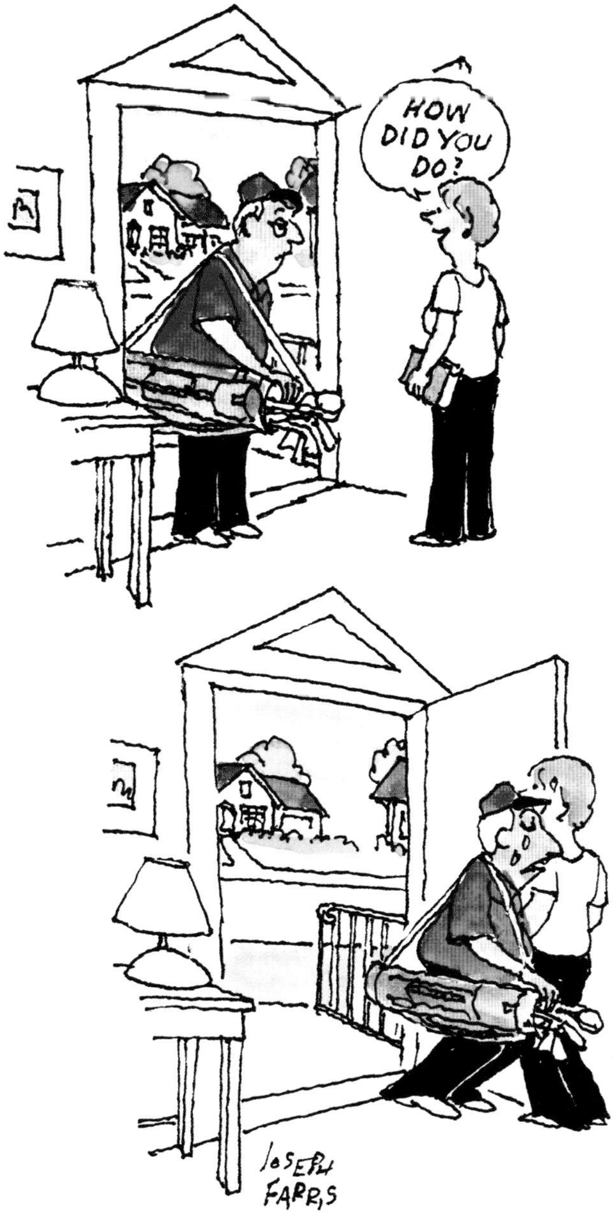
HOW DID YOU DO?
JOSEPH FARRIS

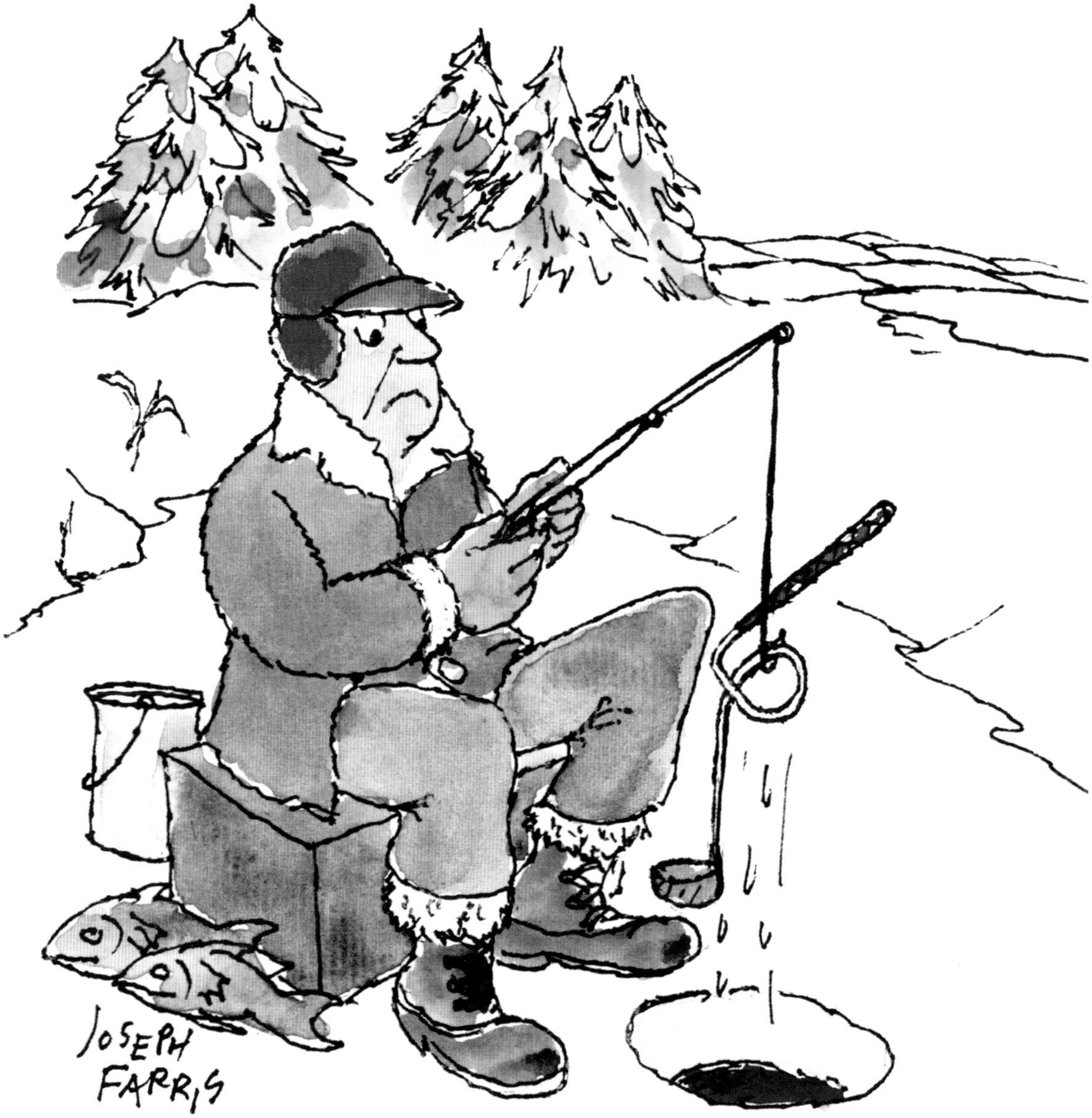
JOSEPH FARRIS

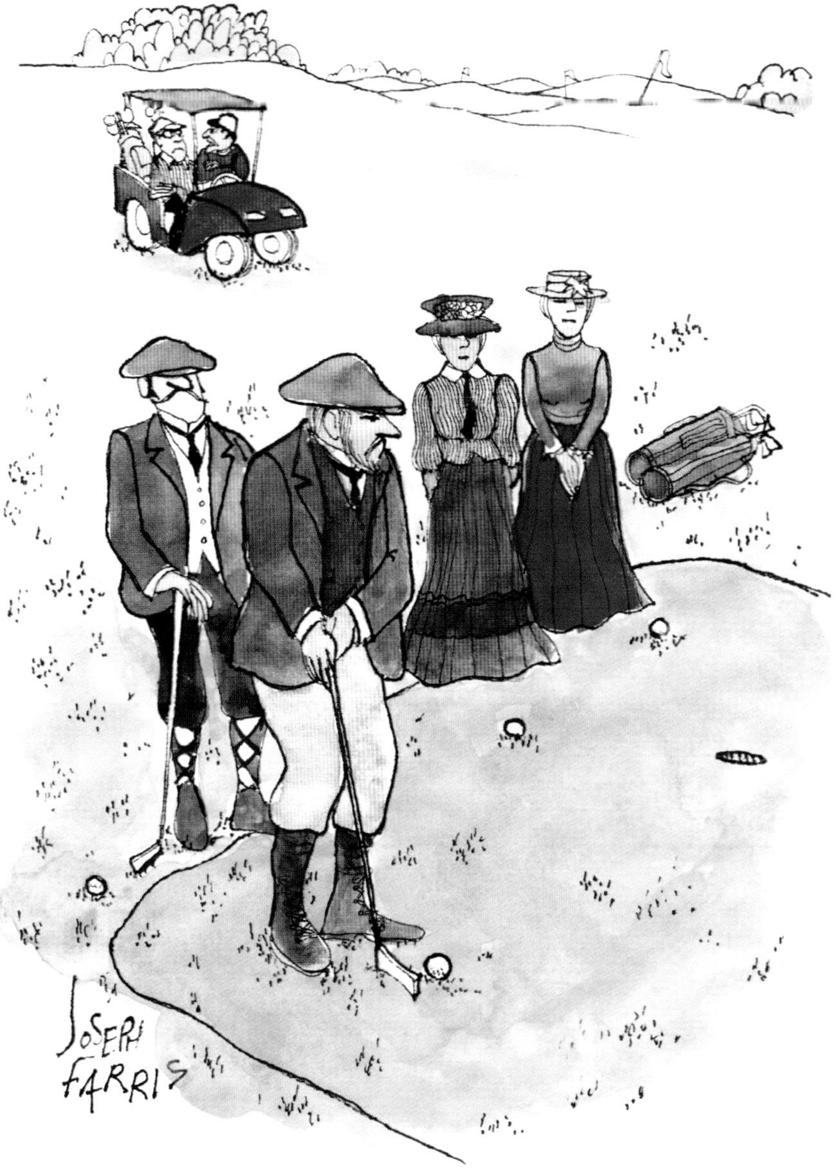
JOSEPH FARRIS

"They're the slowest foursome I've ever seen!"

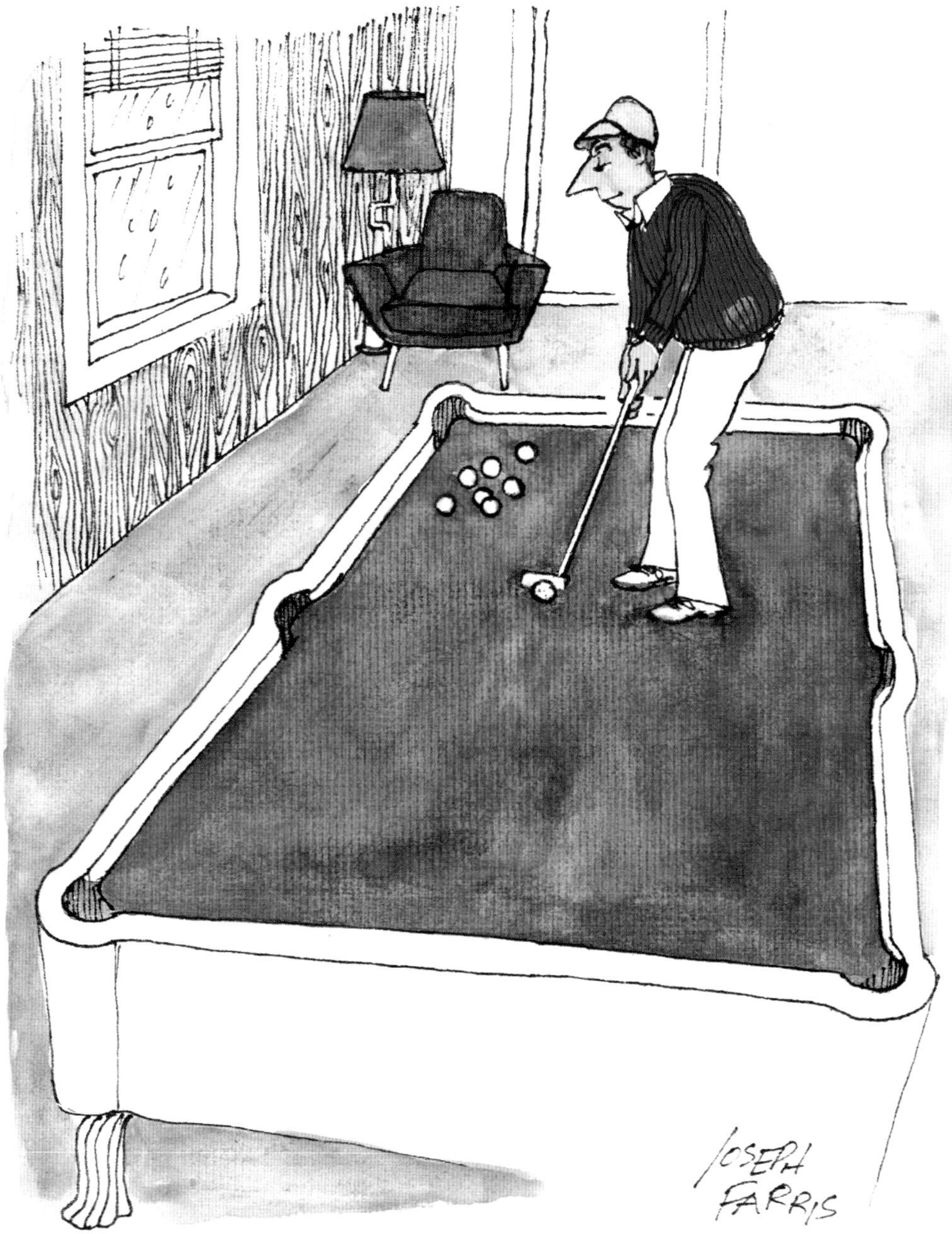
JOSEPH
FARRIS

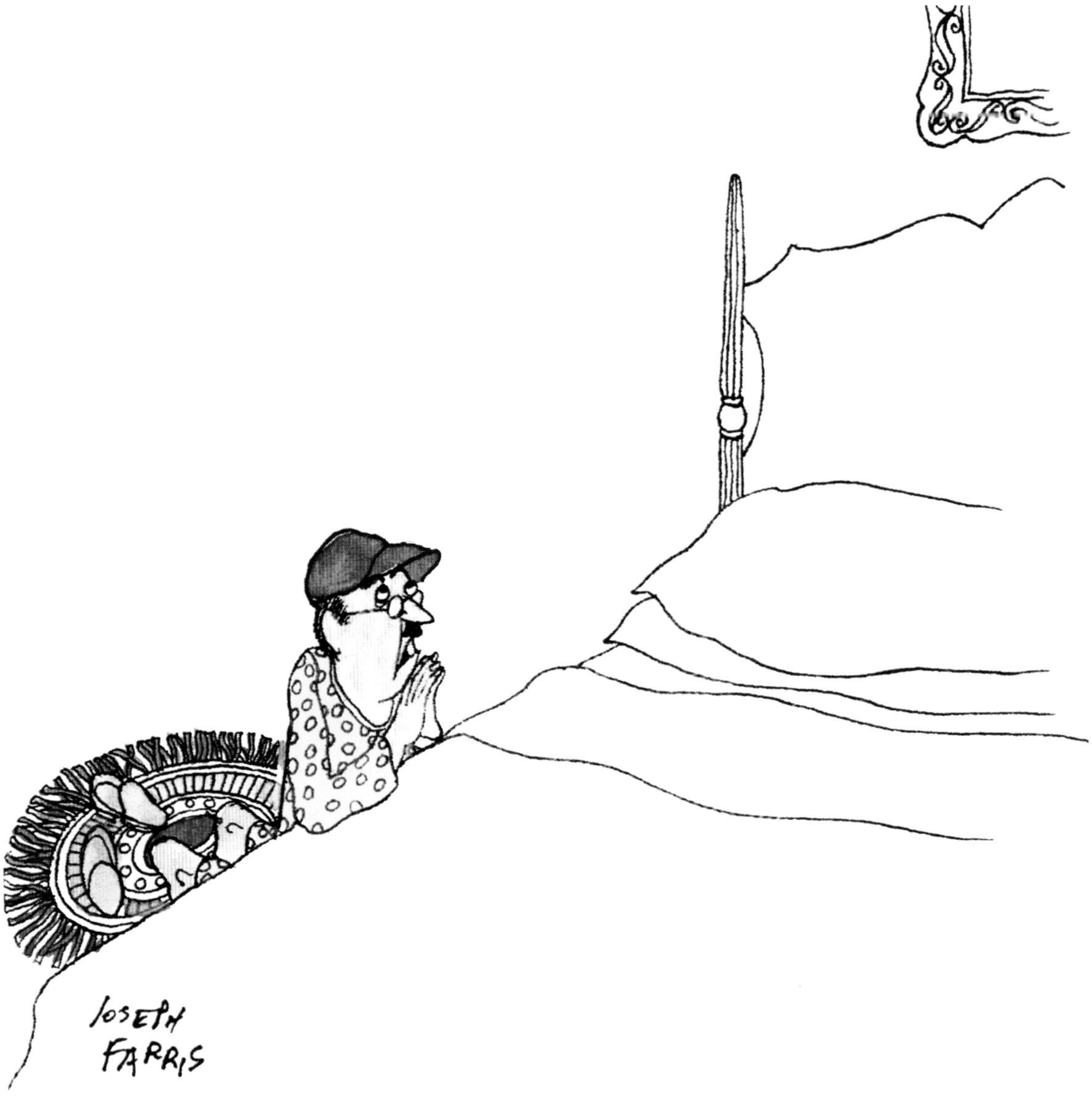
JOSEPH FARRIS

"I've been golfing for over seventy years. Before it's too late, may I have a hole-in-one?

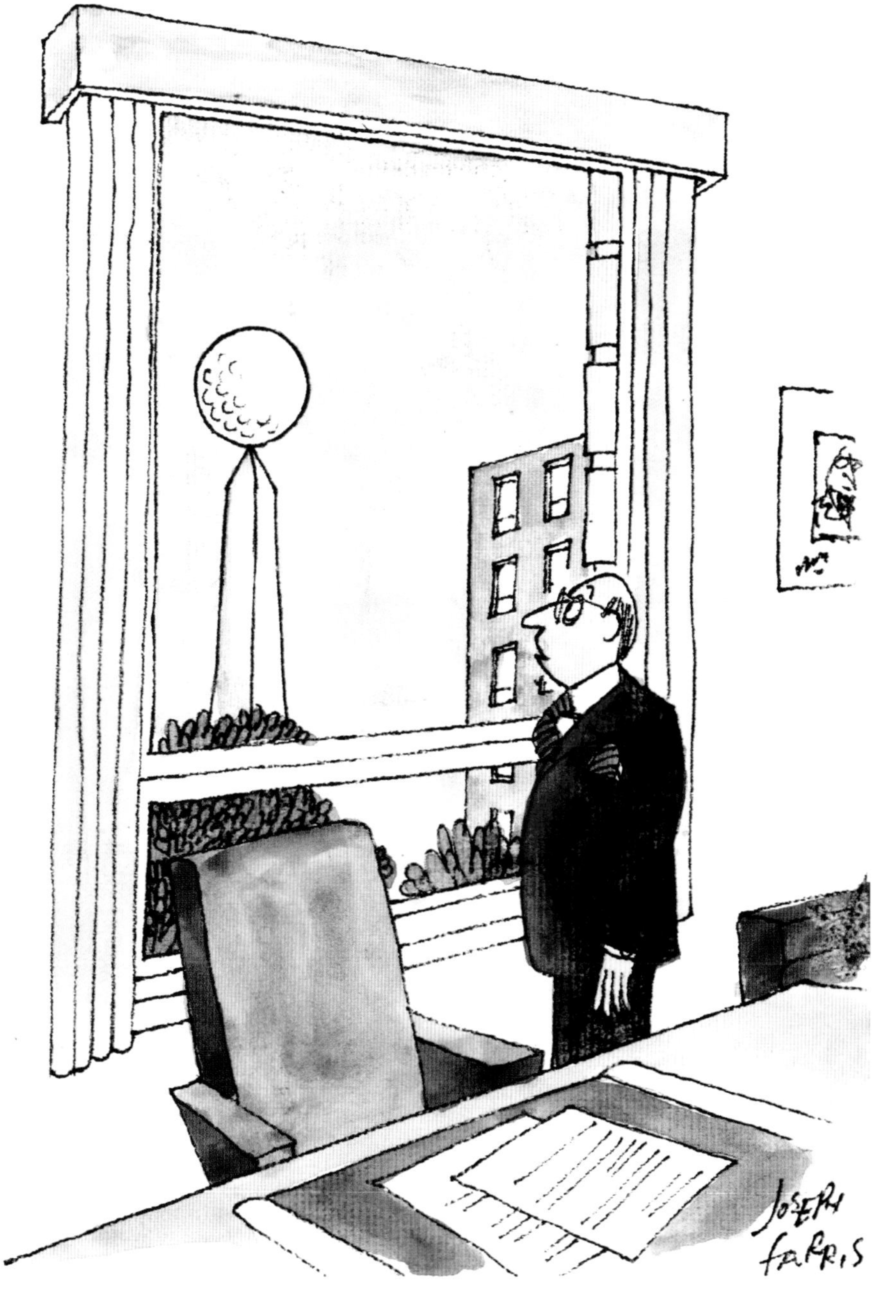
JOSEPH
FARRIS

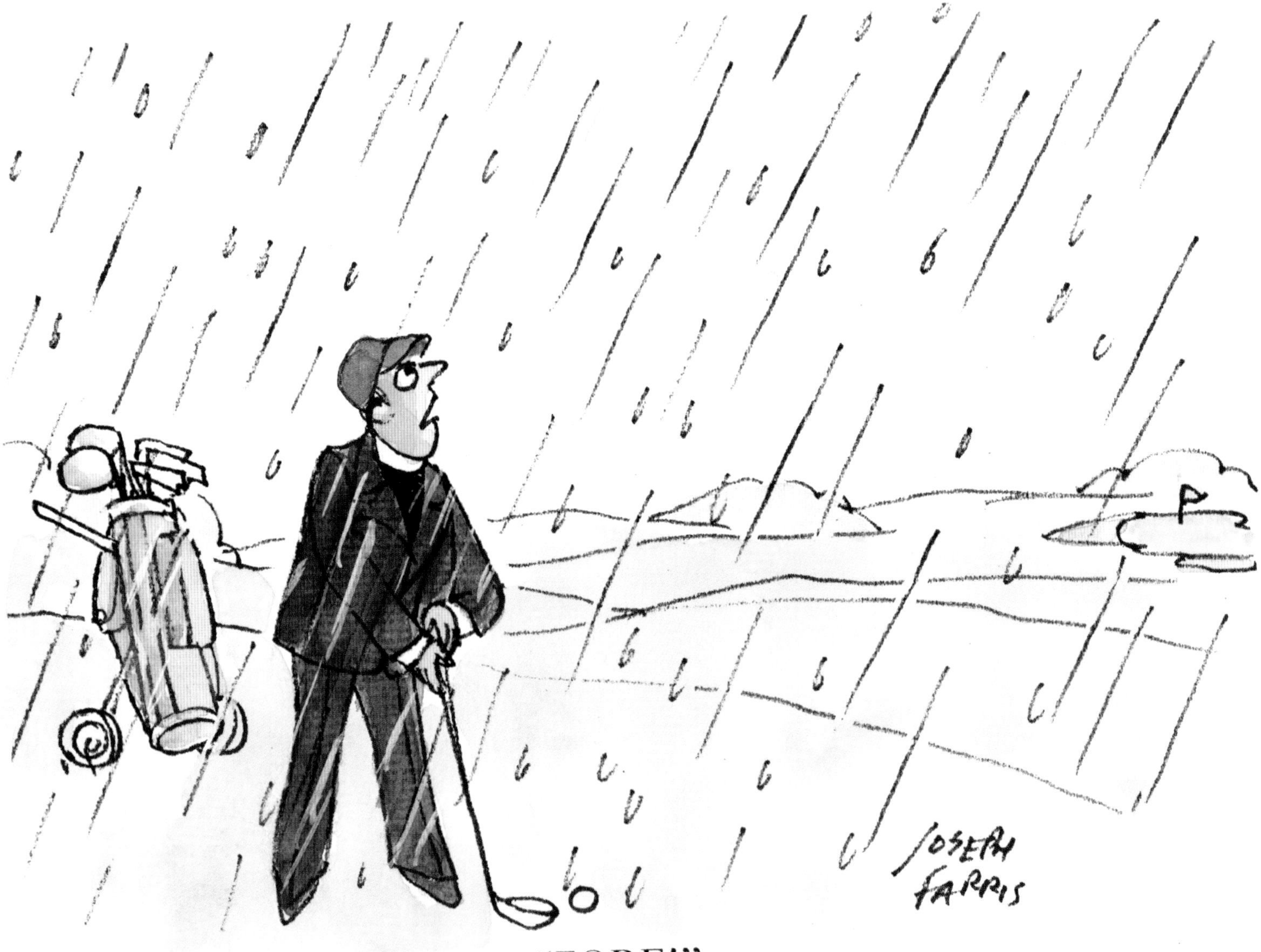
JOSEPH
FARRIS

"FORE!"

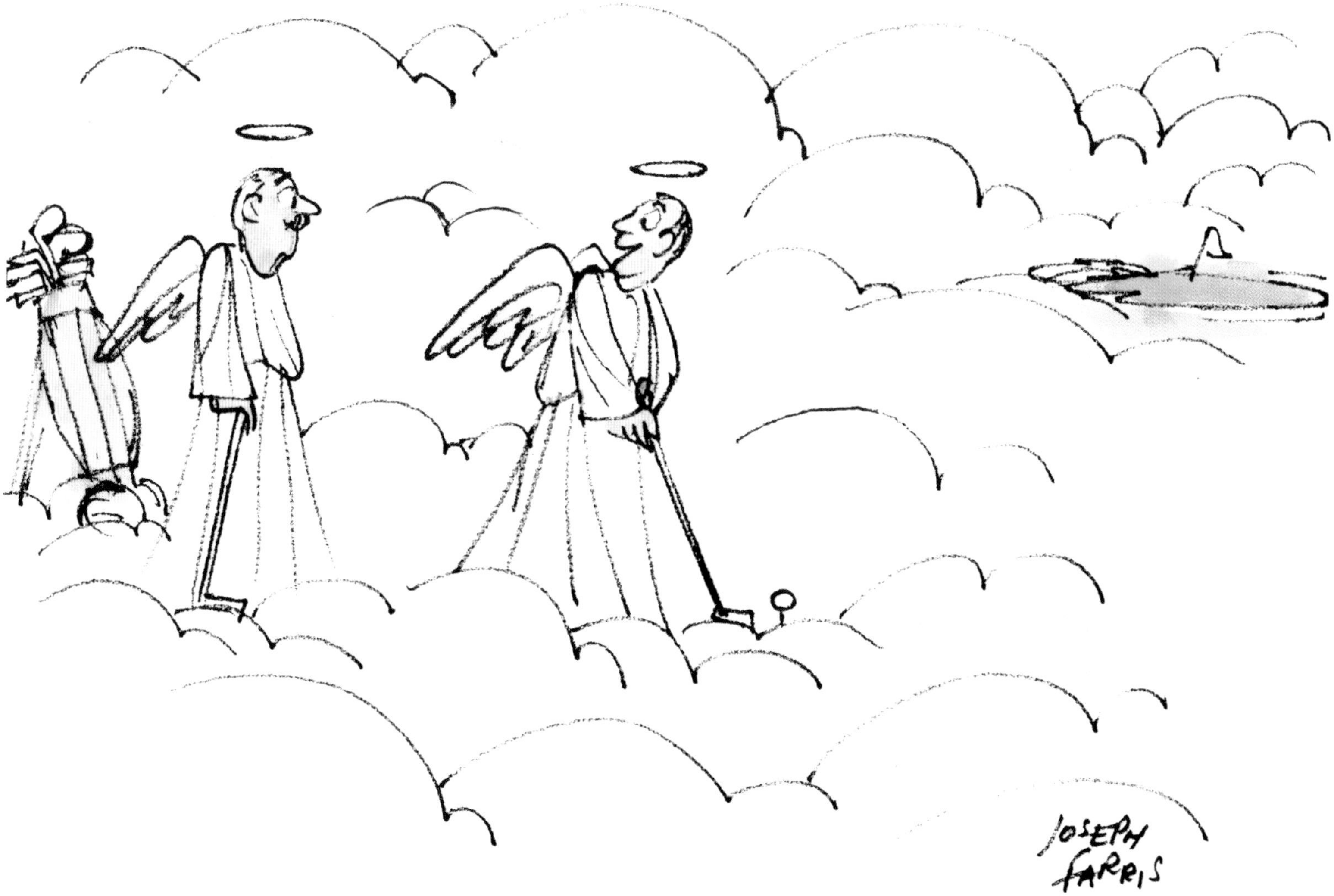
JOSEPH FARRIS

“This really *is* heaven!”

"I deem you first seed."

Joseph Farris

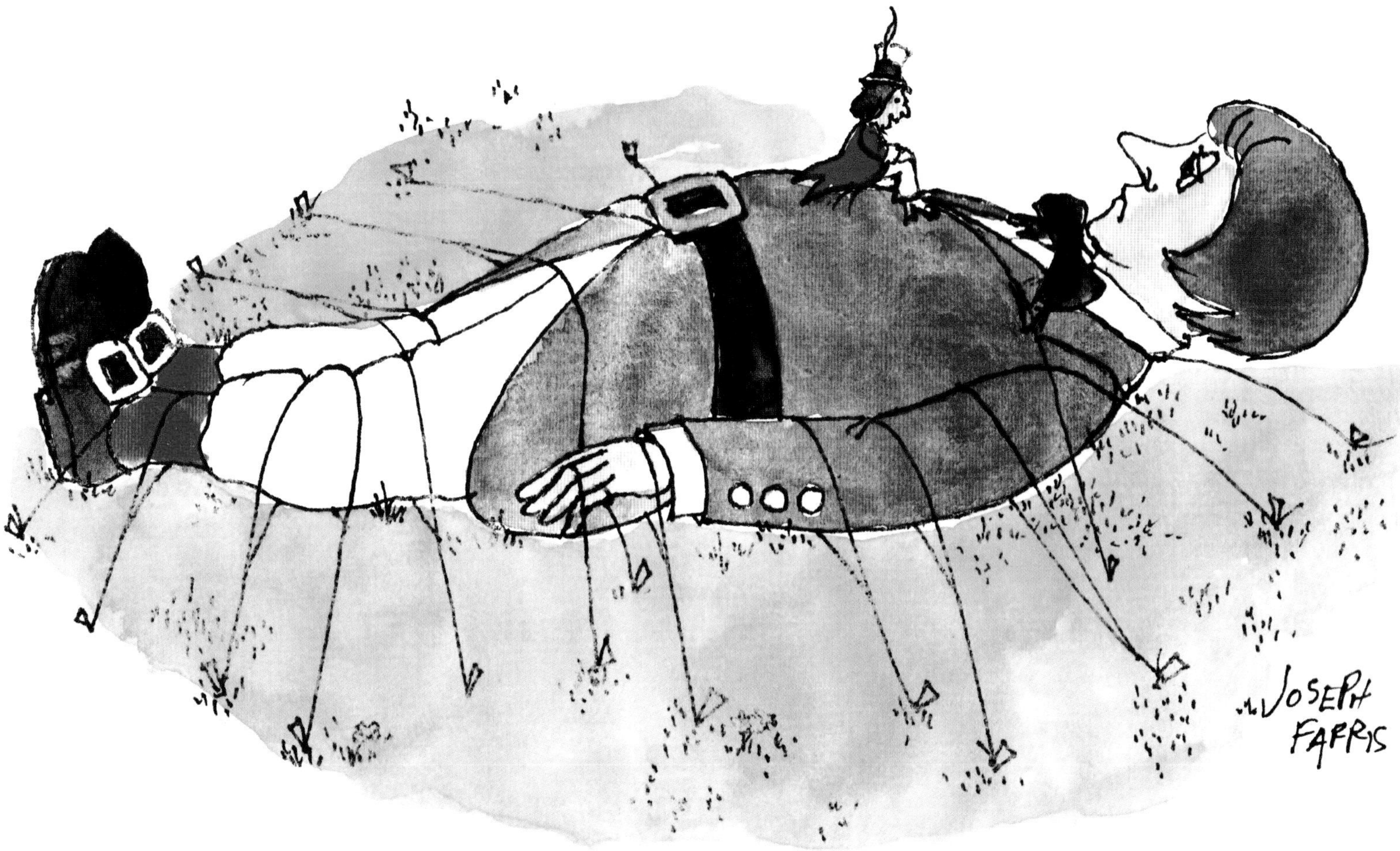
JOSEPH FARRIS

"I'm a golfer's agent, Gulliver. How would you like to train to become a golfer for PGA tours?"

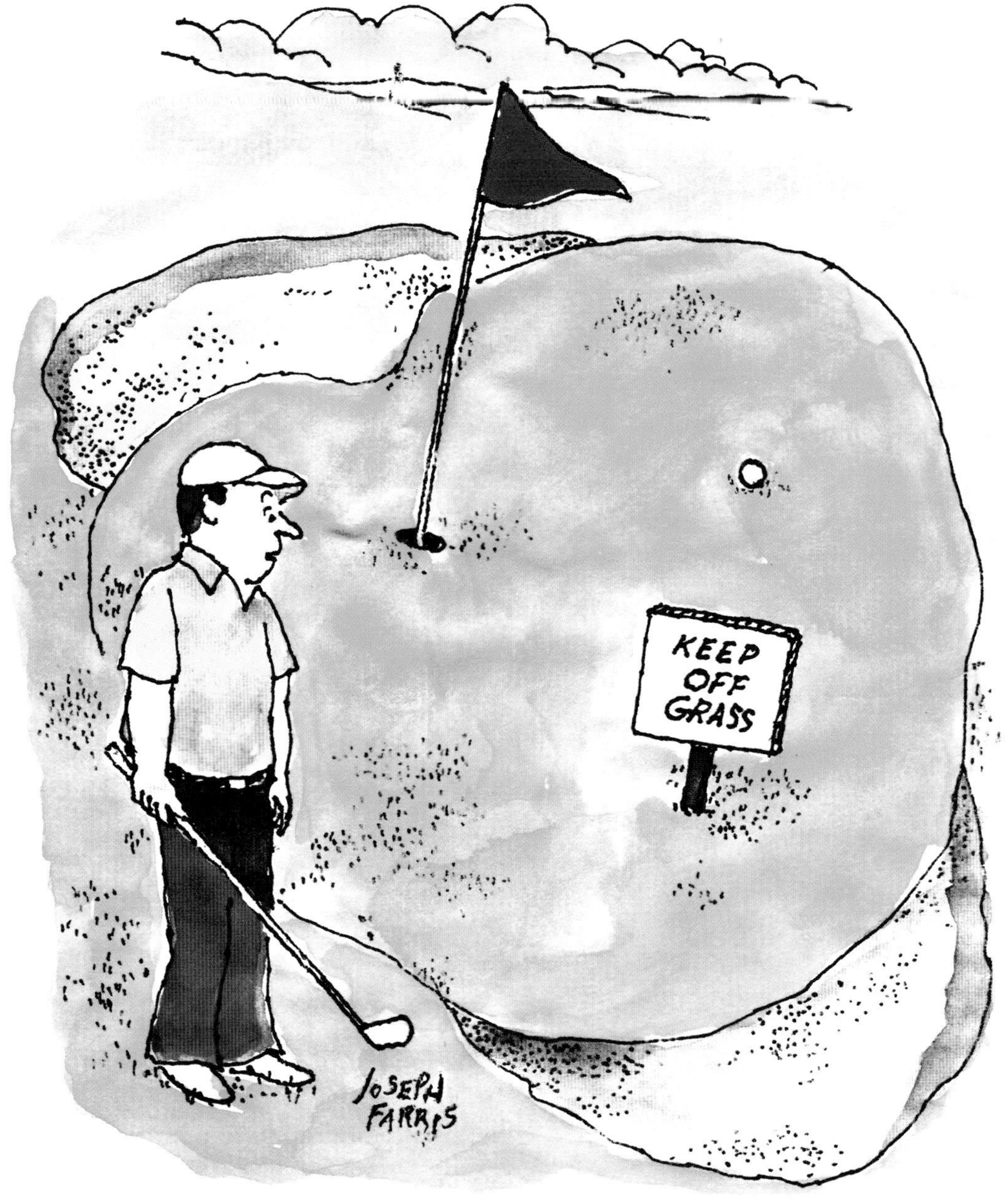
KEEP OFF GRASS
JOSEPH FARRIS

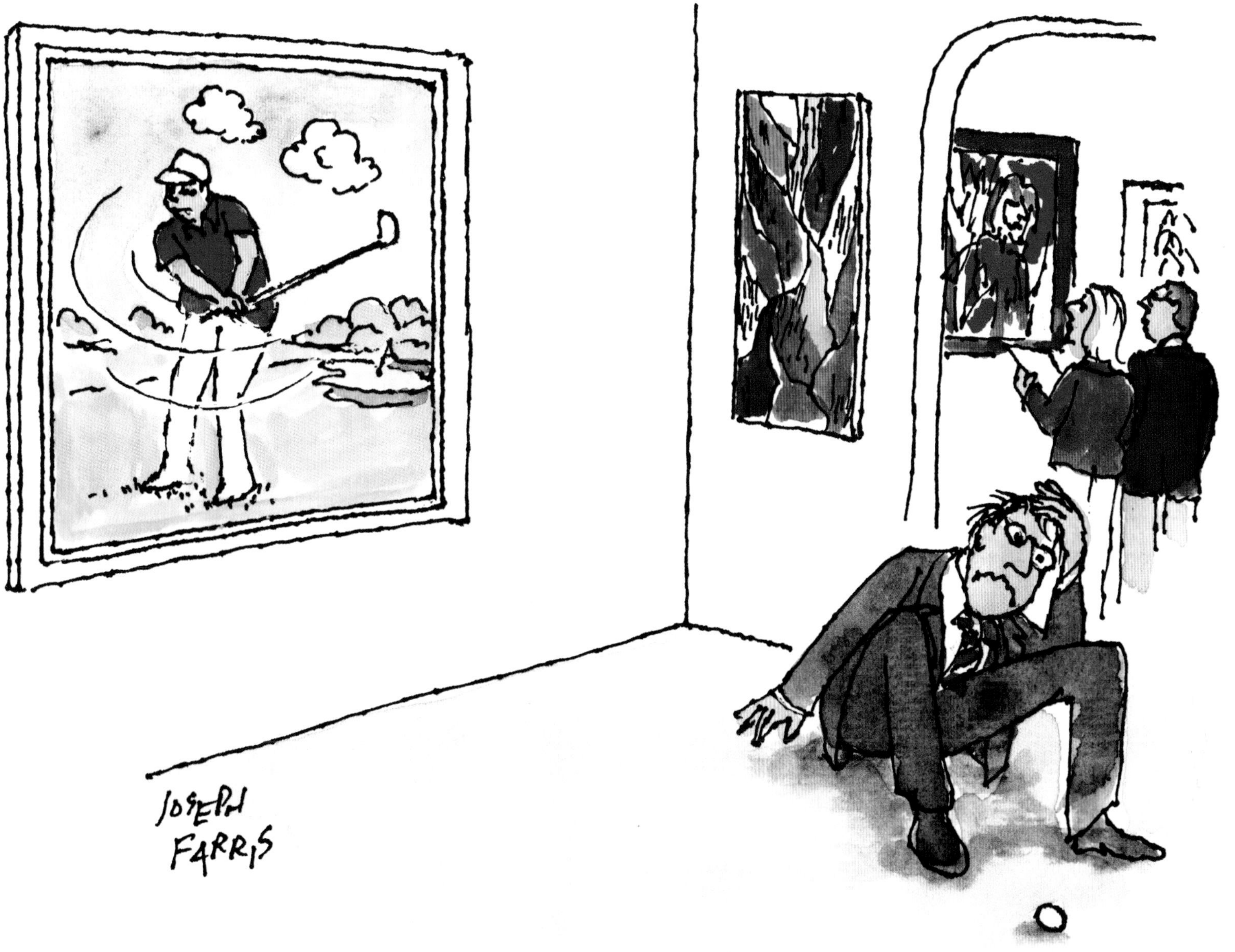
JOSEPH
FARRIS

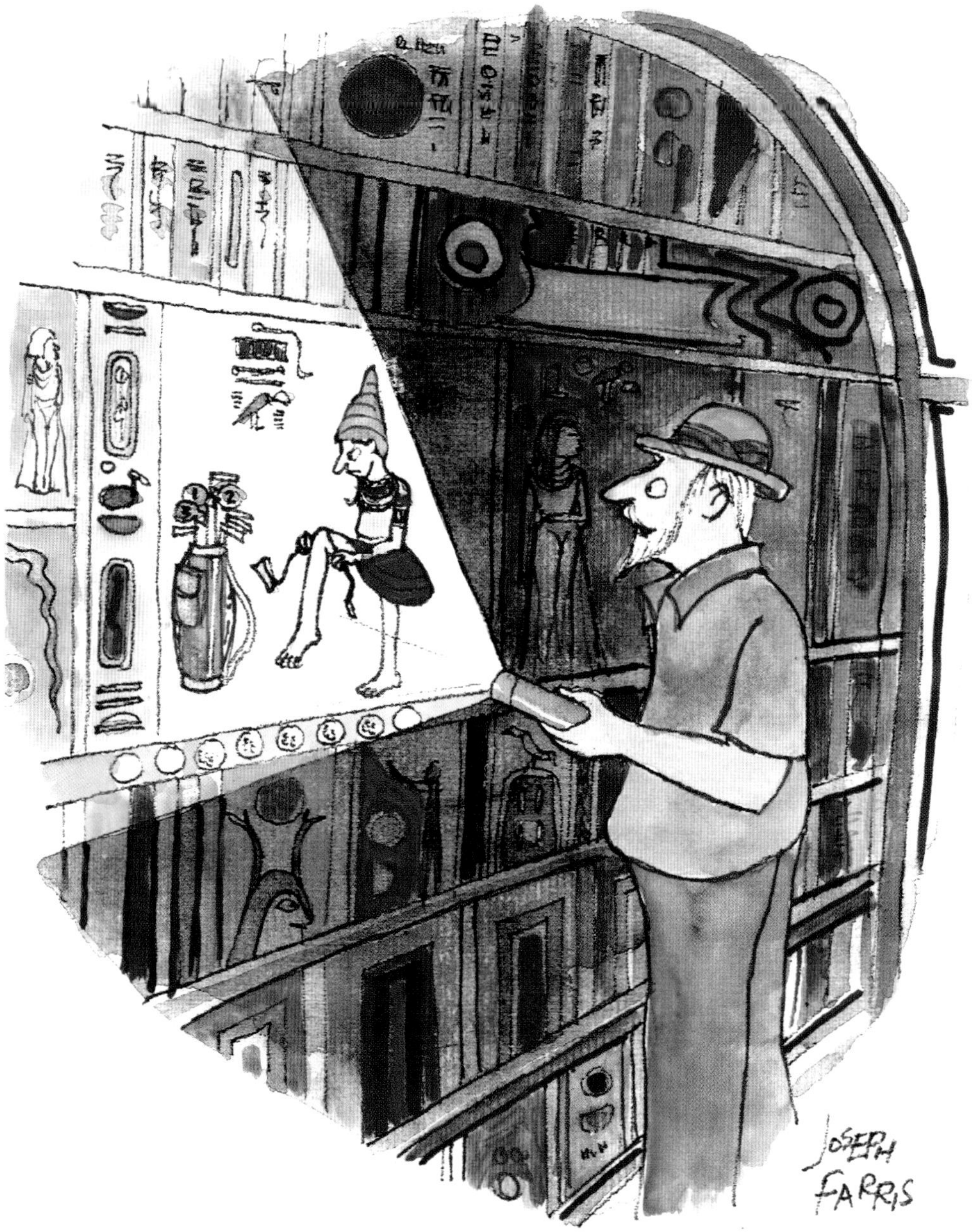
JOSEPH
FARRIS

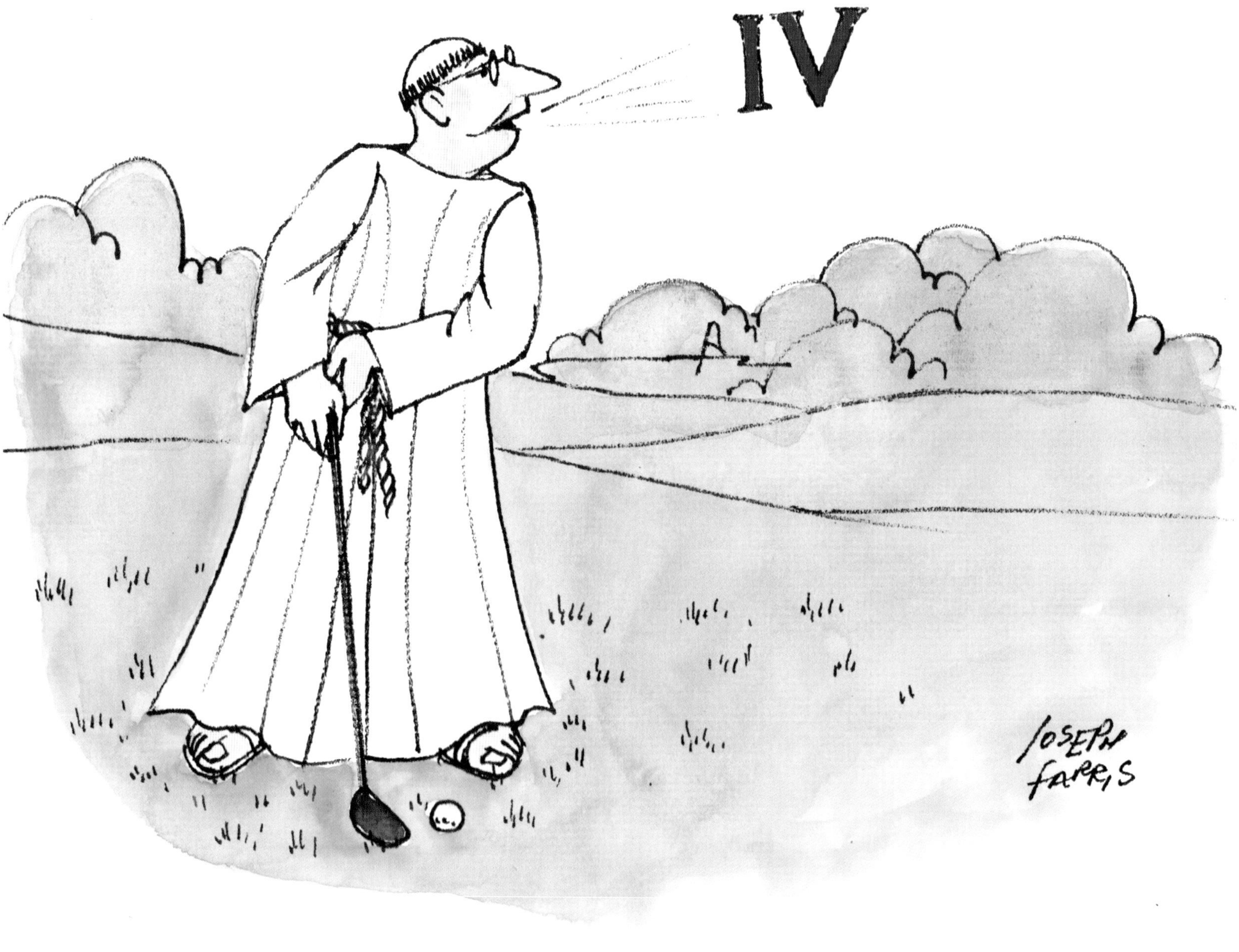
IV
JOSEPH FARRIS

"Let's hit the links."

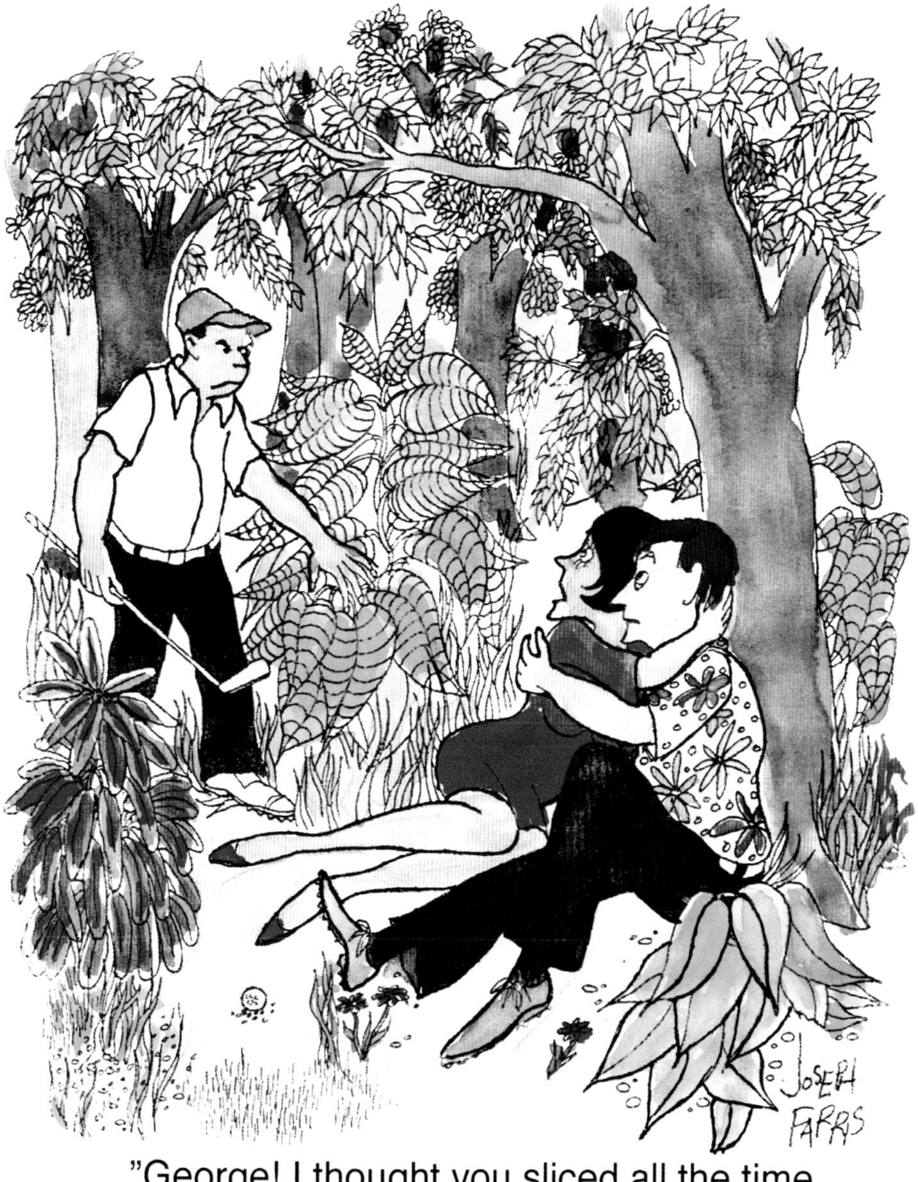
JOSEPH FARRIS

"George! I thought you sliced all the time.
That was a *hook*!"

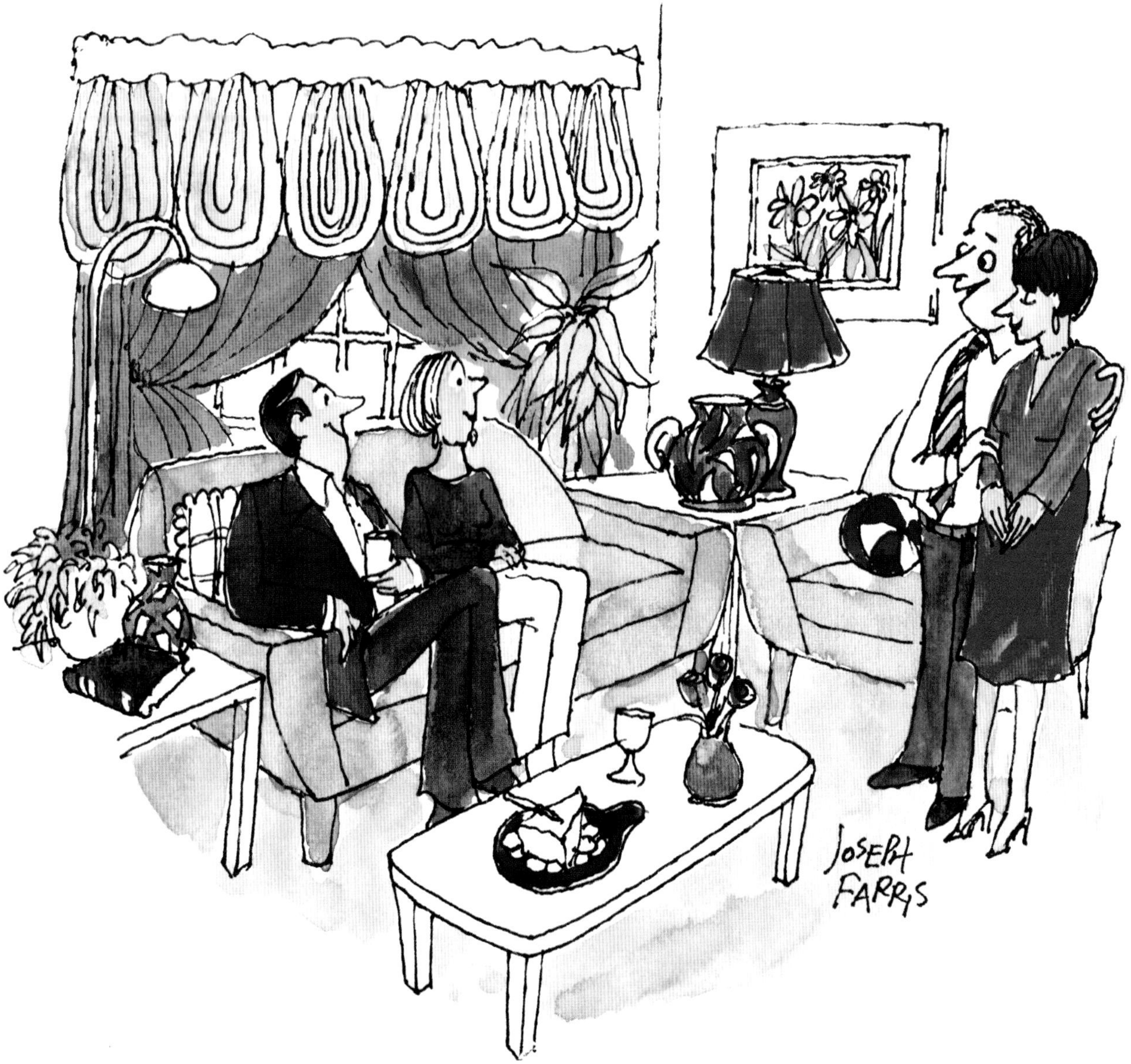
JOSEPH FARRIS

"We met in a bunker on the 9th hole."

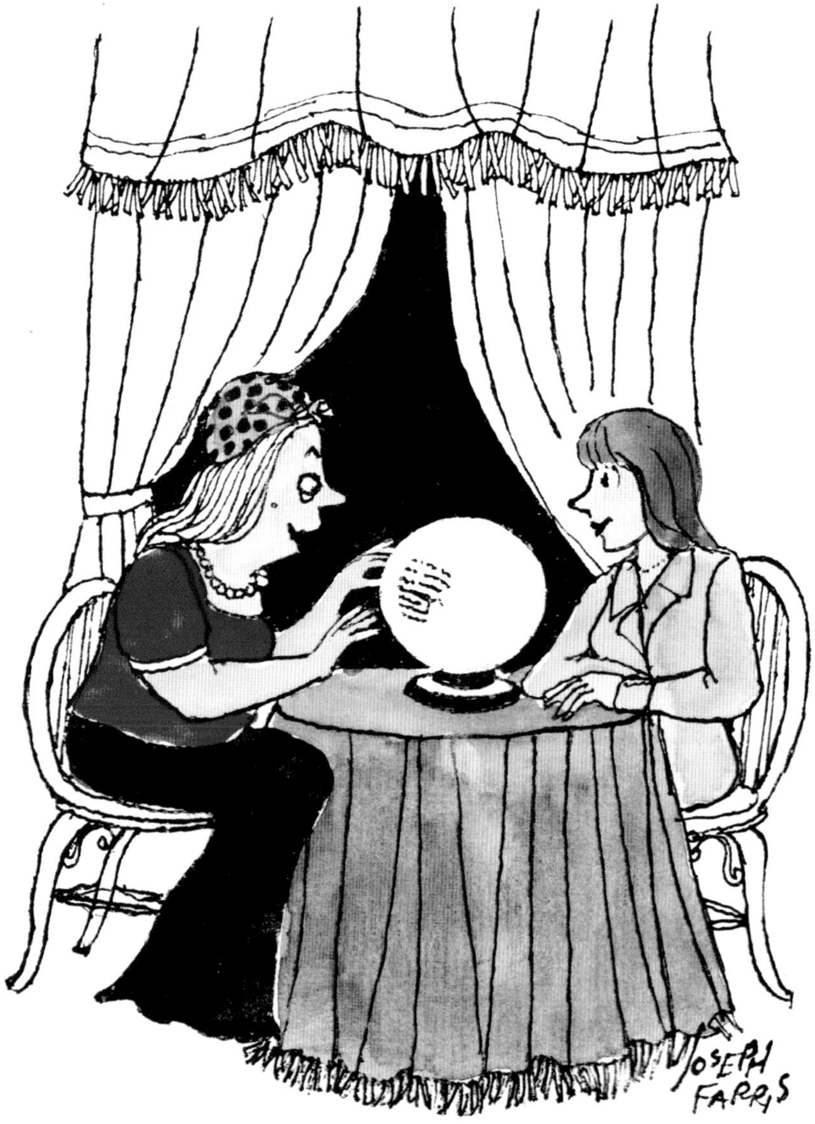
JOSEPH FARRIS

"Good news. You're going to make a hole-in-one on the 14th hole!"

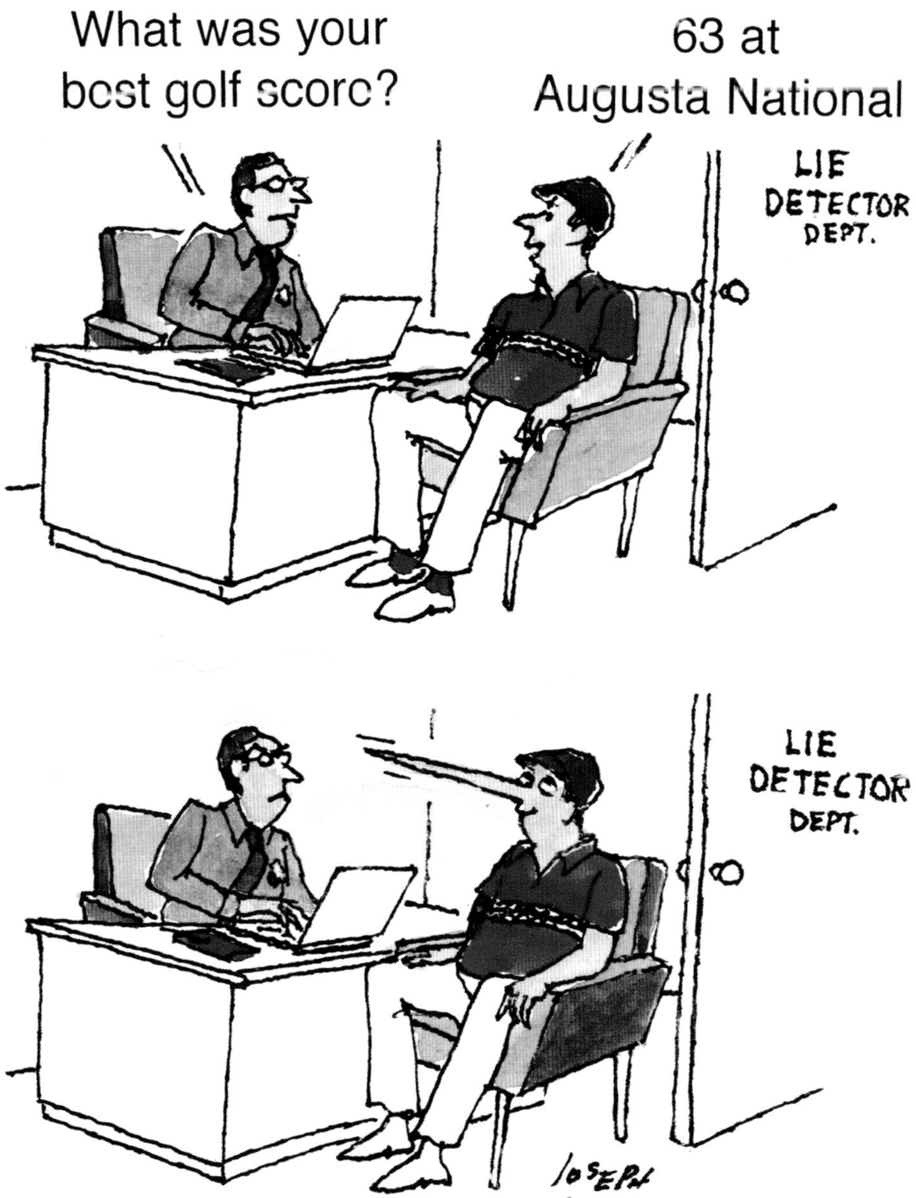
What was your best golf score?
63 at Augusta National
LIE DETECTOR DEPT.
LIE DETECTOR DEPT.
JOSEPH FARRIS

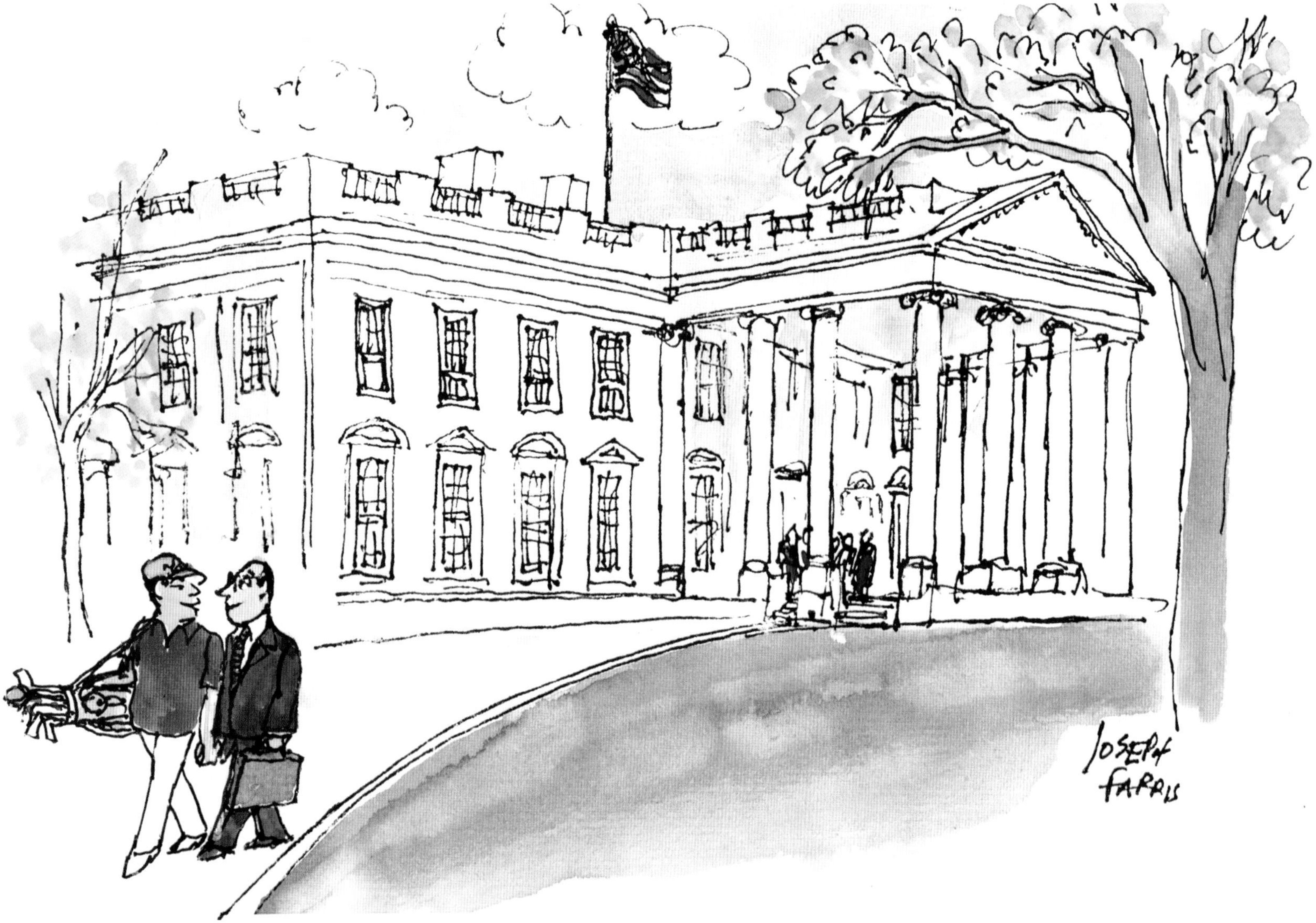
JOSEPH FARRIS

"The President enjoys playing a round with me. I deliberately miss putts so he always beats me."

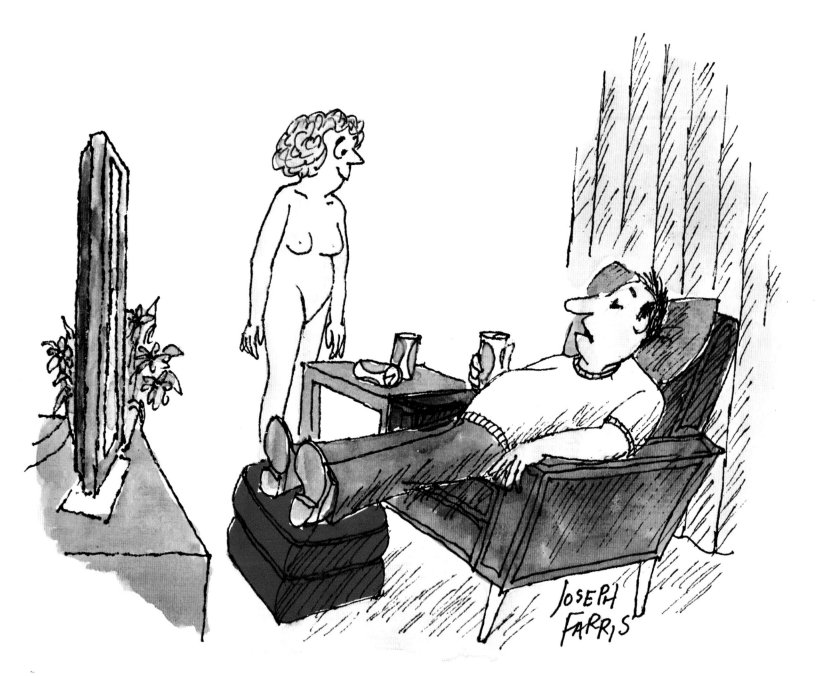

"Not now. I'm watching Tiger Woods.'"

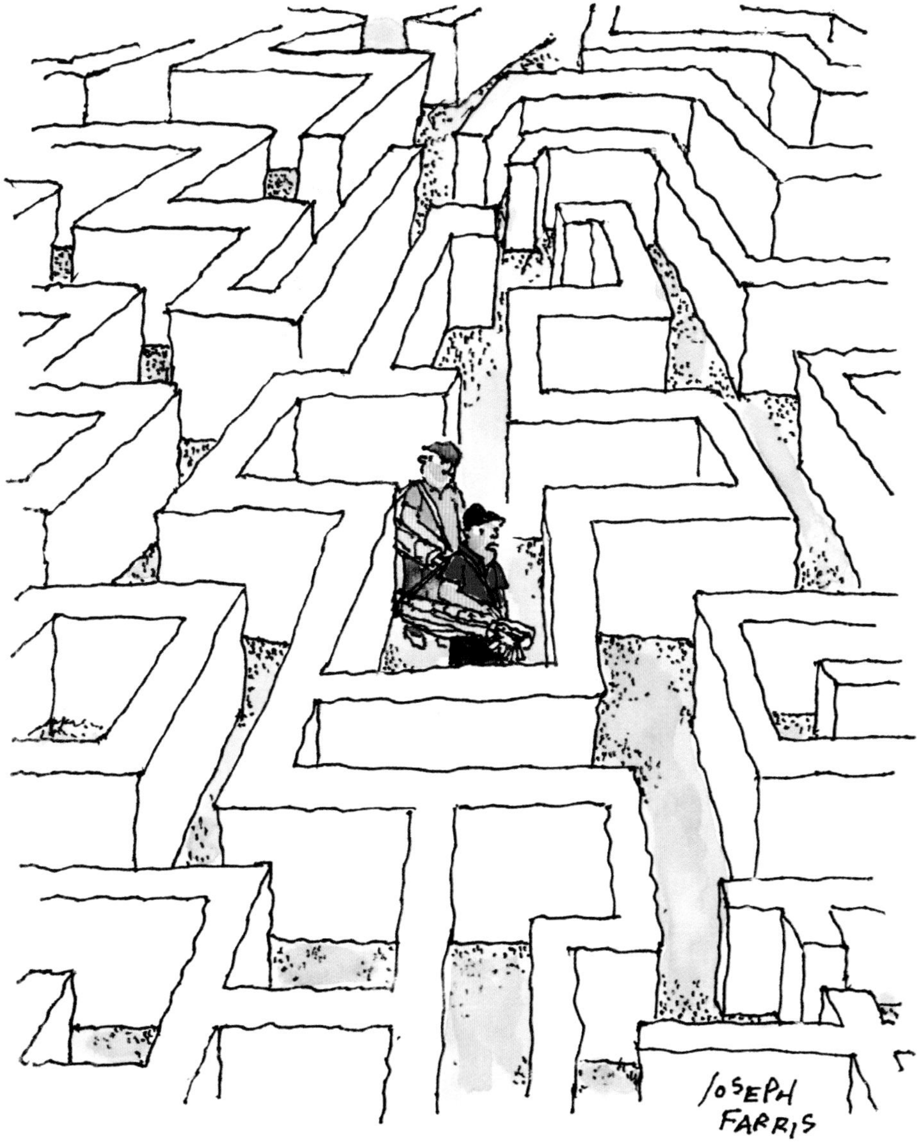
JOSEPH FARRIS

"This is weird! Where in hell is the 13th hole?"

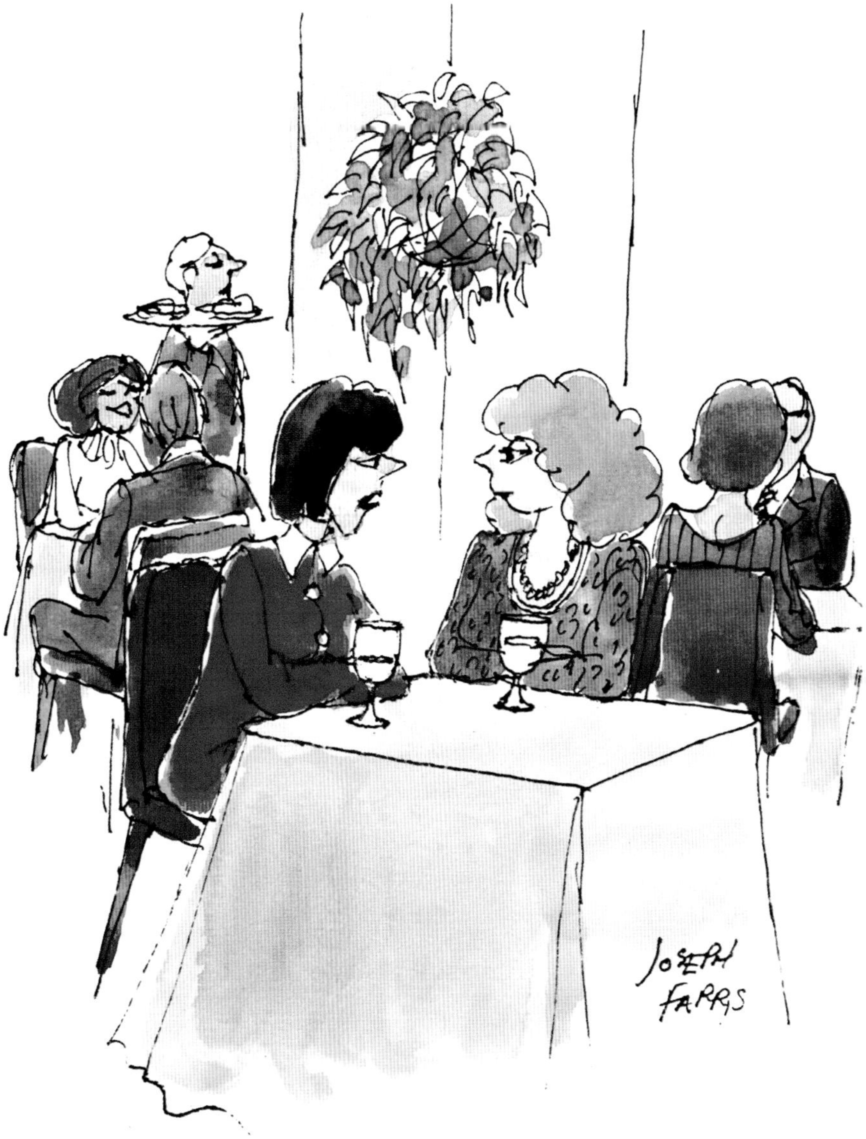
JOSEPH FARRIS

"We met on the first hole and
broke up on the eighteenth."

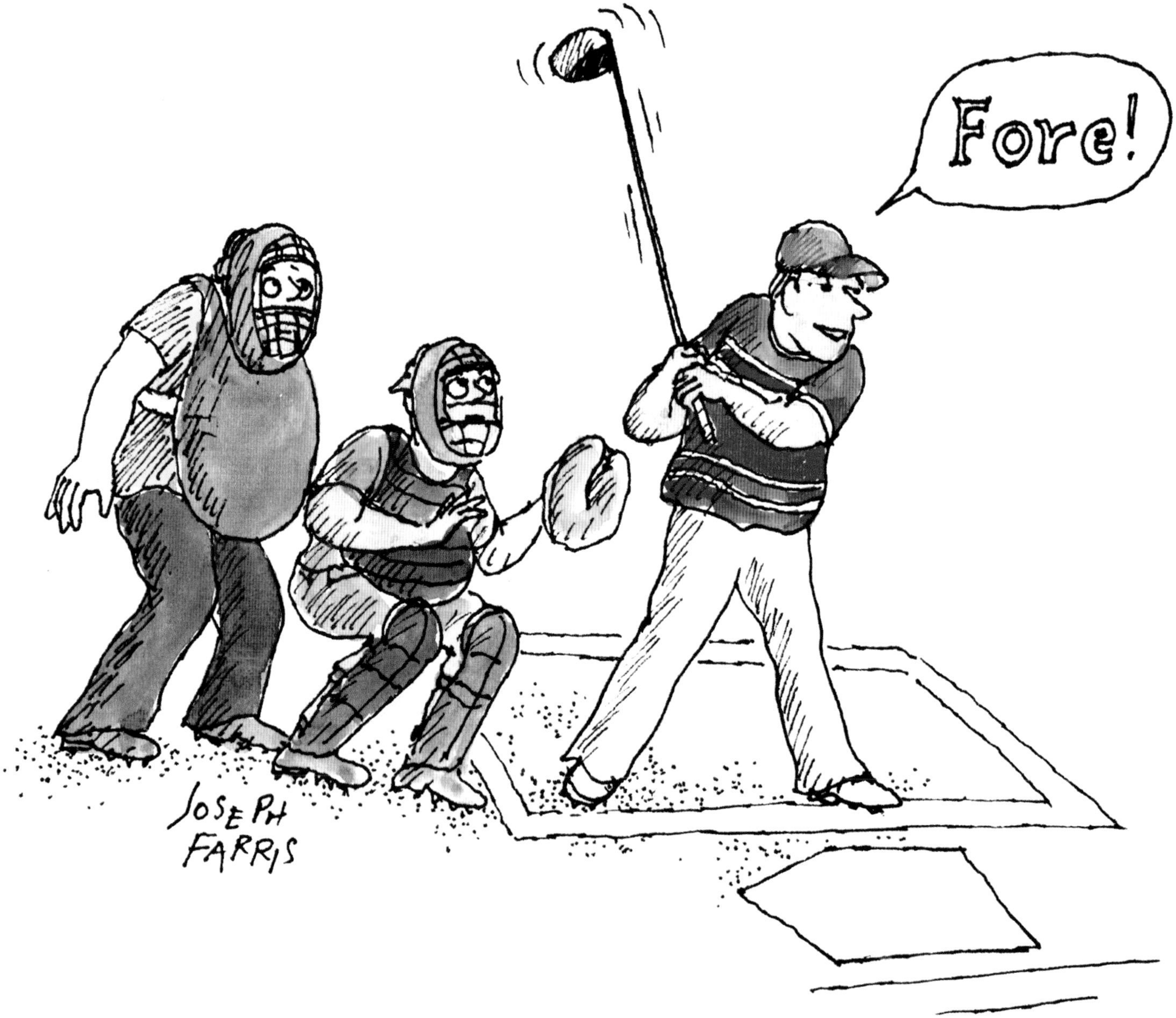
Fore!
JOSEPH FARRIS

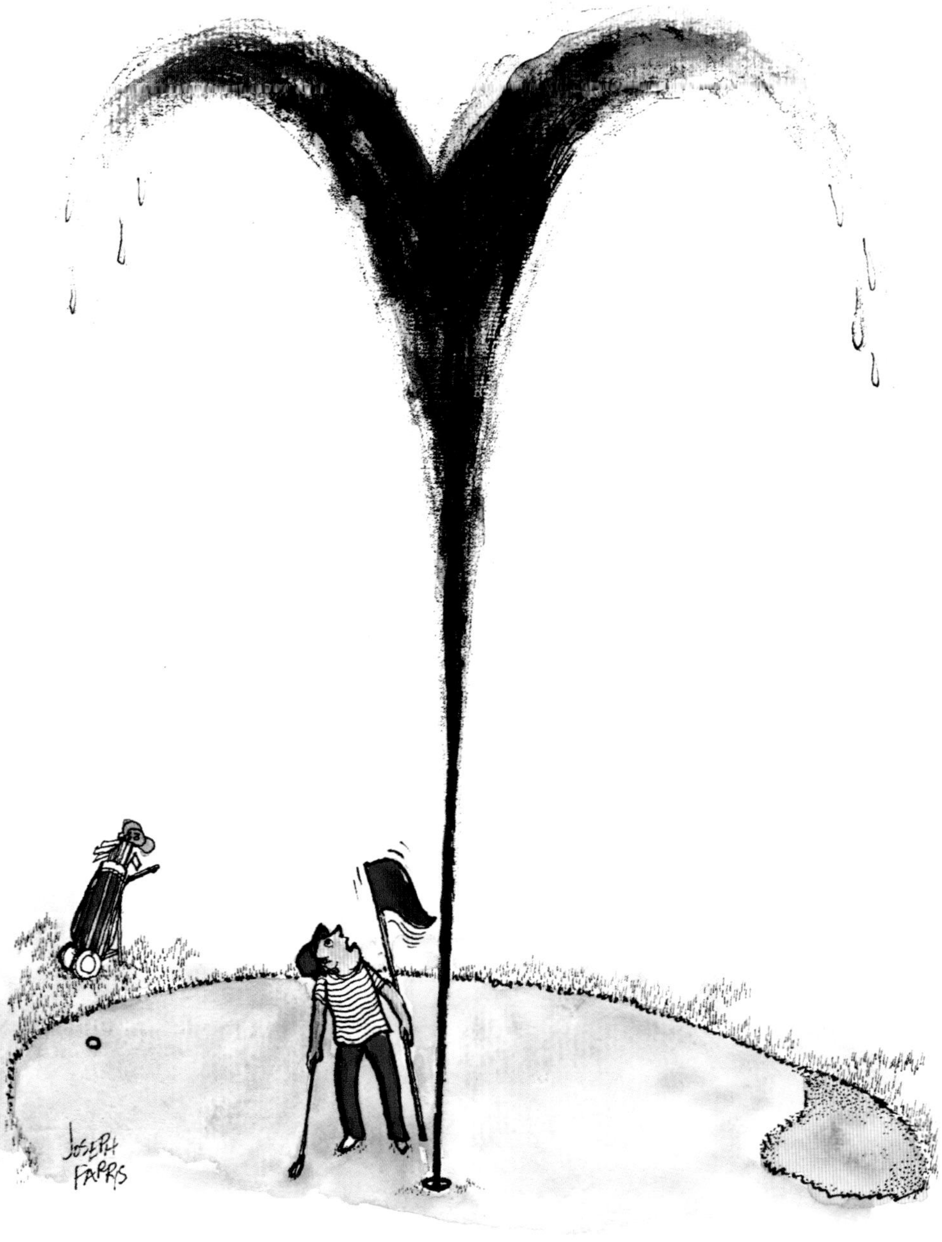
JOSEPH FARRIS

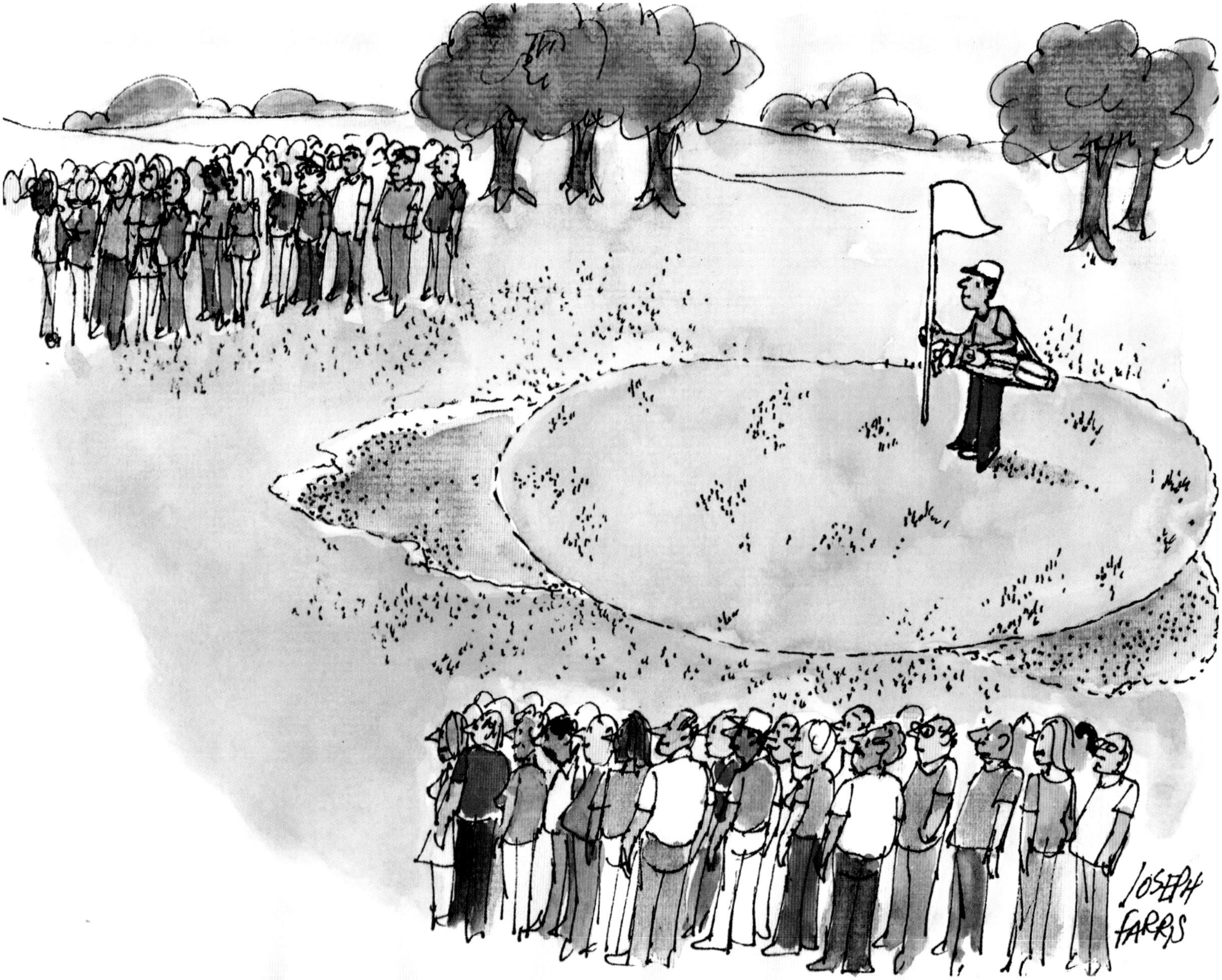
JOSEPH
FARRIS

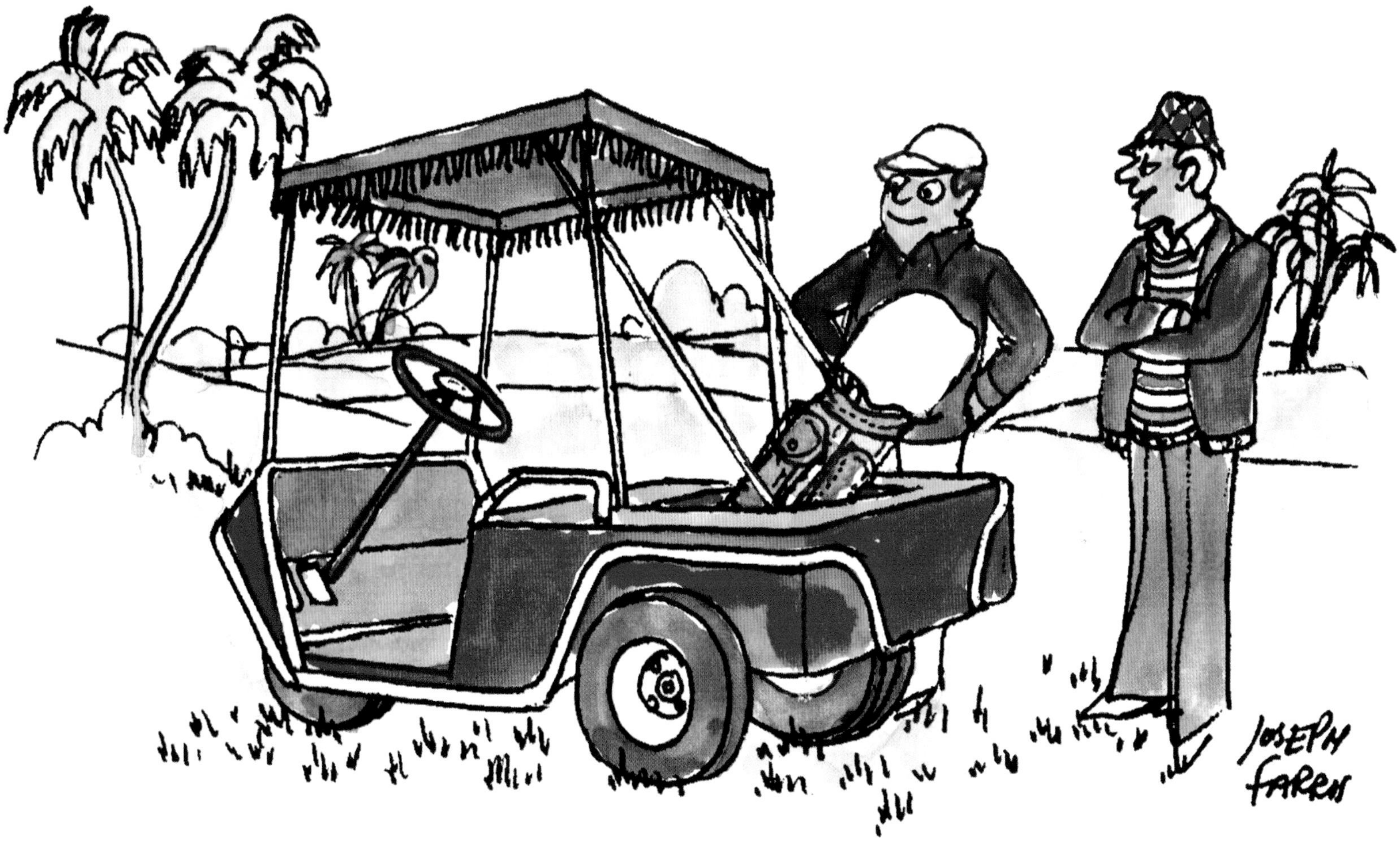
JOSEPH FARRIS

"It's a luxury model and it comes with a guarantee of 48 months or 50,000 holes, whichever comes first."

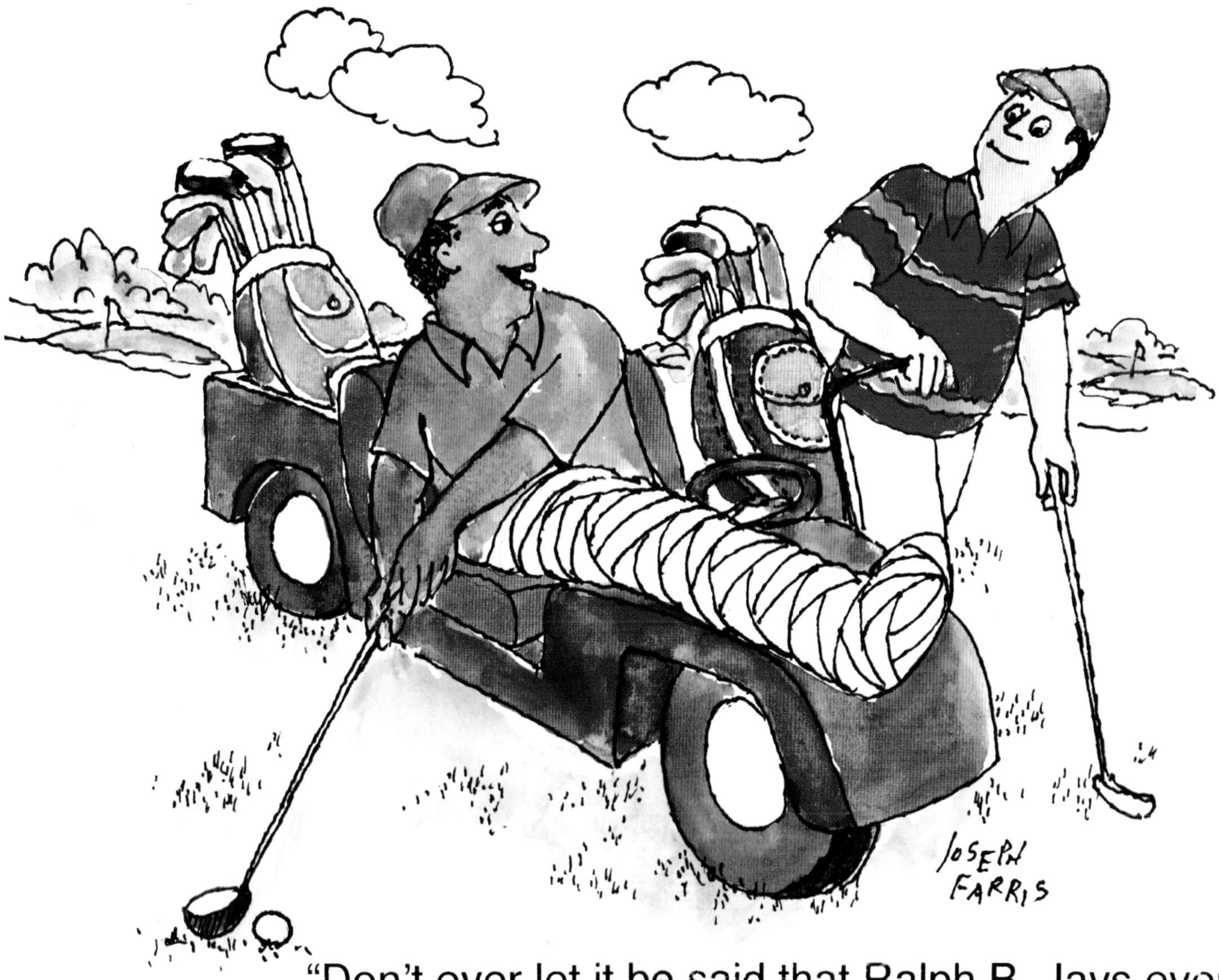
JOSEPH FARRIS

"Don't ever let it be said that Ralph B. Jays ever finked out on a golf date."

"A HOLE IN ONE!"

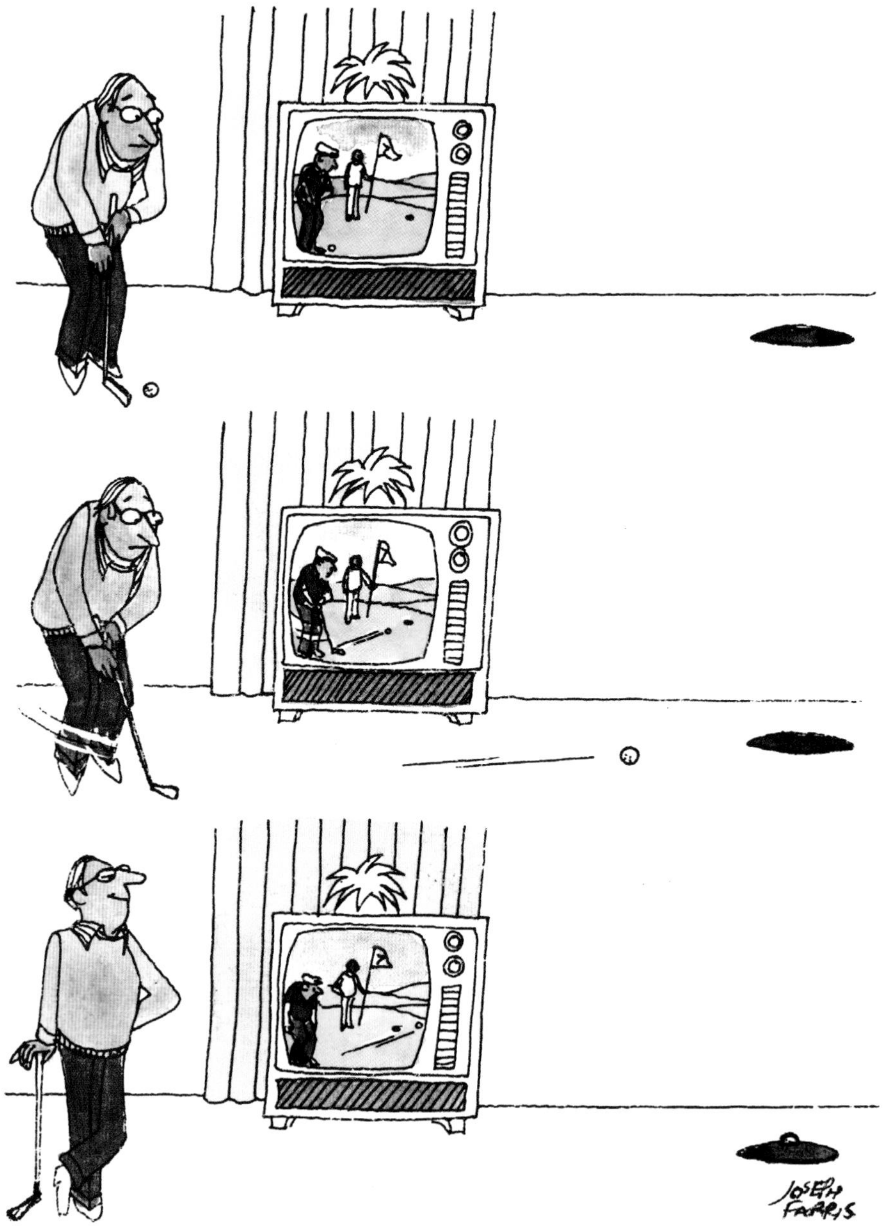
JOSEPH FARRIS

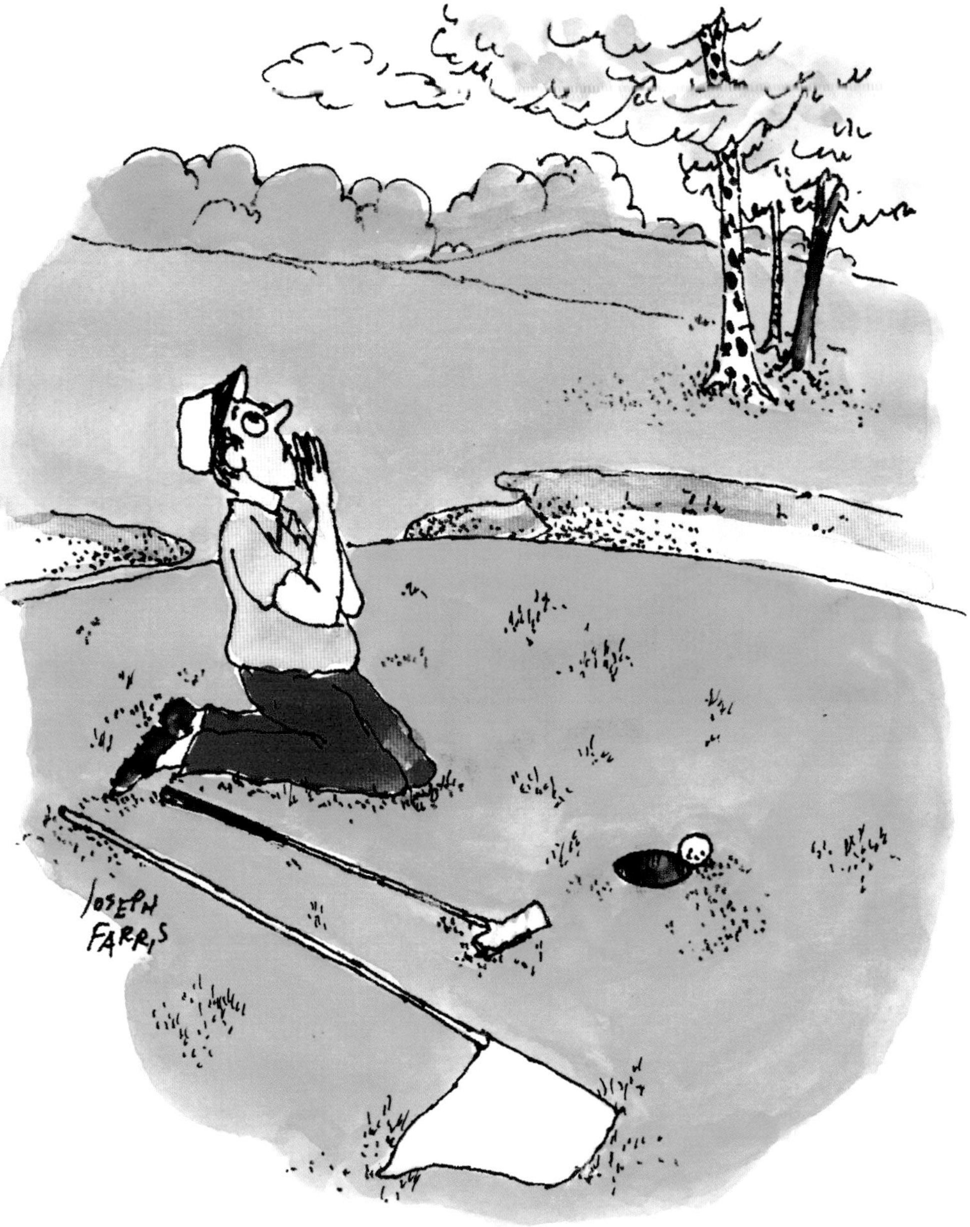
JOSEPH FARRIS

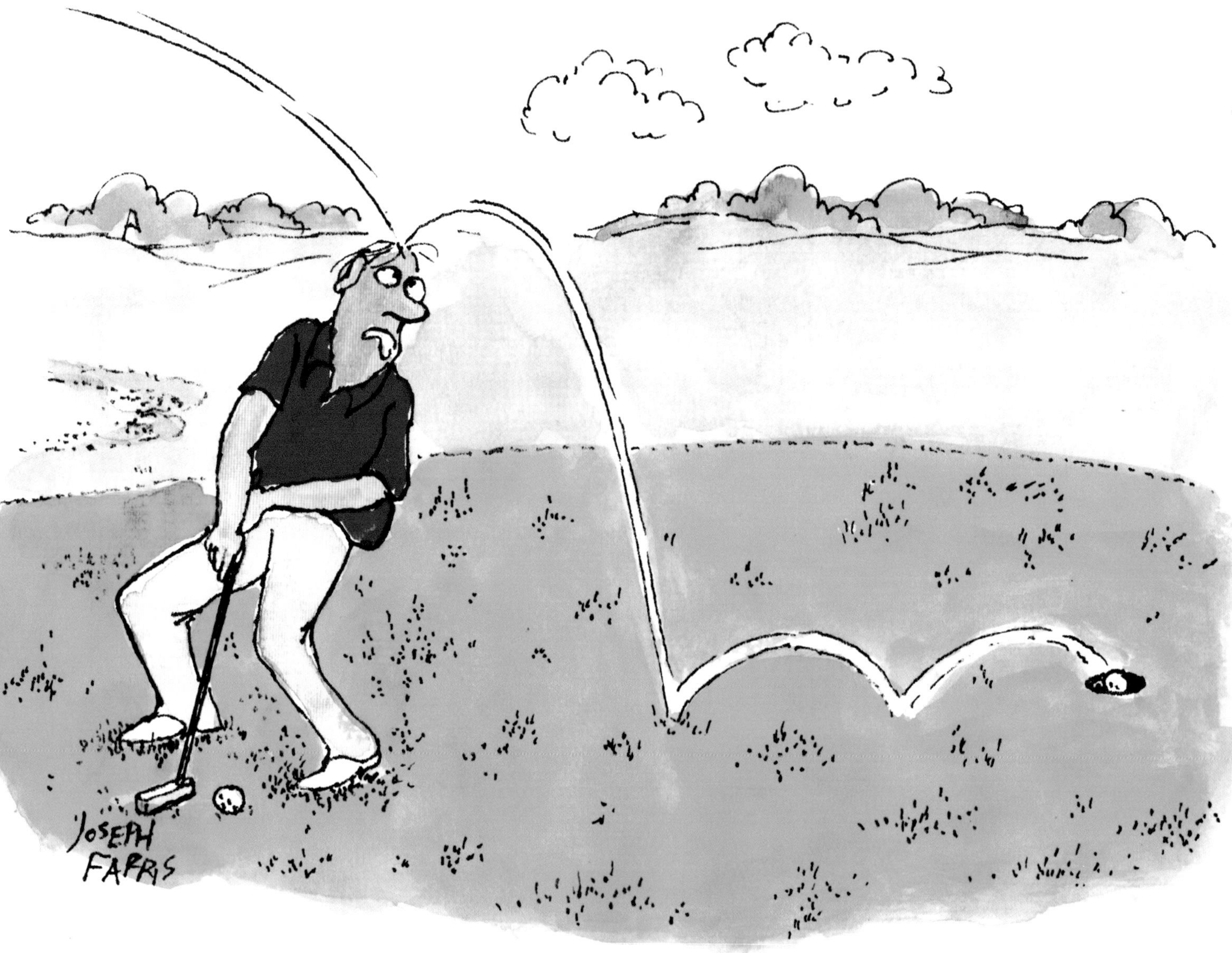
JOSEPH
FARRIS

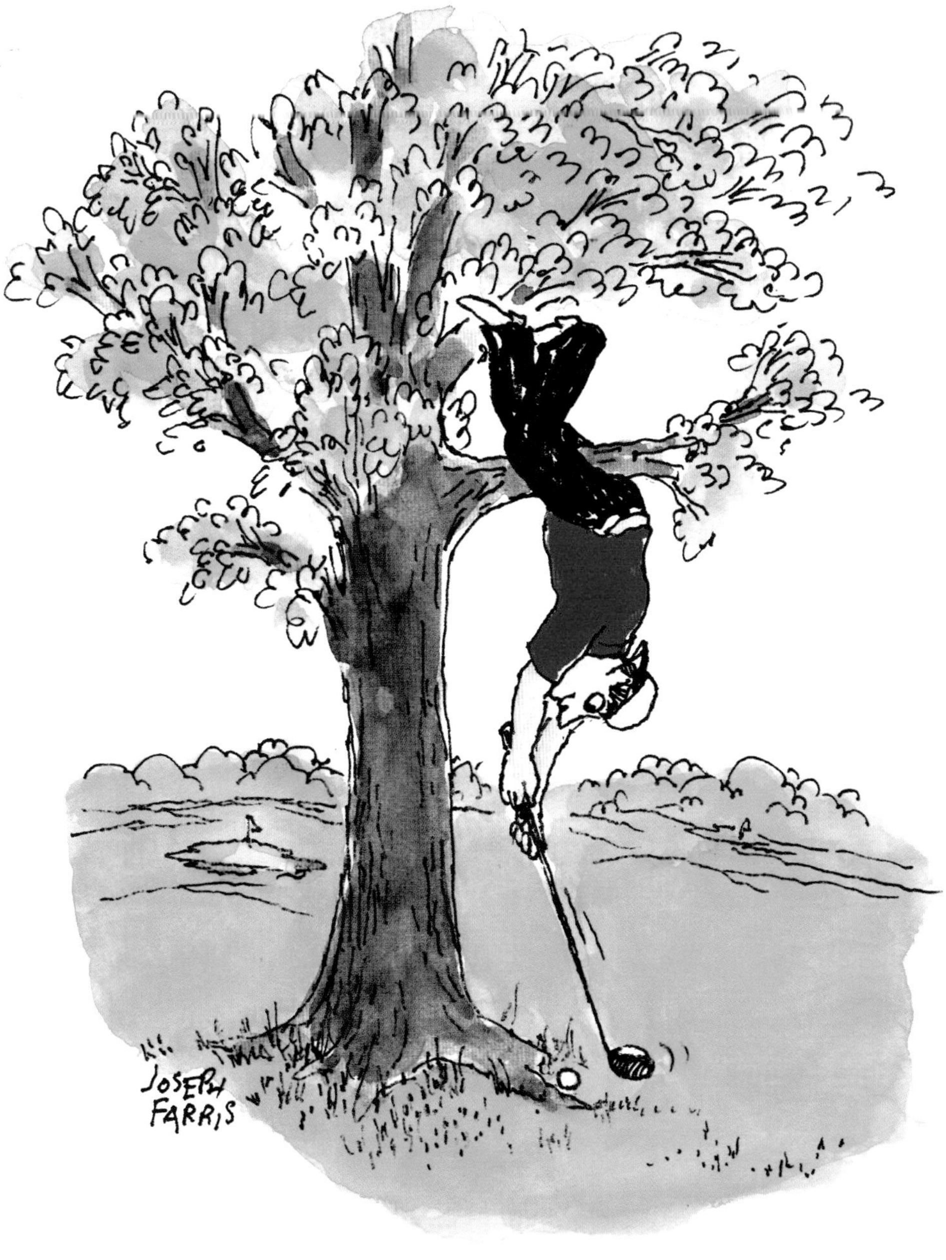
JOSEPH
FARRIS

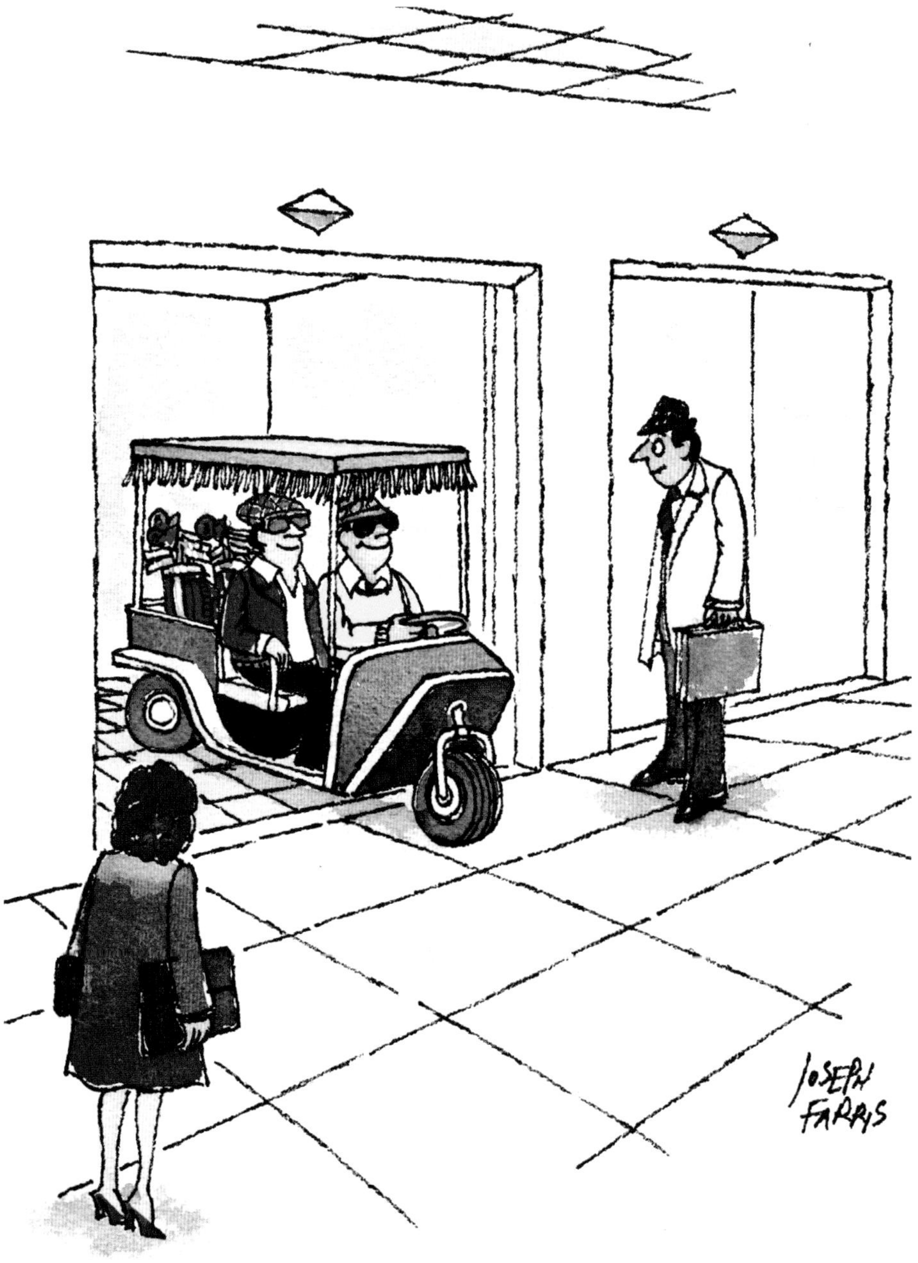
JOSEPH FARRIS

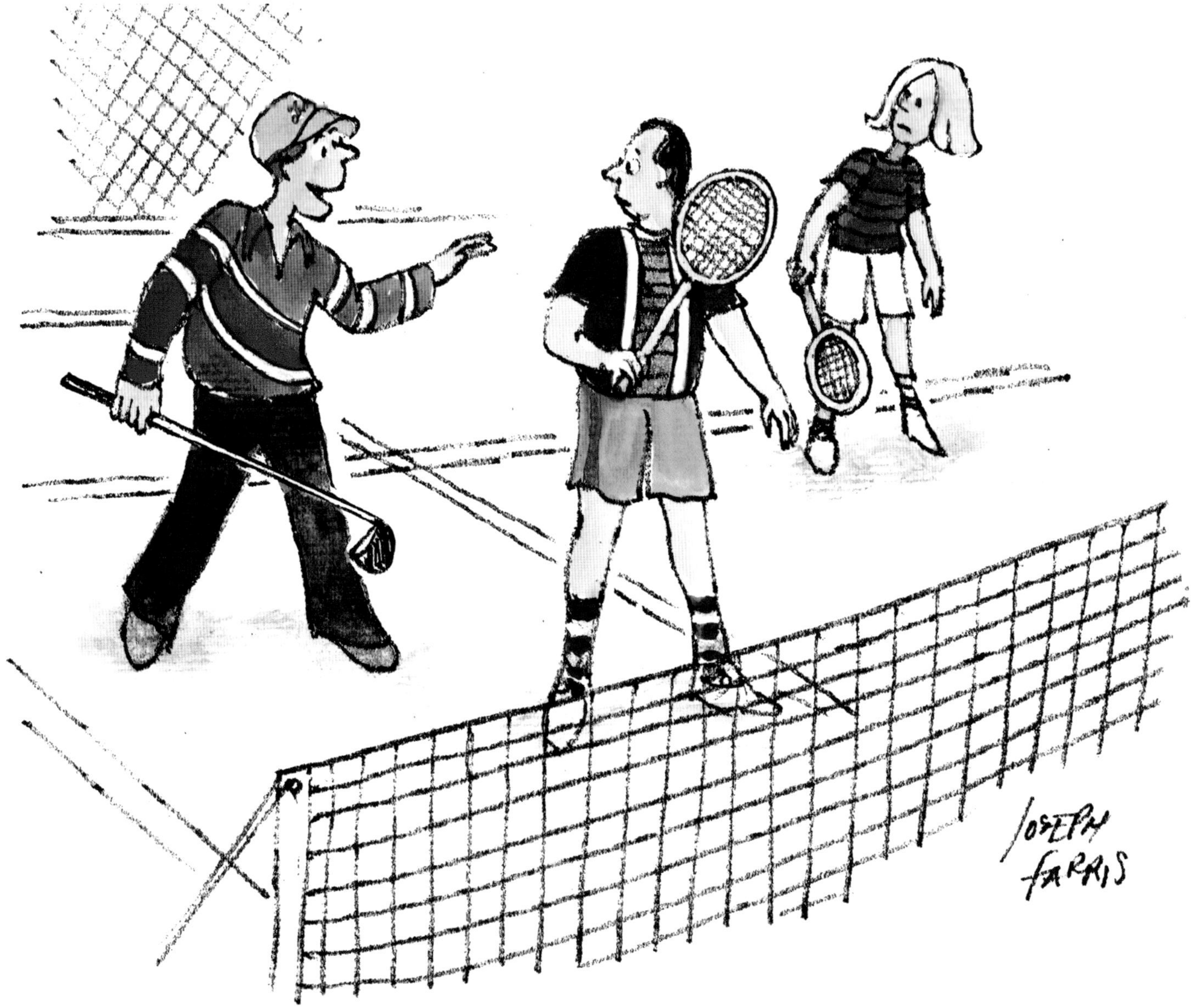
JOSEPH FARRIS

“Golf anyone?”

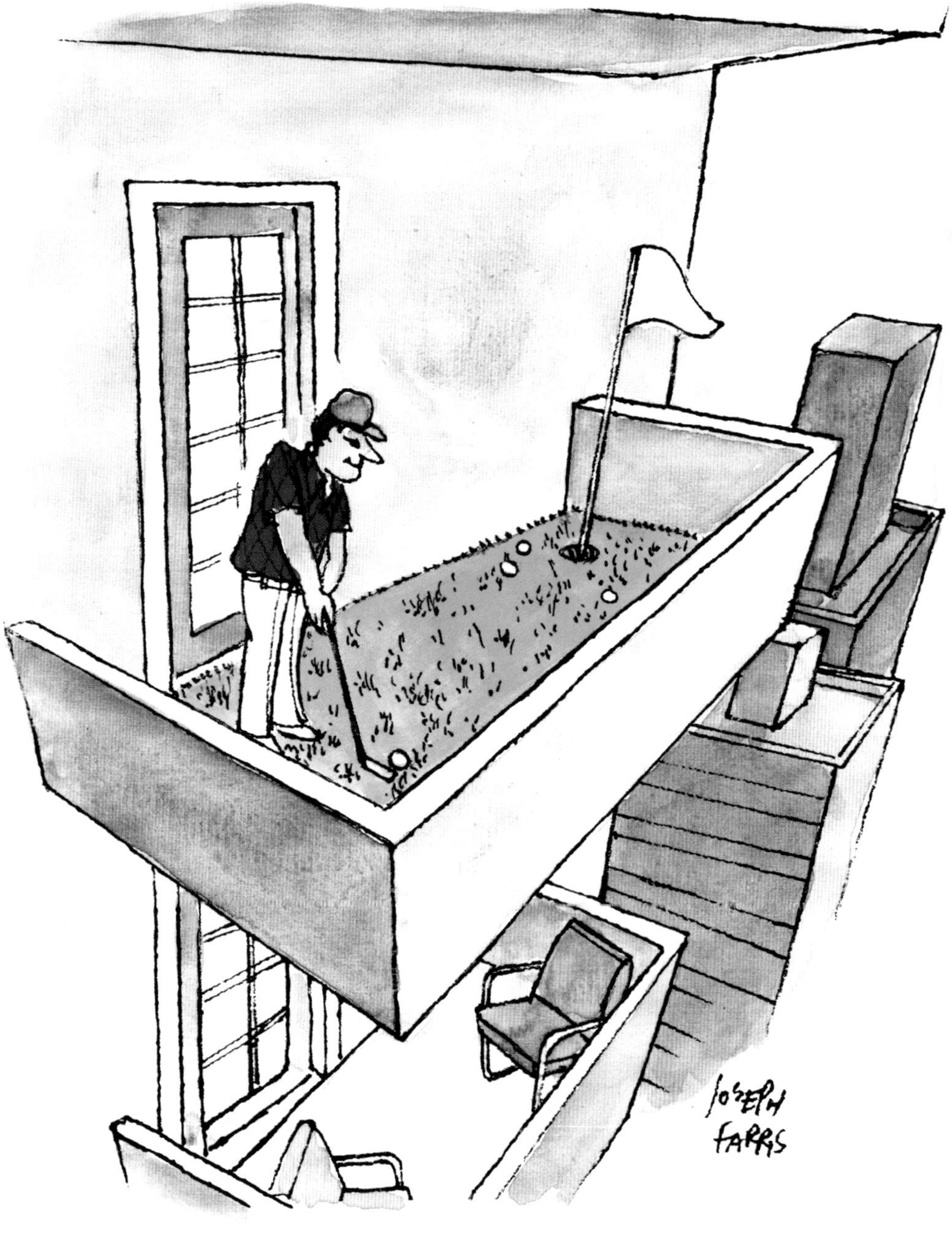
JOSEPH
FARRIS

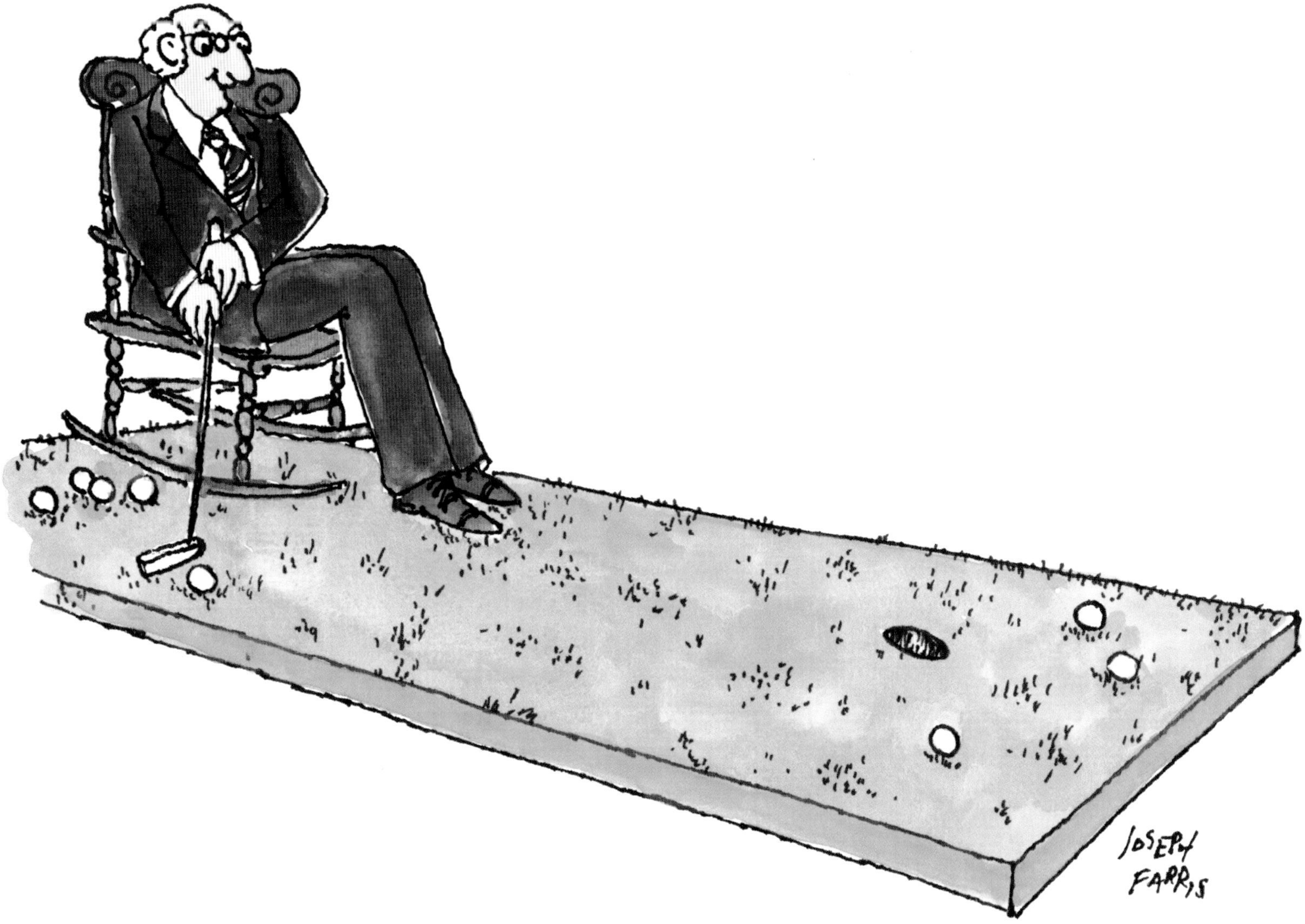
JOSEPH FARRIS

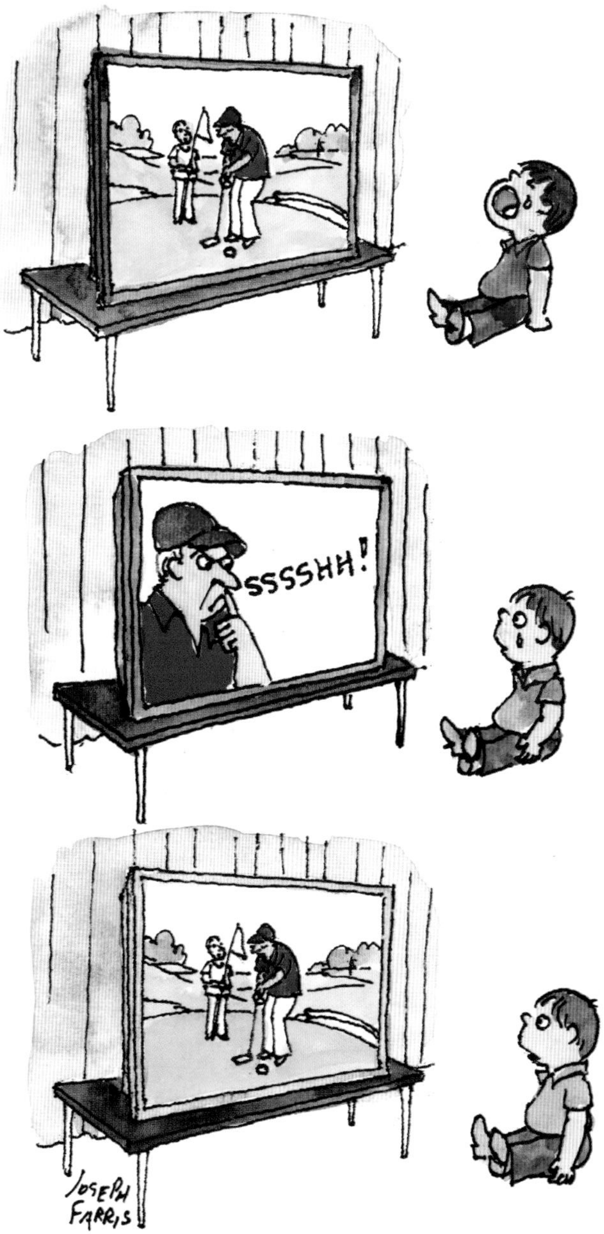
SSSSHH!
JOSEPH FARRIS

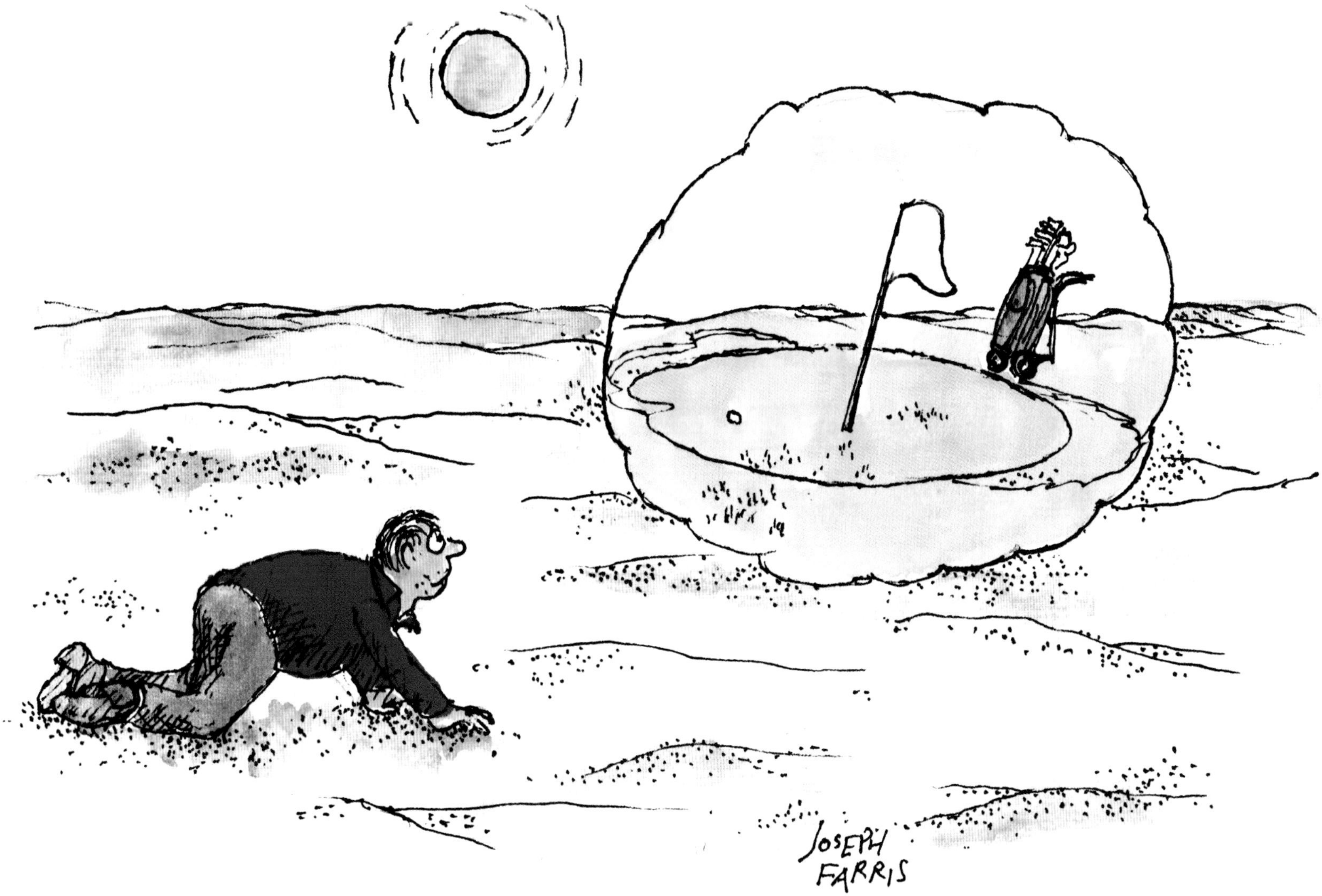
JOSEPH
FARRIS

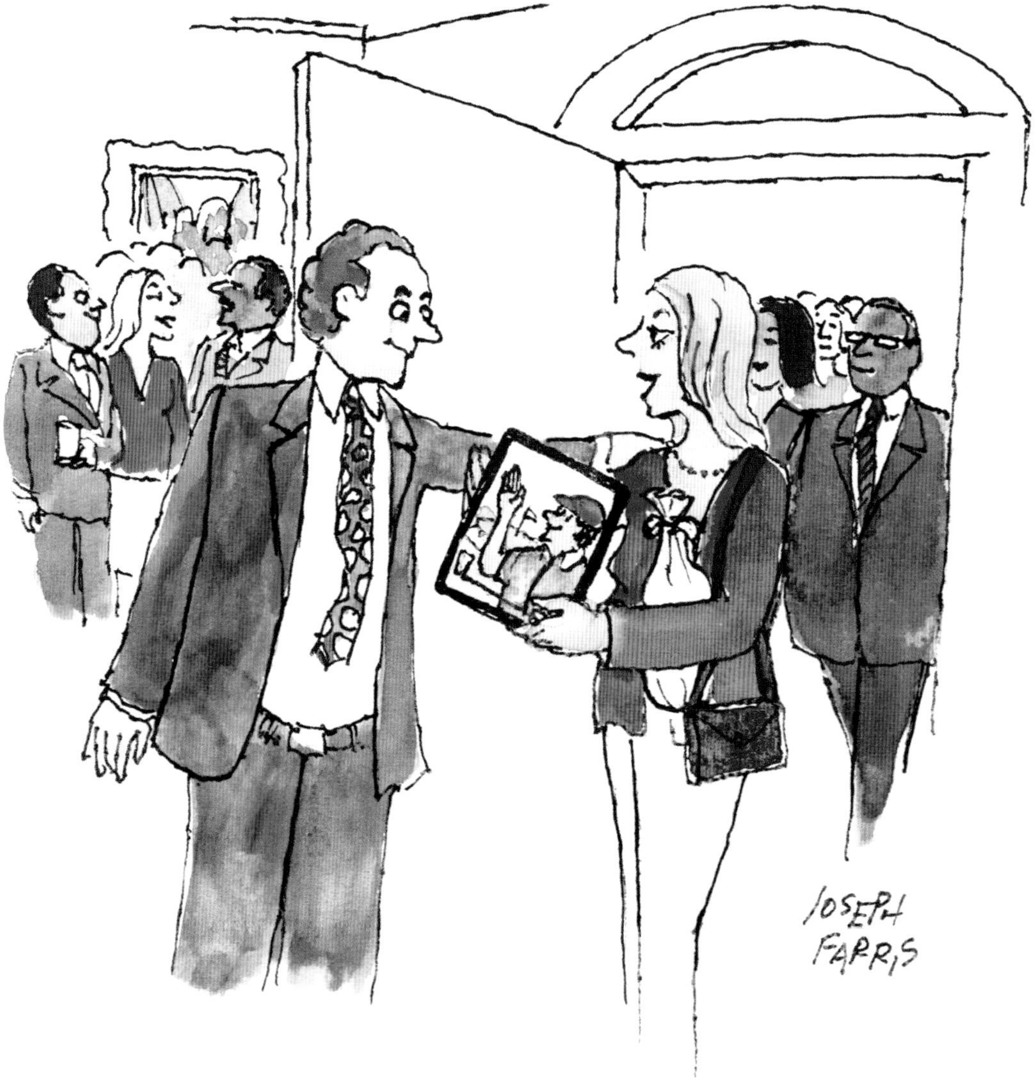
JOSEPH
FARRIS

"Tom couldn't make it. He had a golf date but he's here digitally."

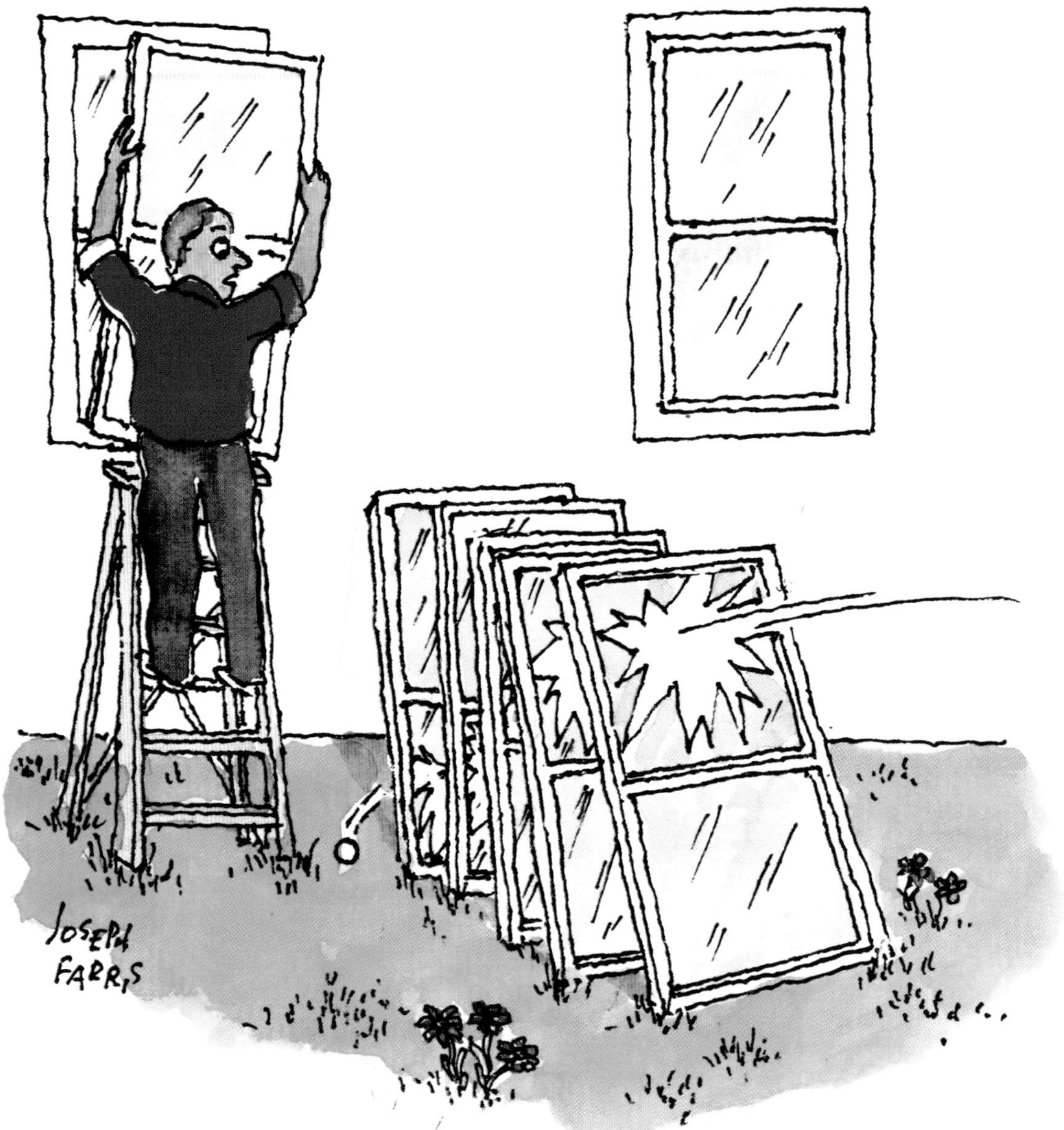
JOSEPH FARRIS

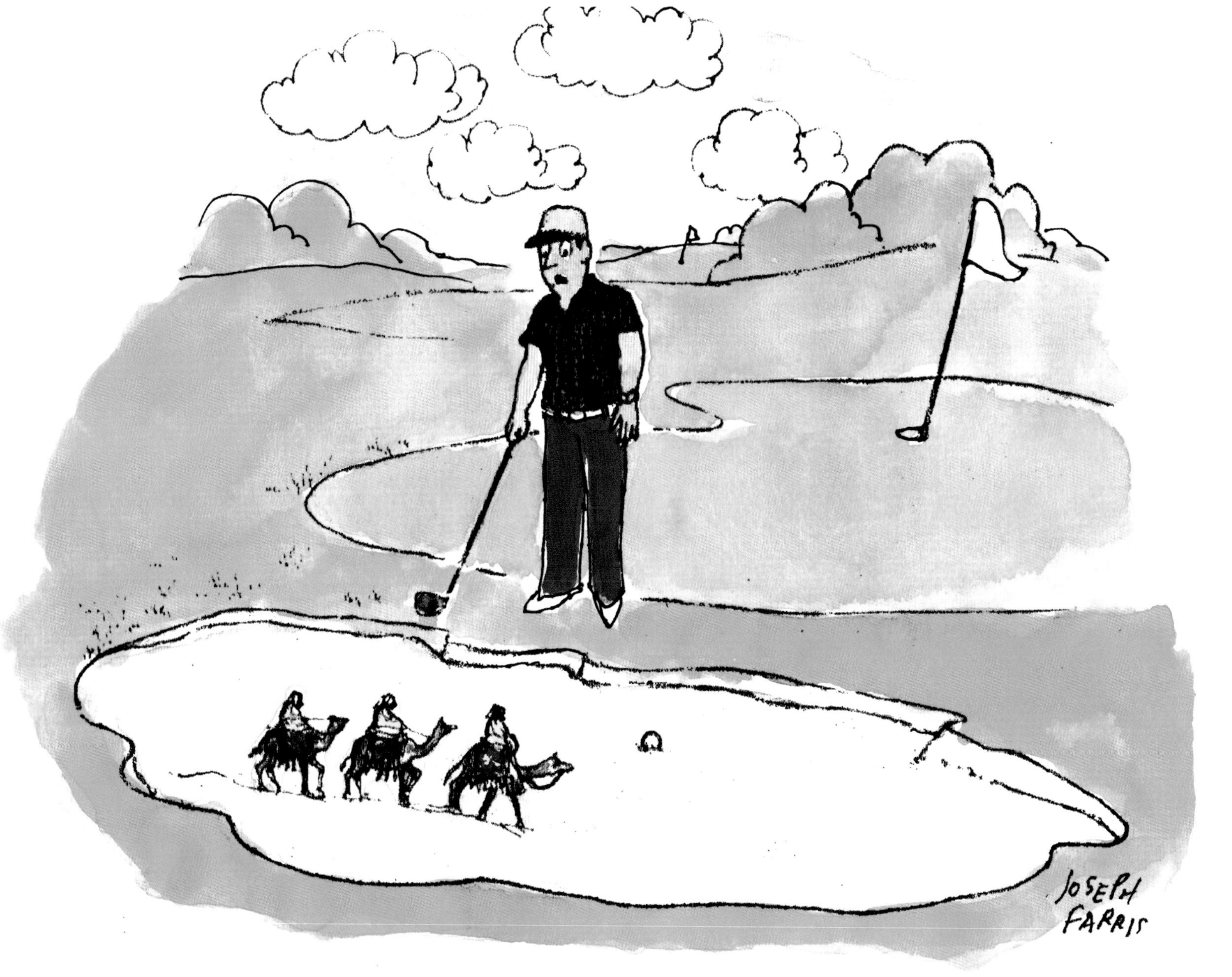
JOSEPH
FARRIS

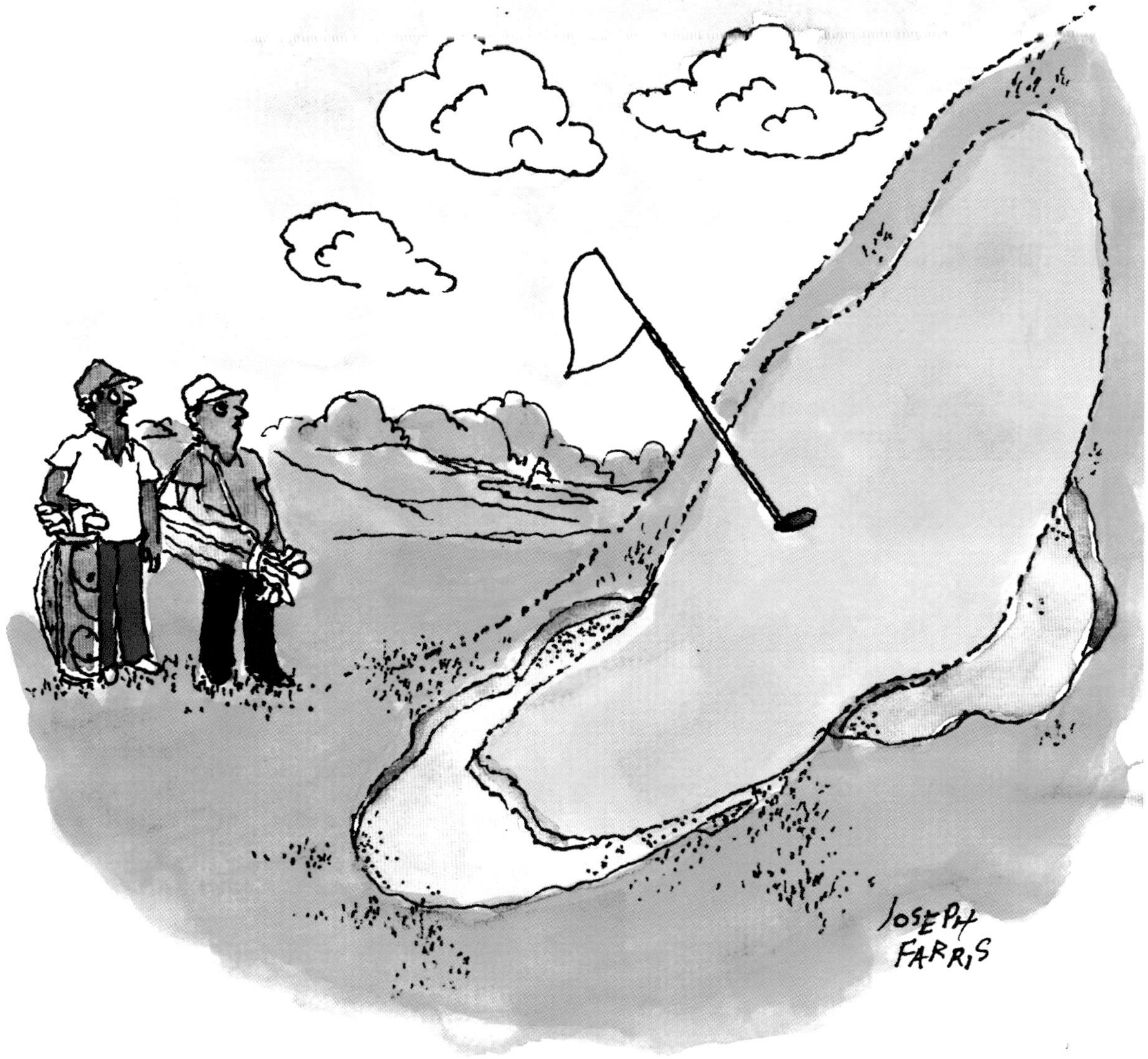
JOSEPH FARRIS

"Now you see why this is a par 14 hole."

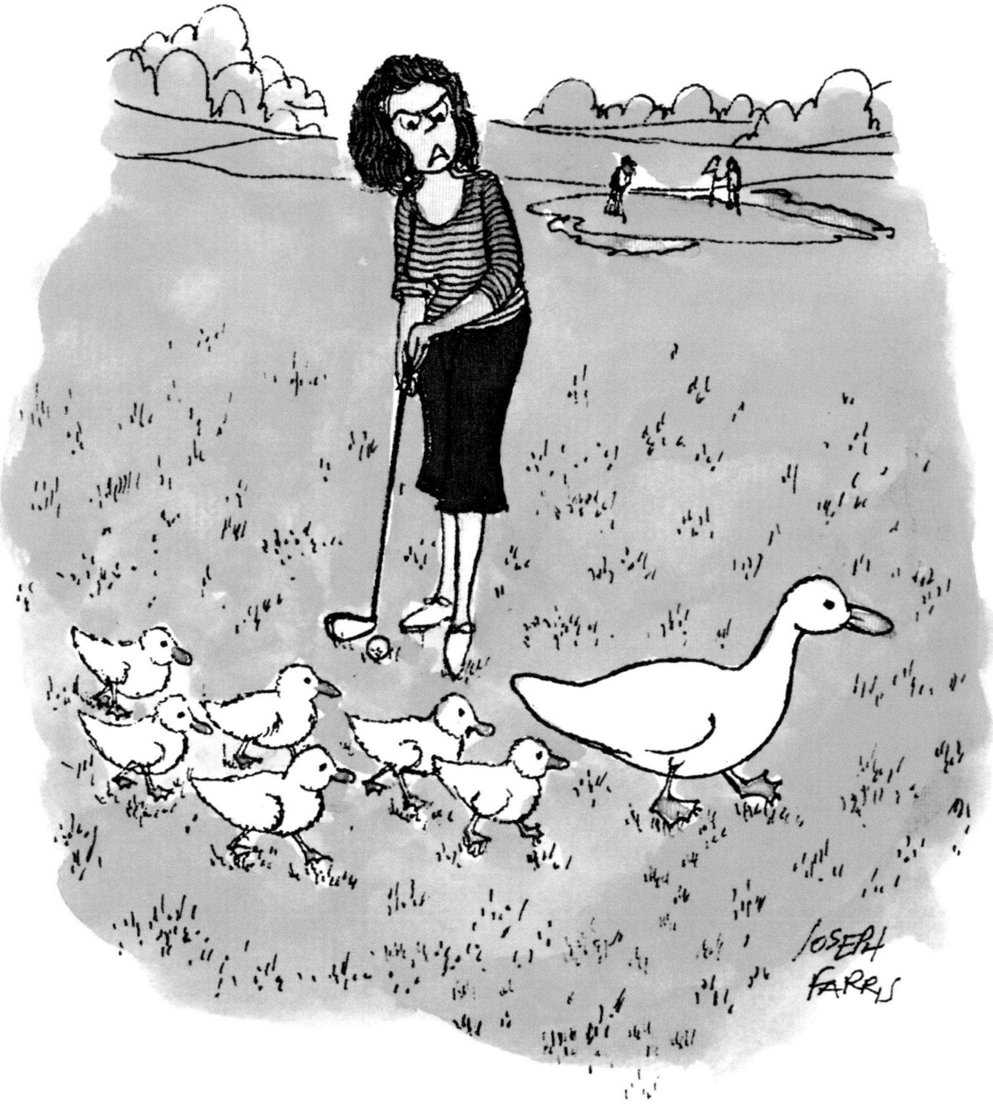
JOSEPH FARRIS

"Fore!"

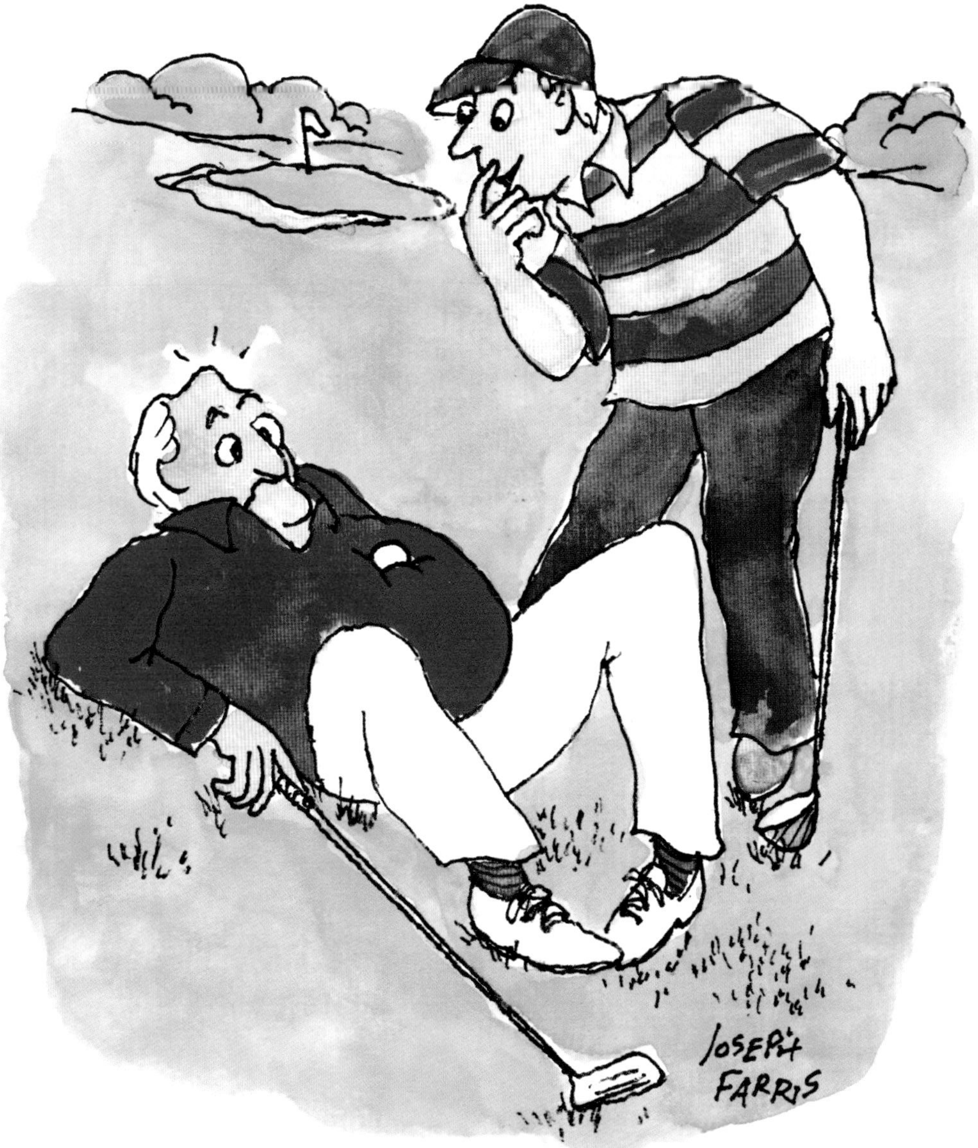
JOSEPH
FARRIS

"I'm terribly sorry but may I play it as it lies?"

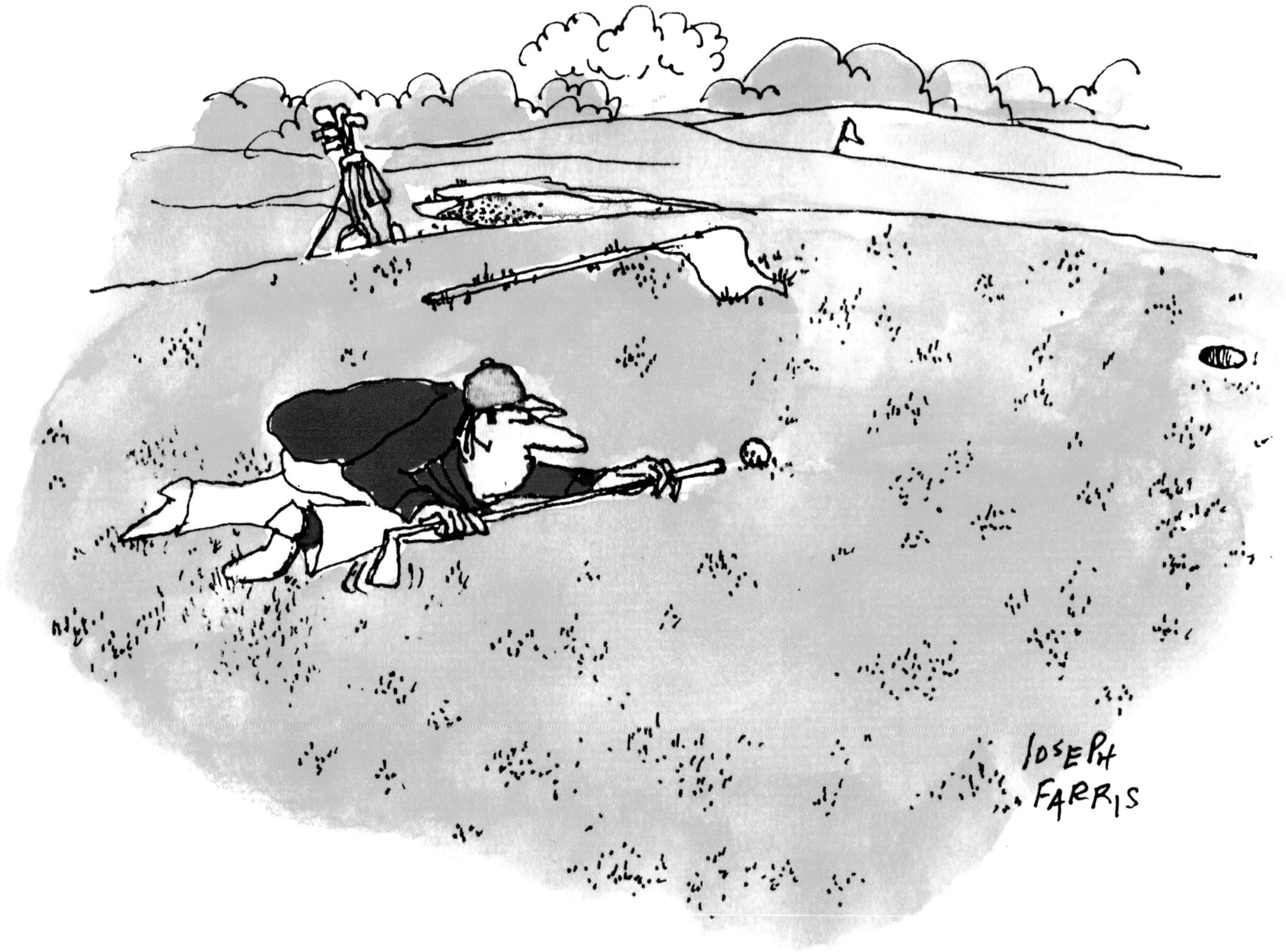
JOSEPH
FARRIS

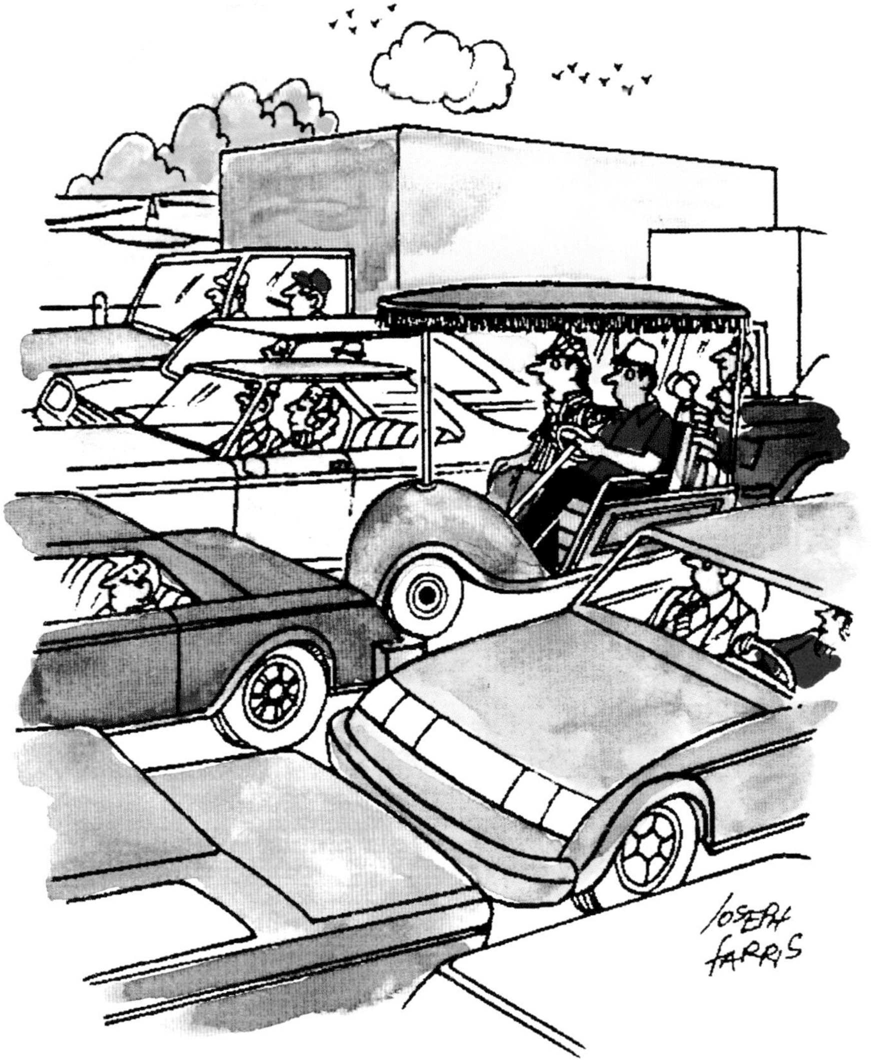
JOSEPH
FARRIS

“I think we took a wrong turn
between the 7th and 8th holes.”

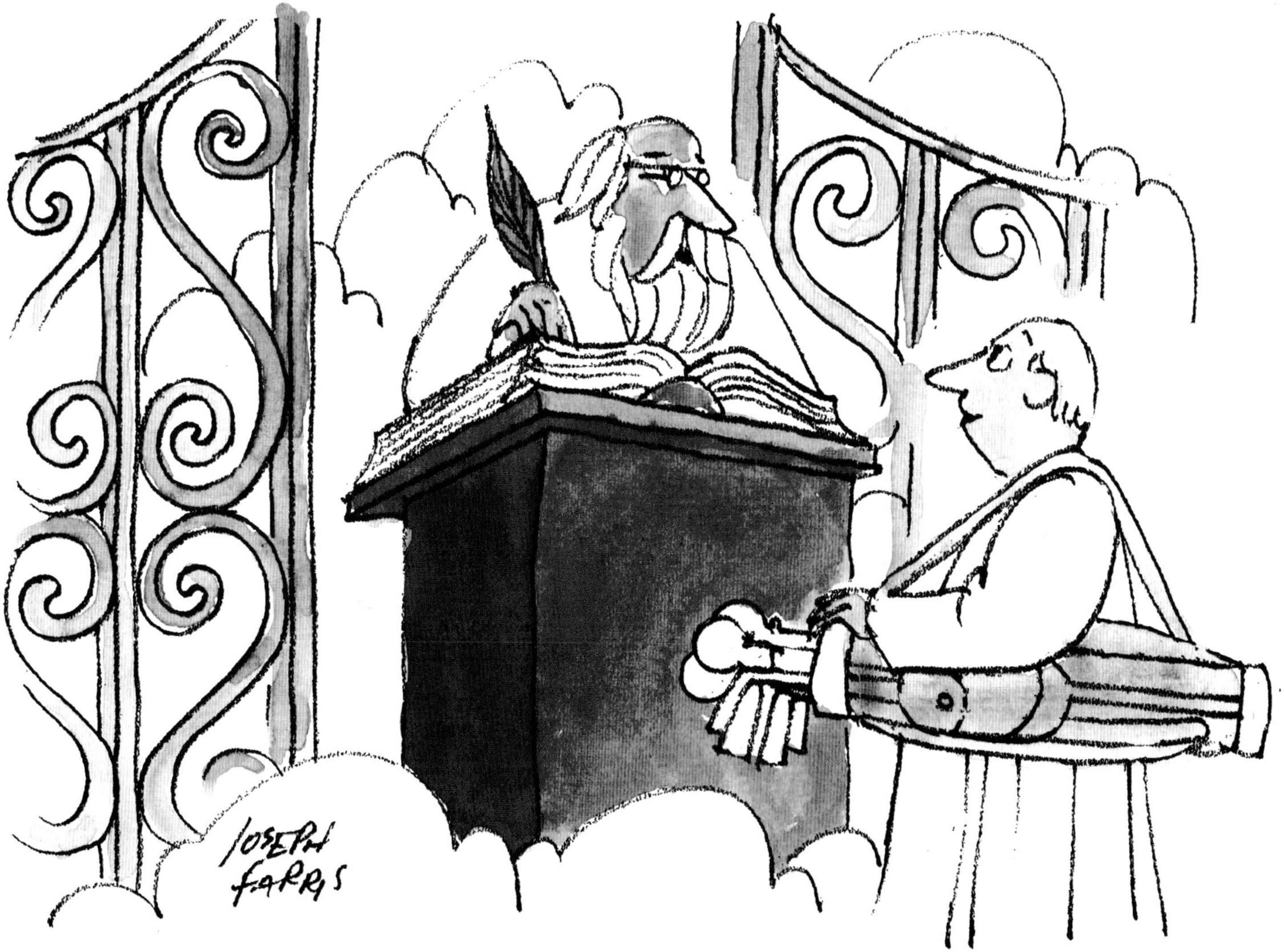
JOSEPH FARRIS

"Yes, Bobby Jones is here and gives lessons but he's booked up for eternity."

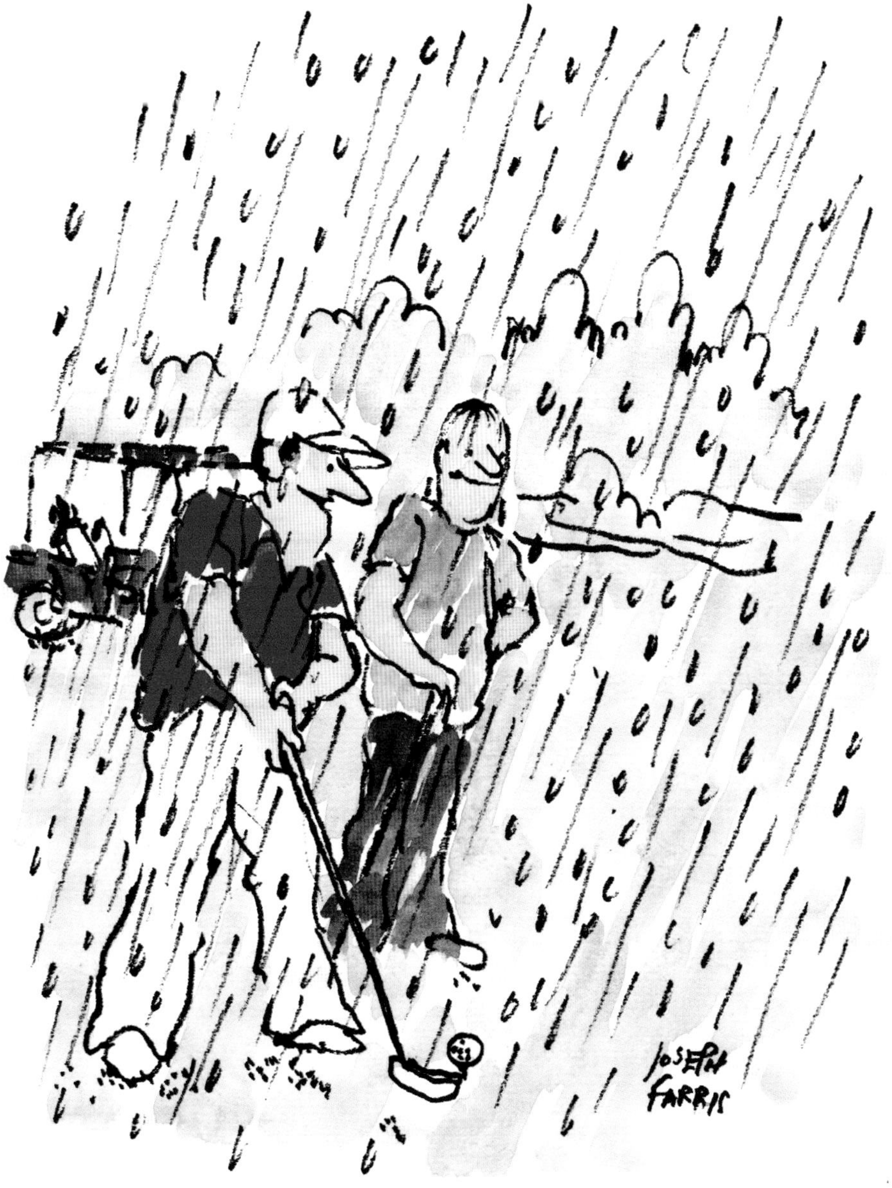
JOSEPH
FARRIS

“The weather was much too rotten to go to work.”

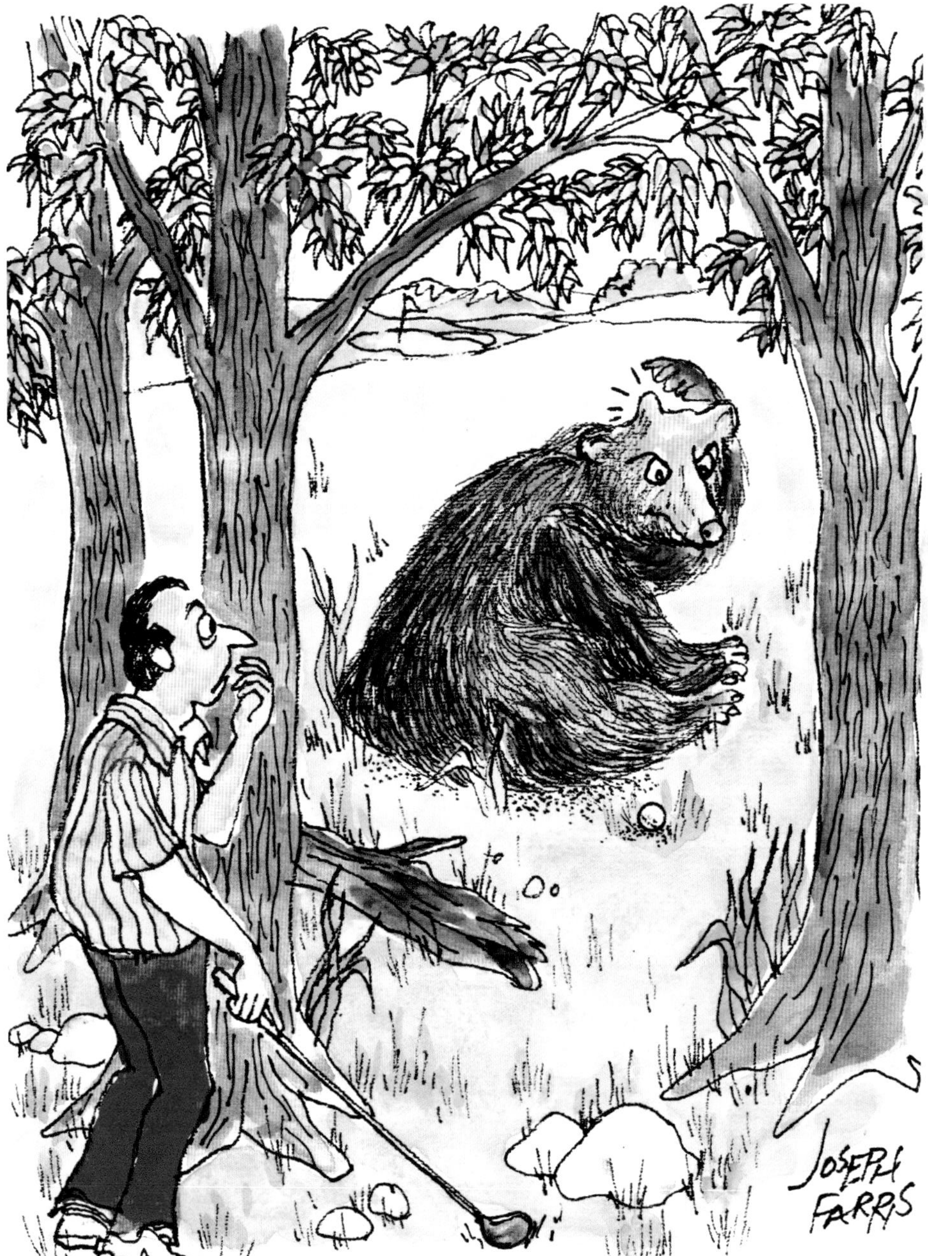
JOSEPH FARRIS

"I've been practicing my putting and lost
my ball somewhere in your damn garden!"

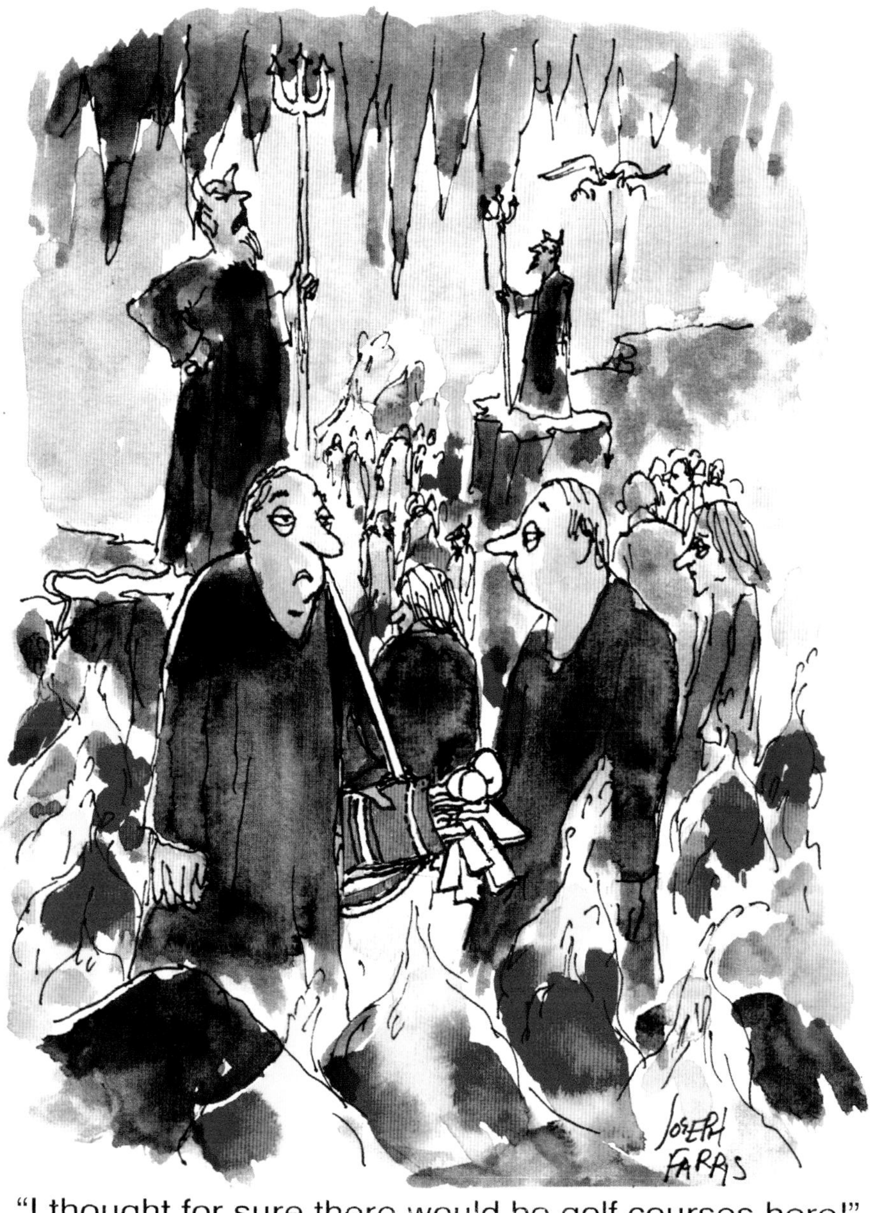
JOSEPH FARRIS

"I thought for sure there would be golf courses here!"

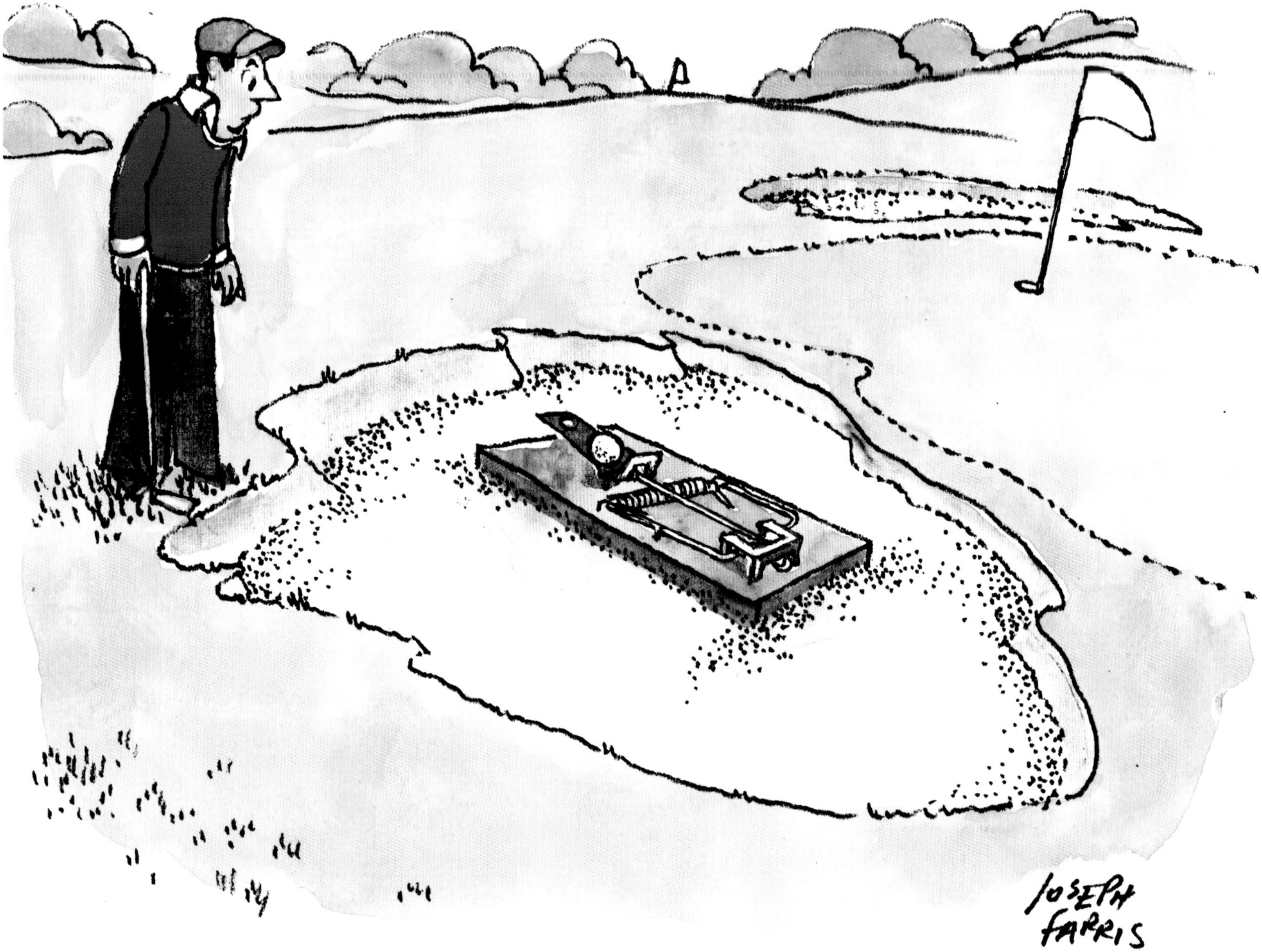
JOSEPH FARRIS

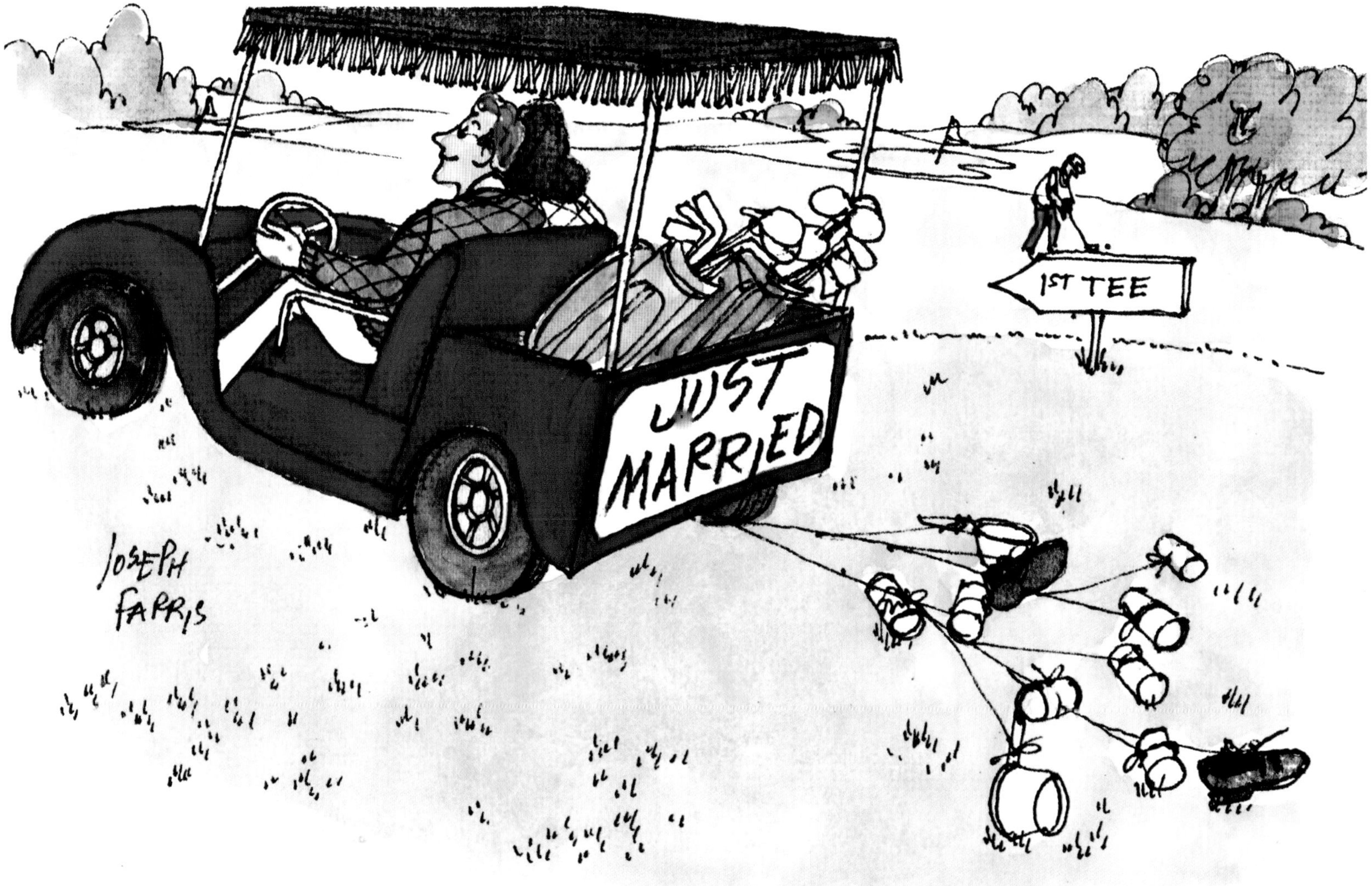

1ST TEE
JUST MARRIED
JOSEPH FARRIS

"Sorry, Tom, but I can't join you for a round of golf and dinner today. How about next week sometime?"

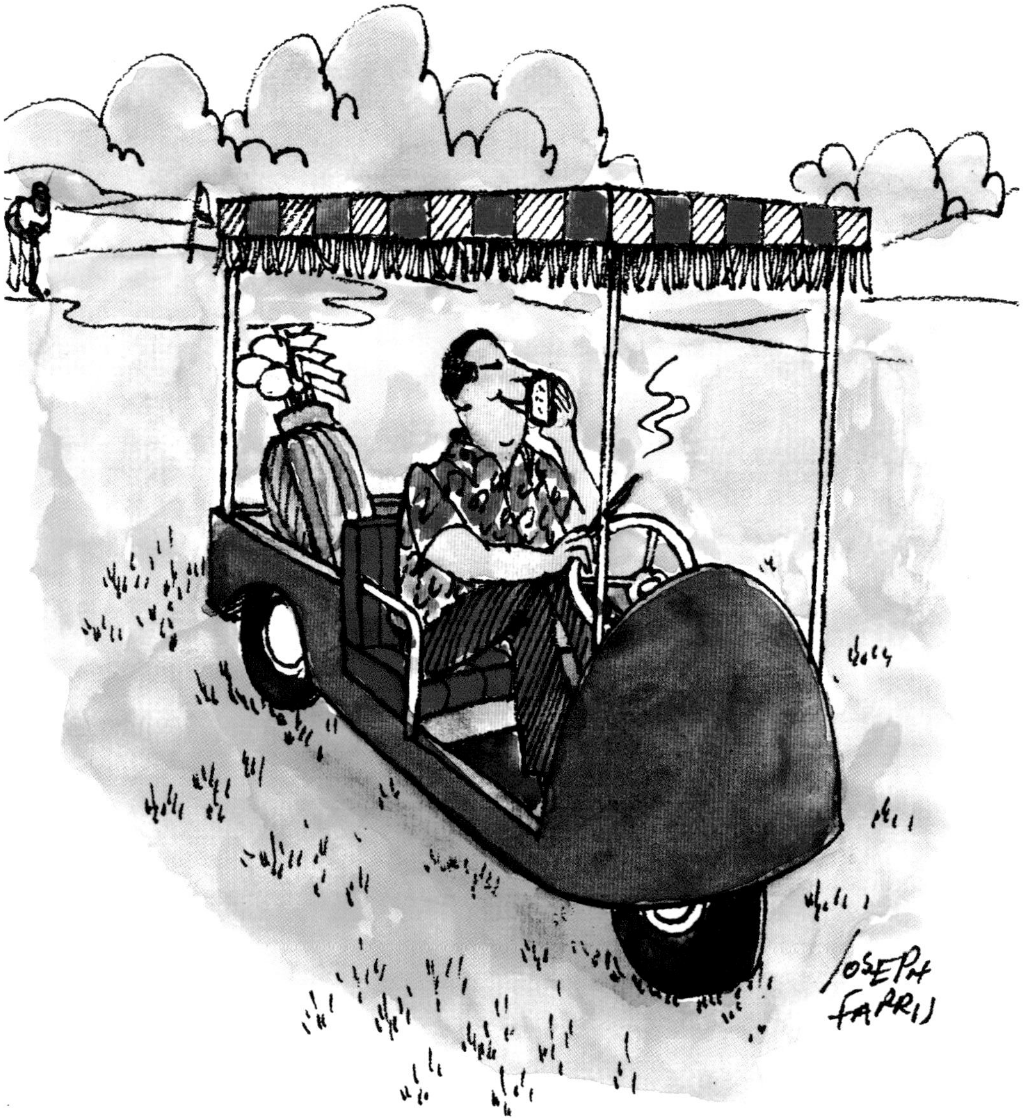
JOSEPH FARRIS

"Sorry, I didn't get back to you sooner, Barry, but I'm up to my ears in work."

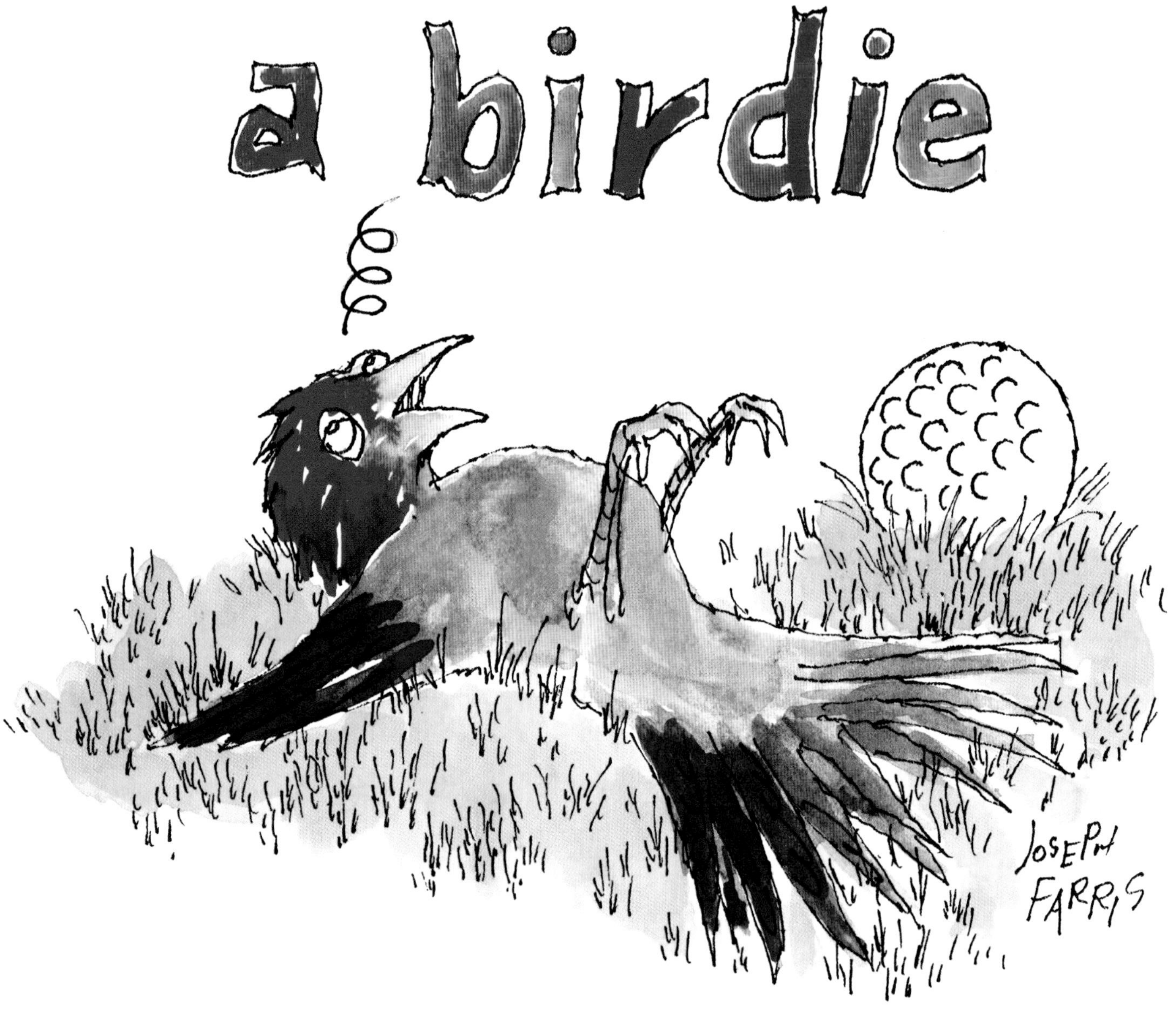
a birdie
JOSEPH FARRIS

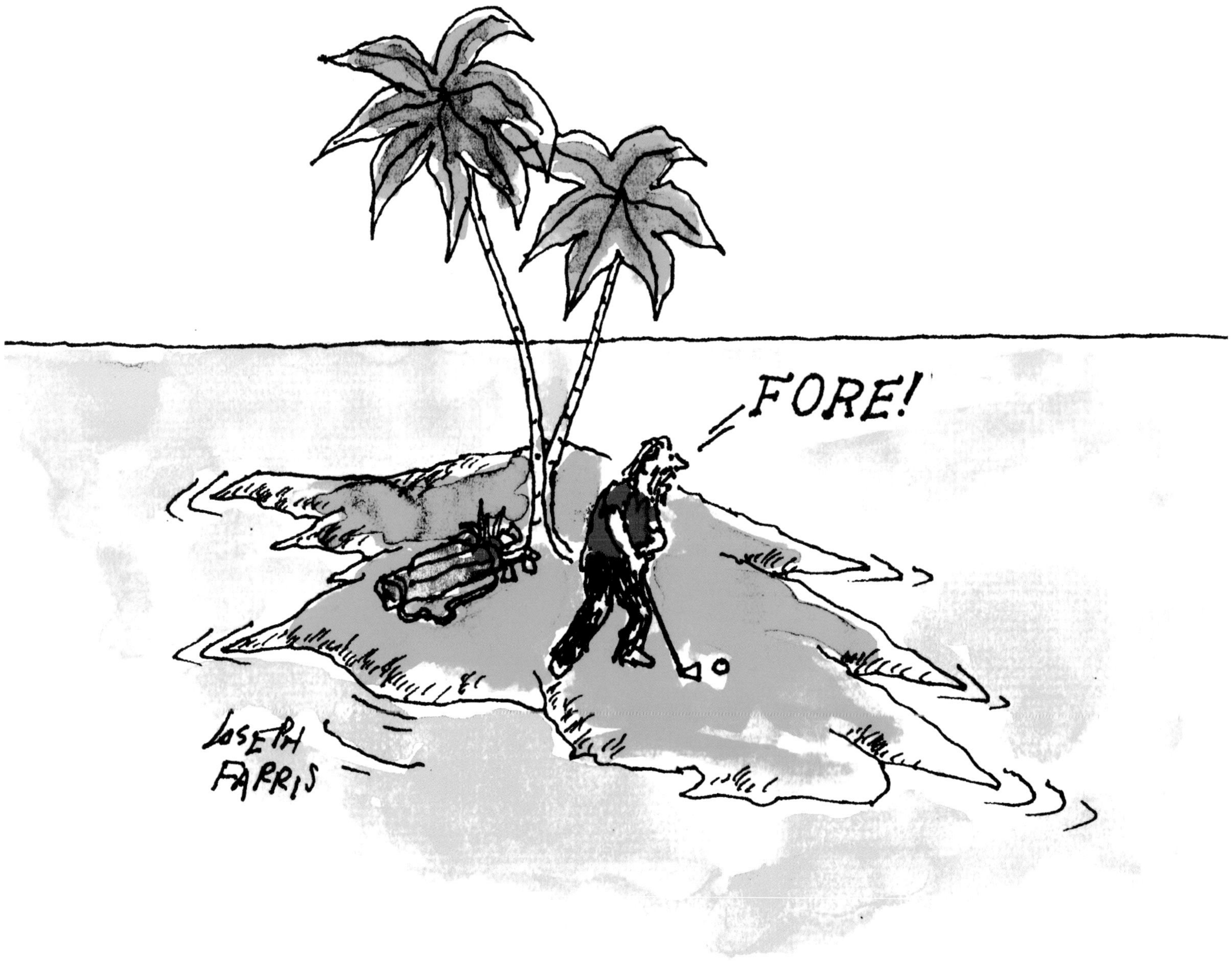
FORE!
JOSEPH FARRIS

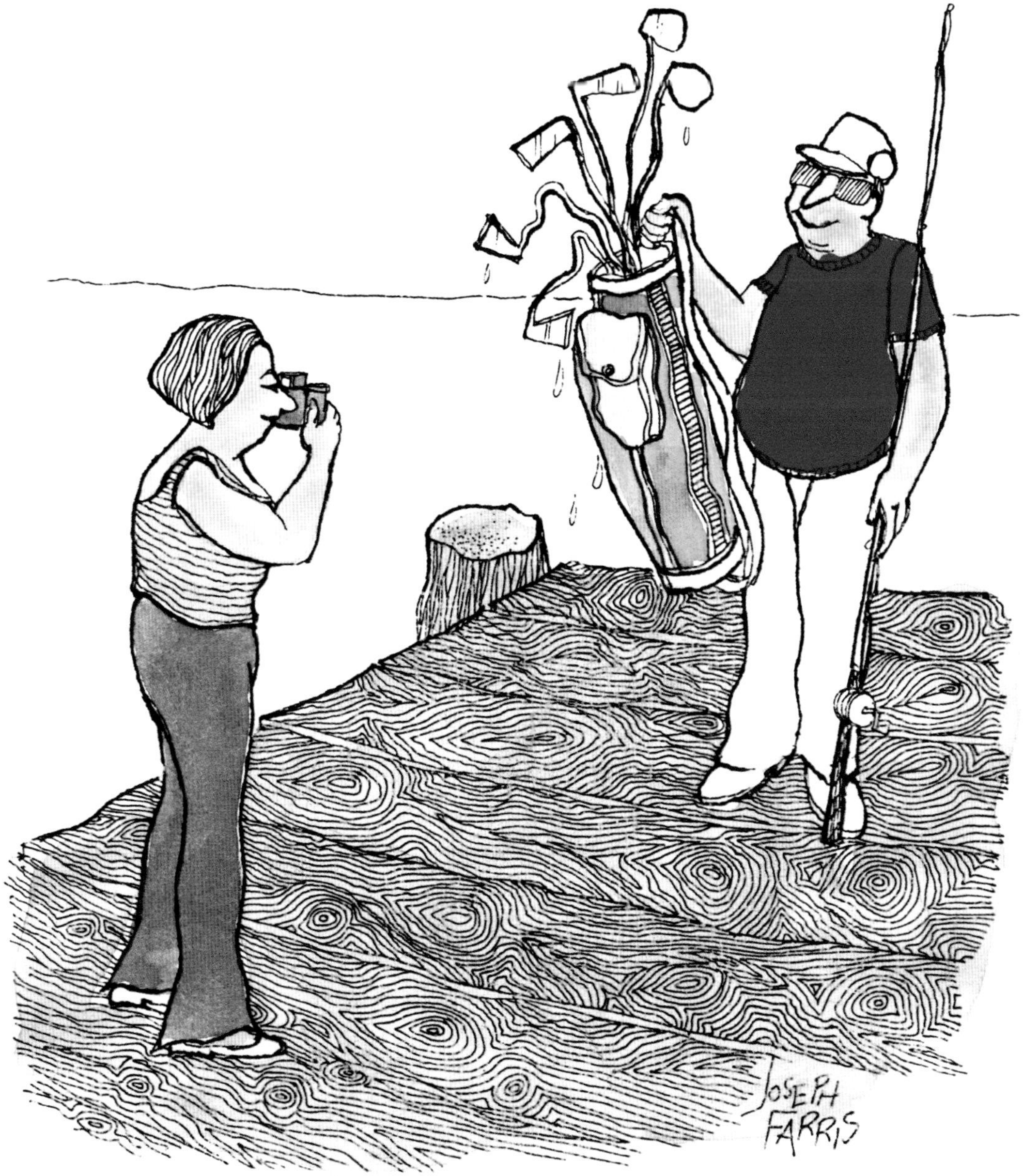
JOSEPH FARRIS

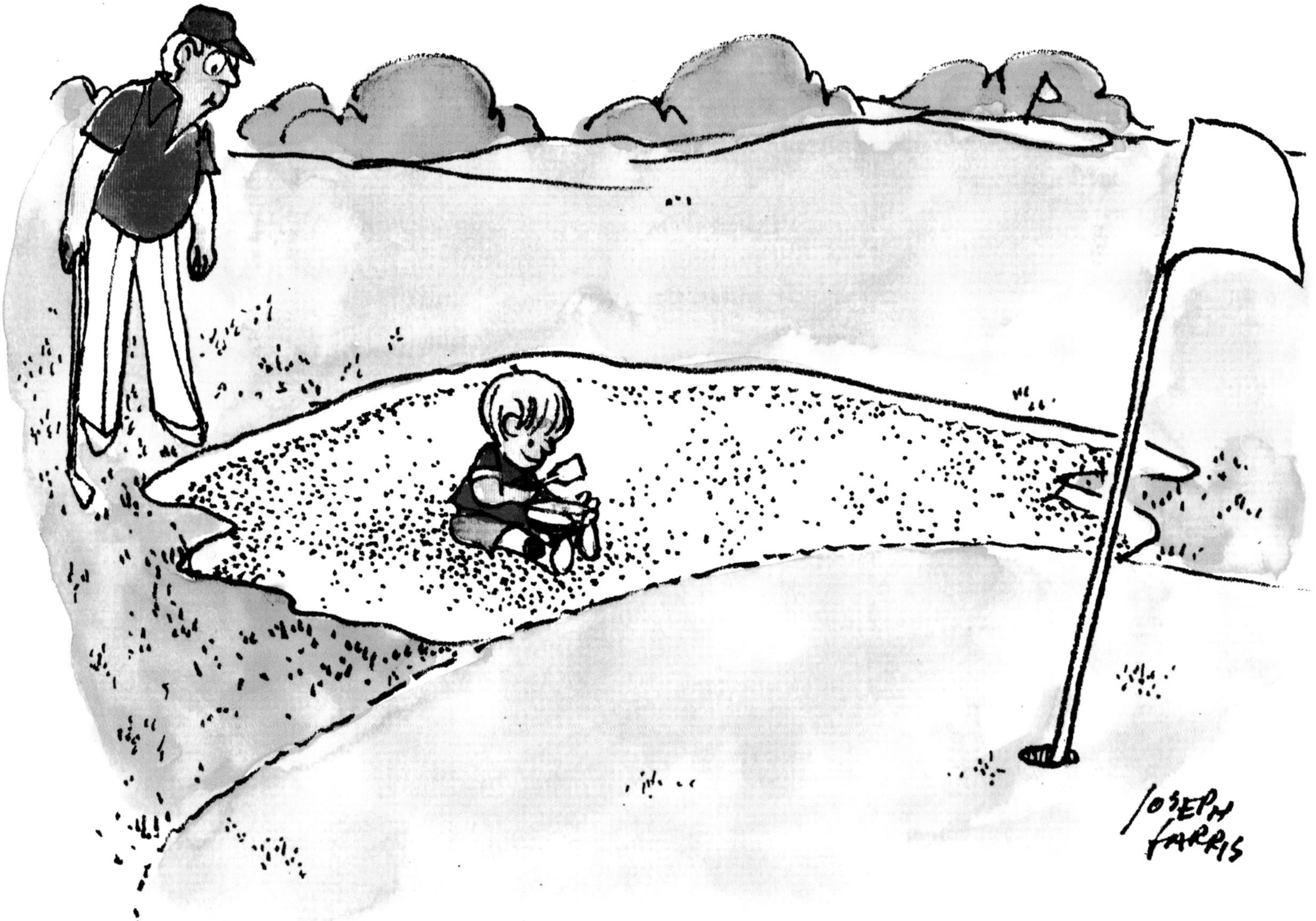
JOSEPH FARRIS

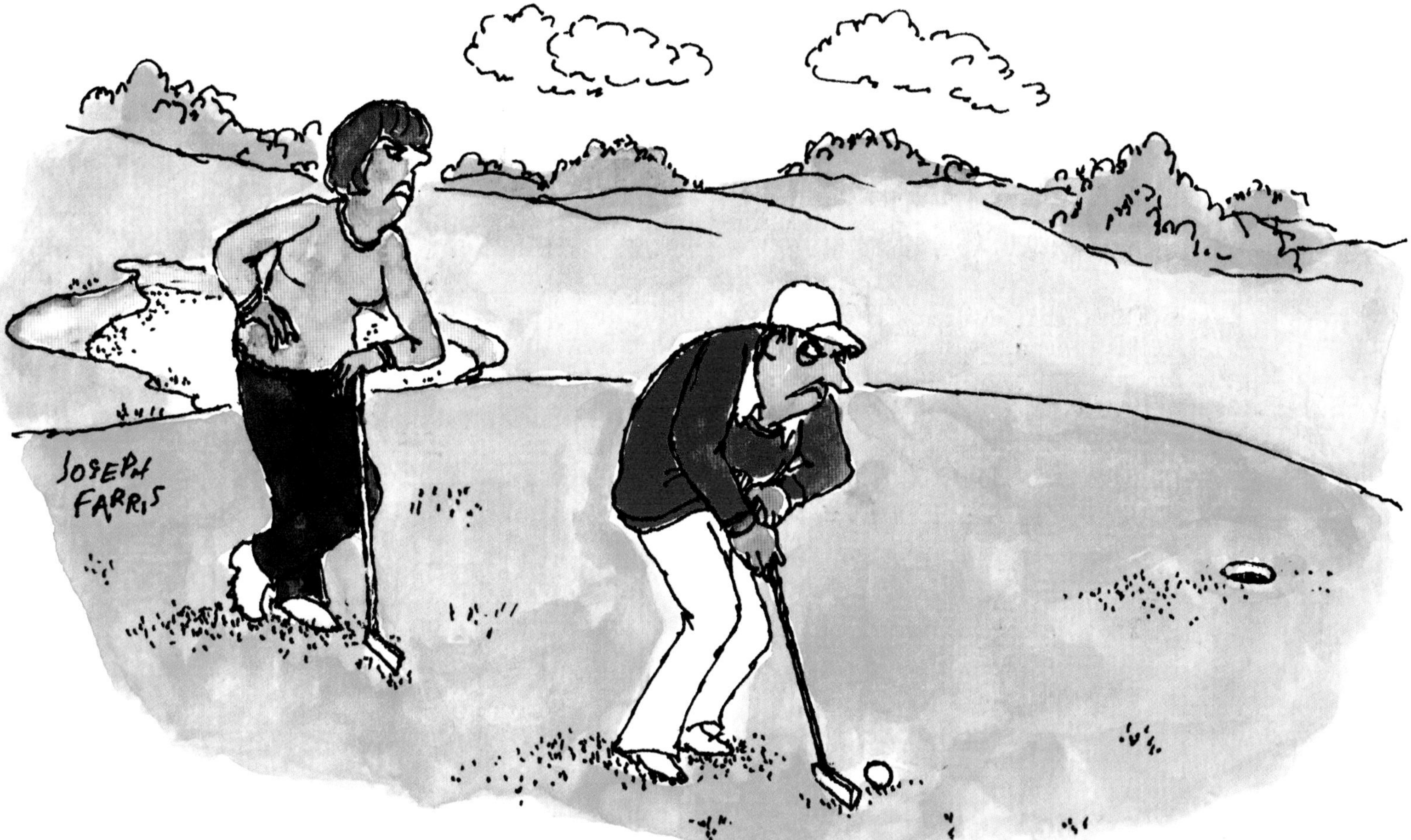
JOSEPH
FARRIS

"We need to talk!"

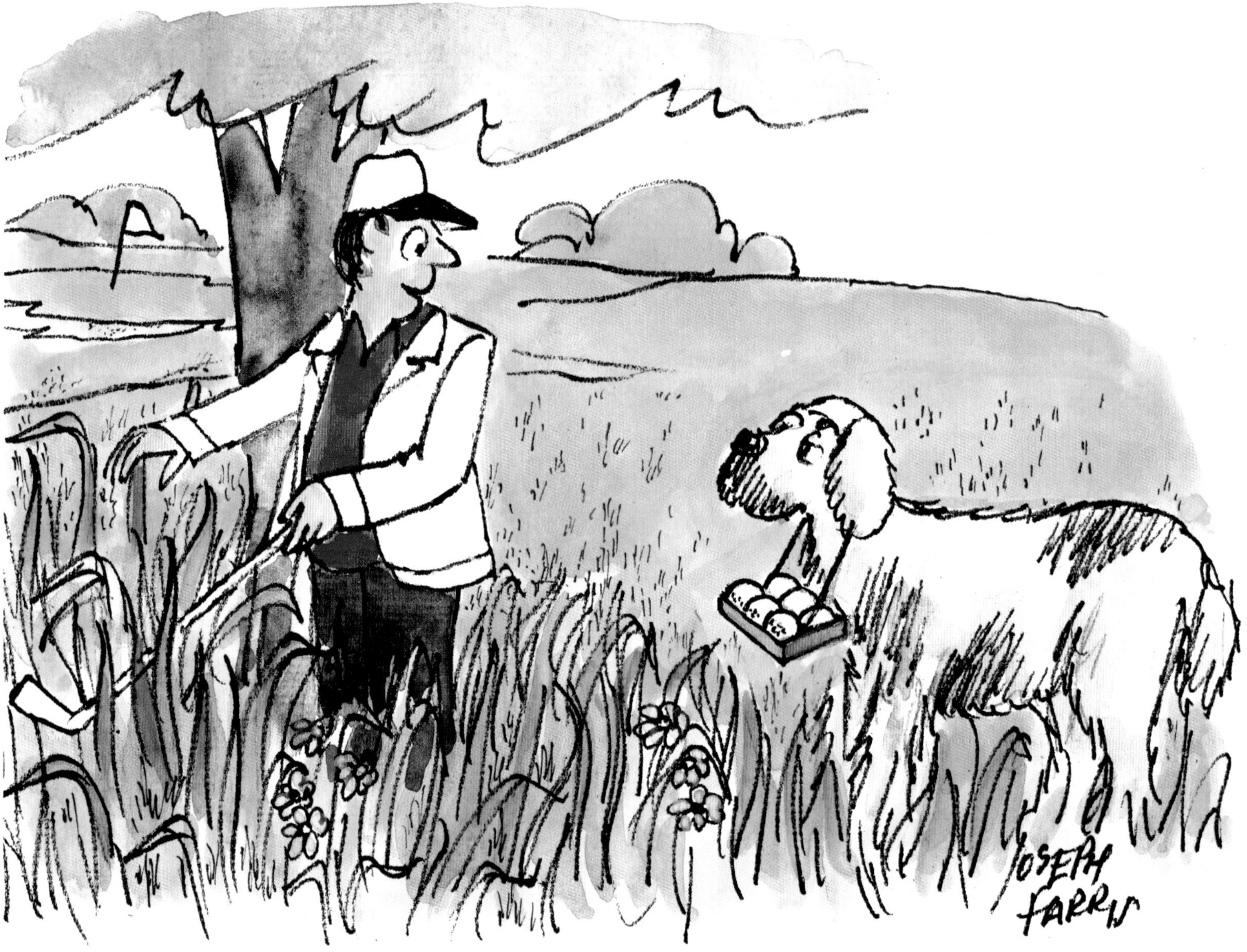
JOSEPH FARRIS

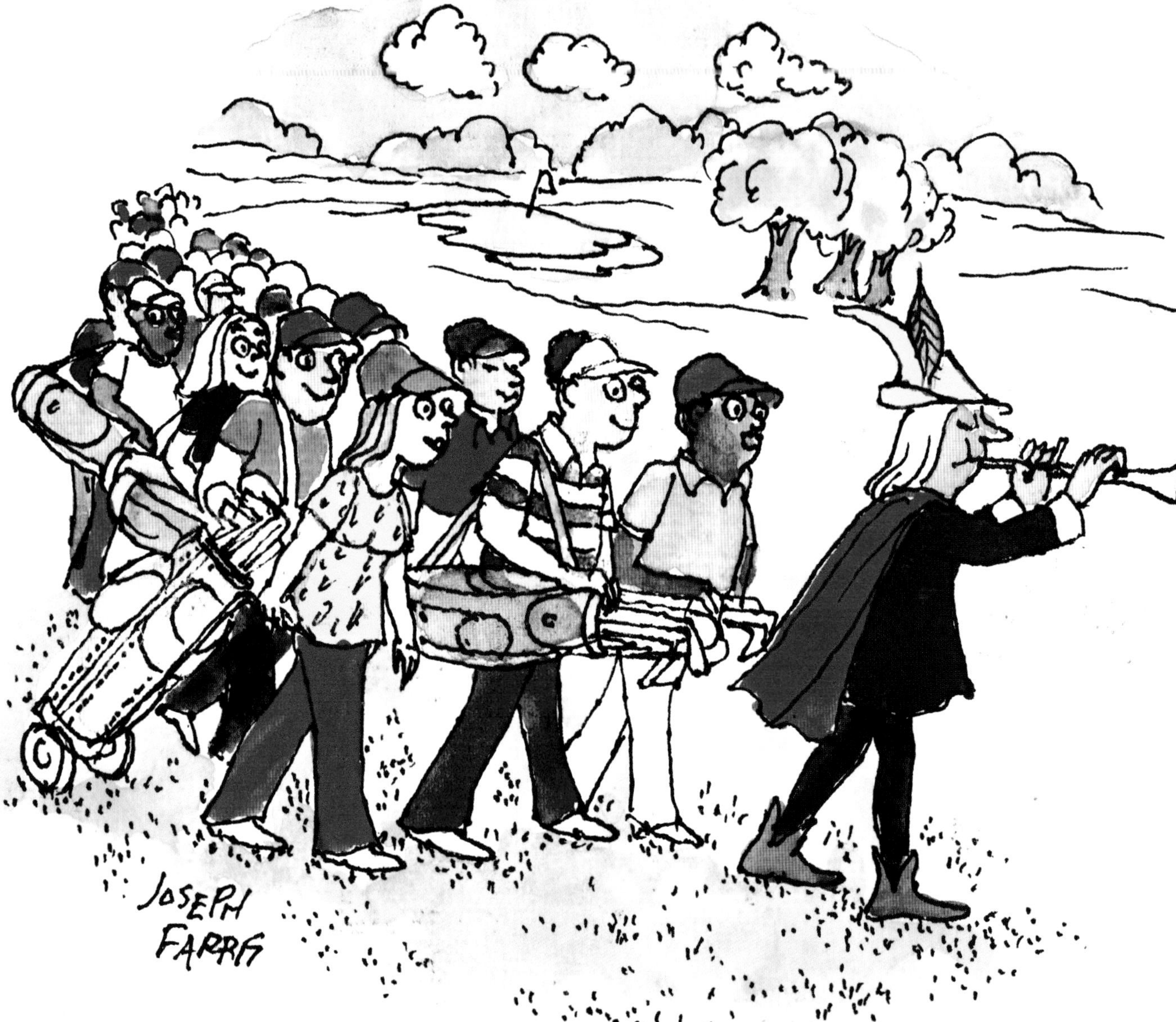
JOSEPH
FARRIS

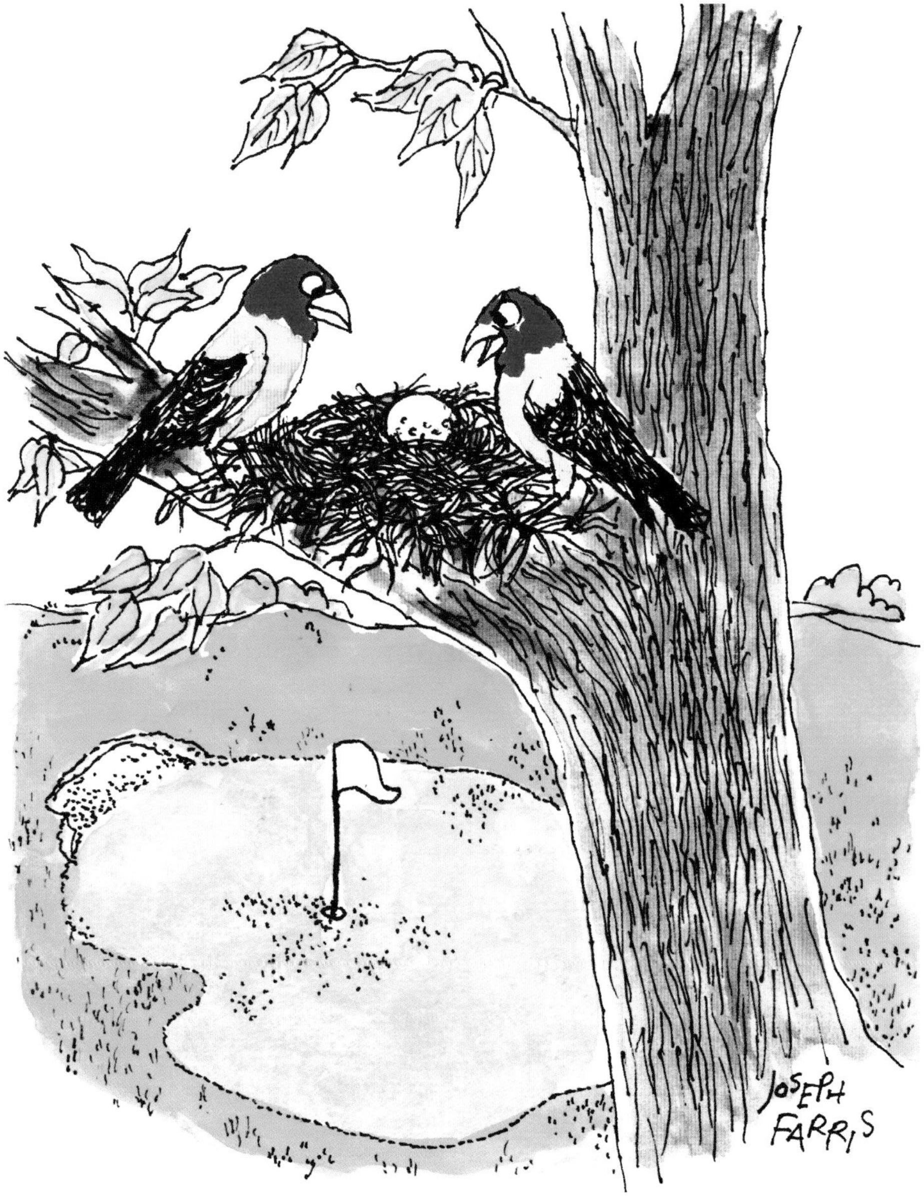
JOSEPH FARRIS

"I've been sitting on it for days and nothing happens!"

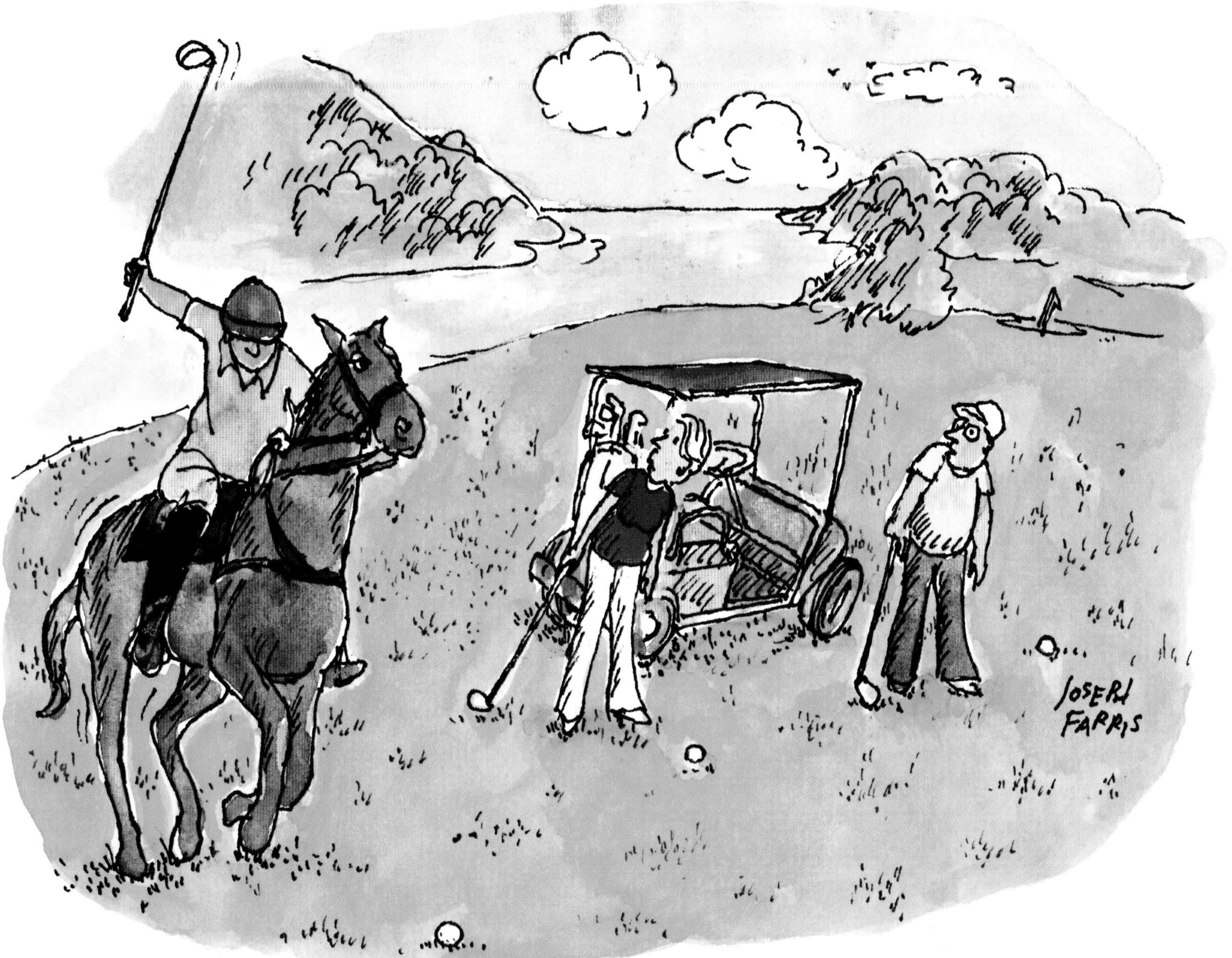
JOSEPH FARRIS

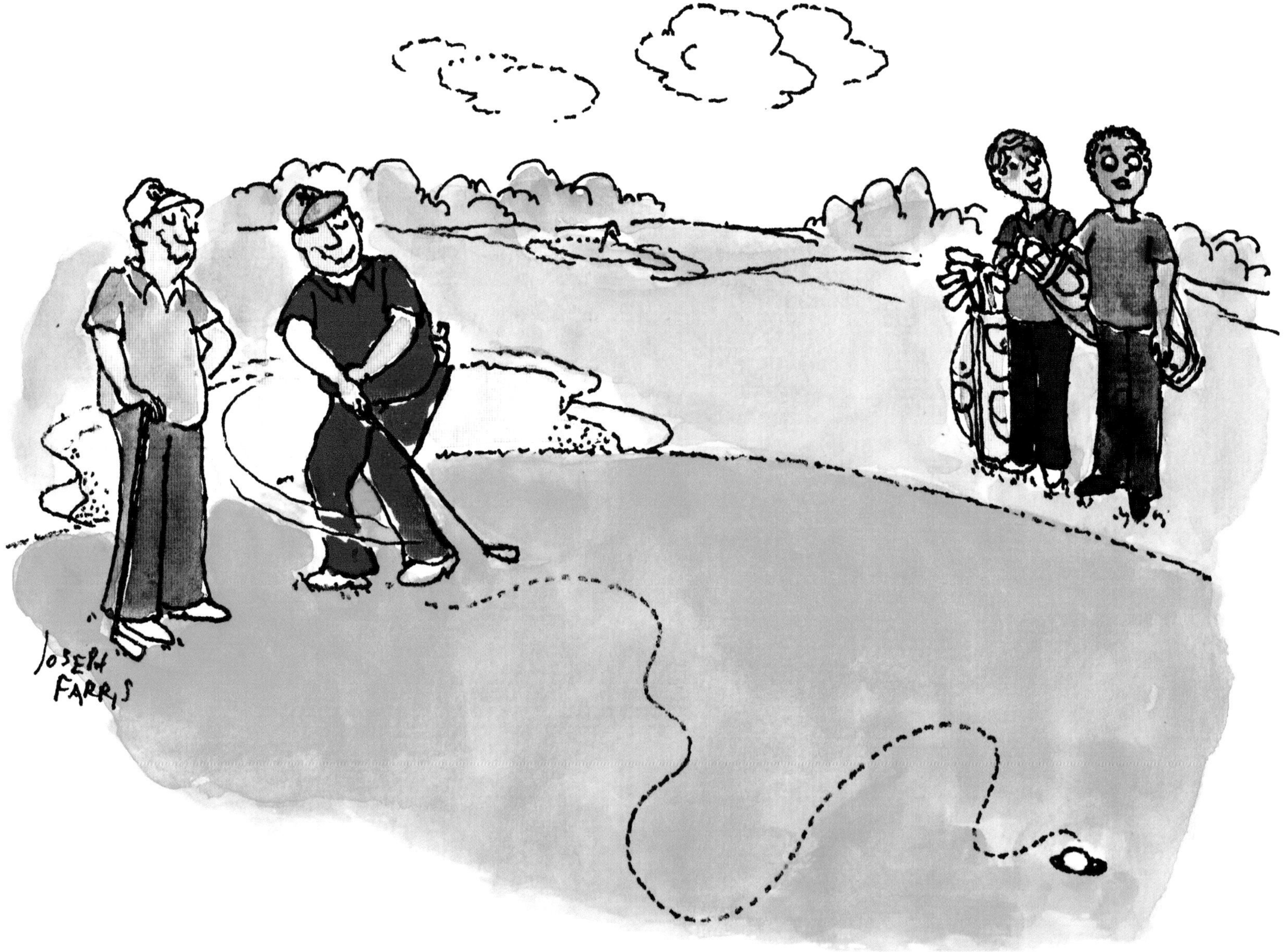
JOSEPH
FARRIS

"He's the best soused putter I've ever seen."

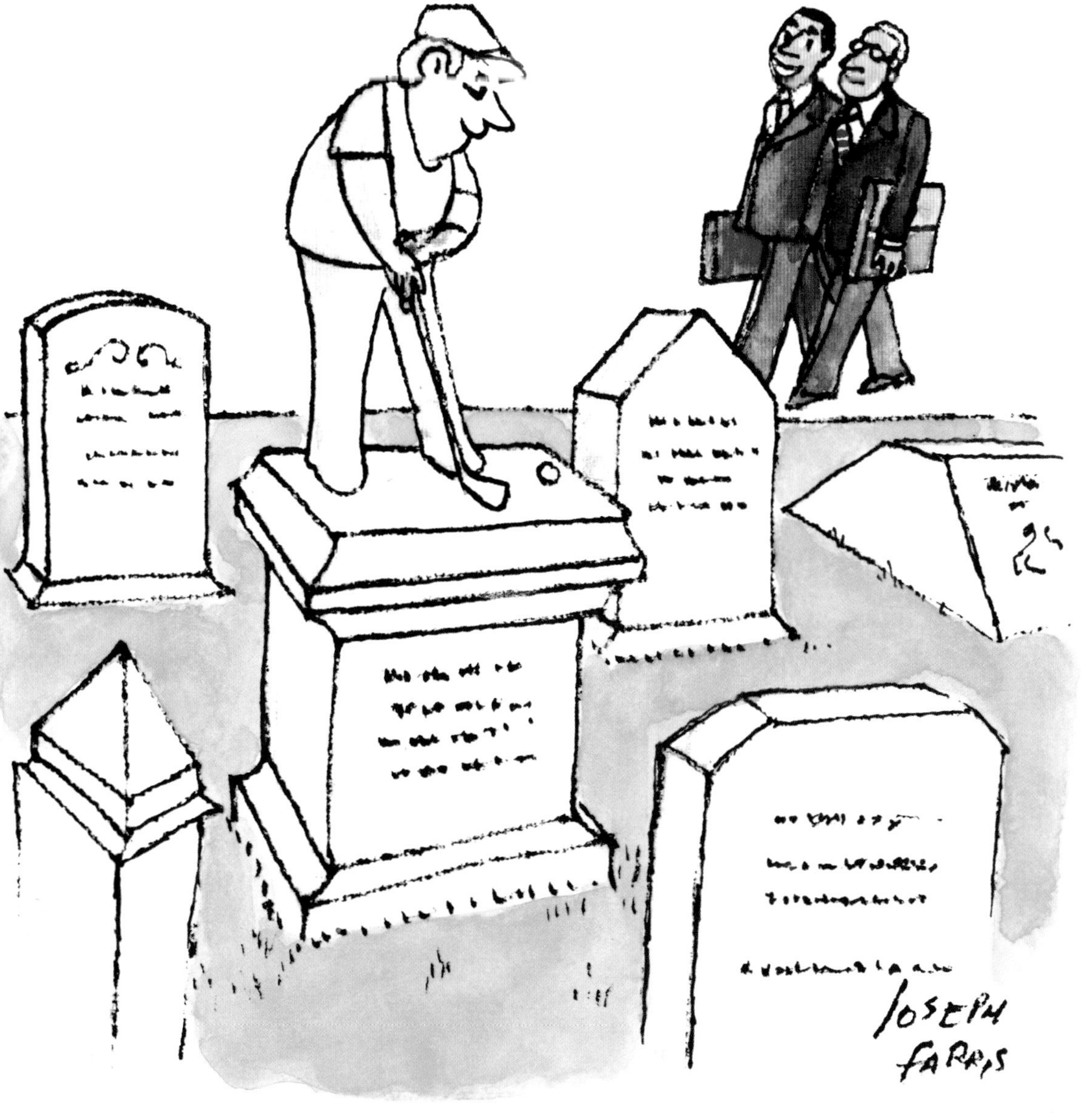
JOSEPH FARRIS

"He lived and died for golf."

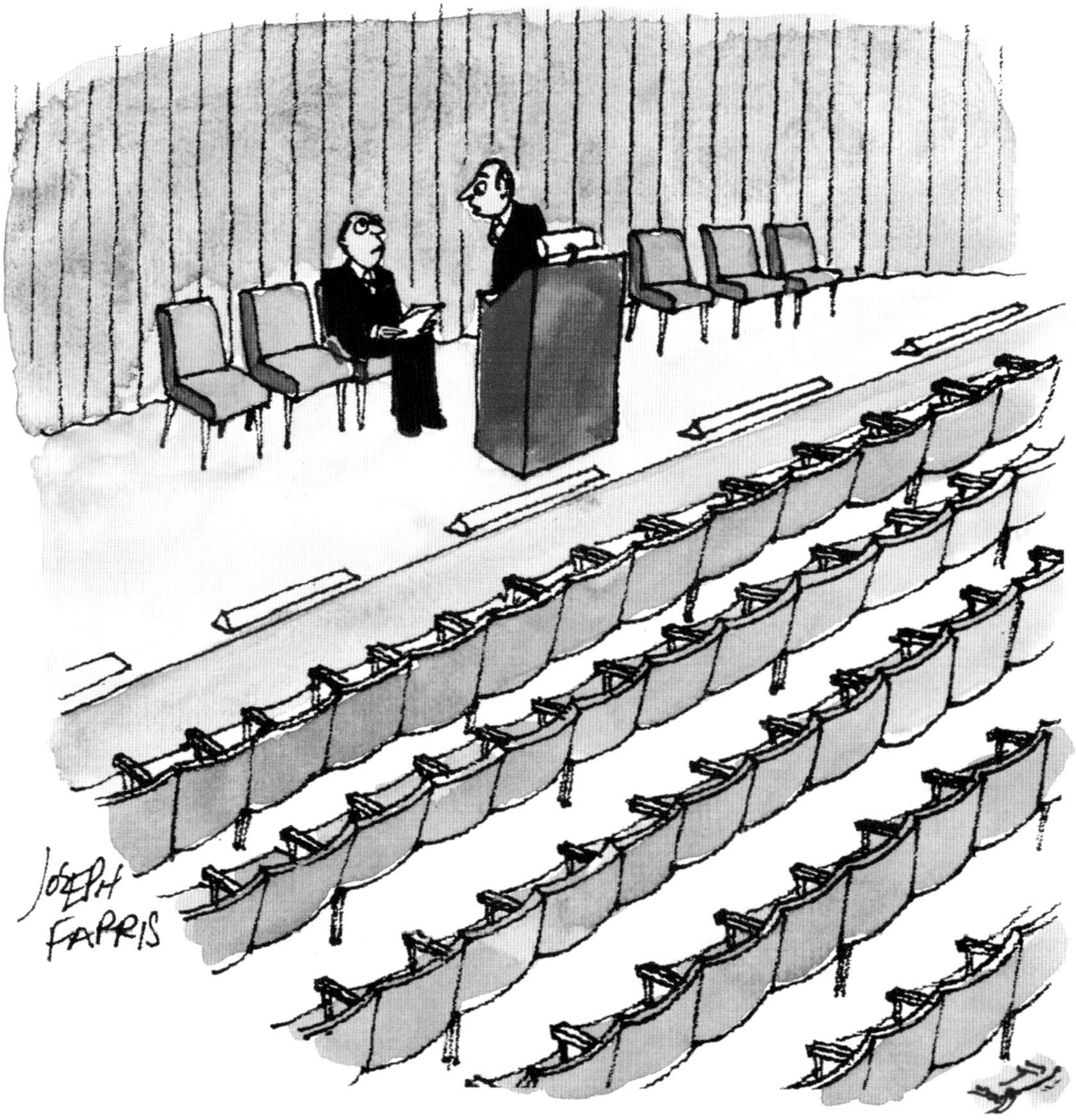
JOSEPH FARRIS

“We made the mistake of scheduling your speech the same time as the Master’s tournament.”

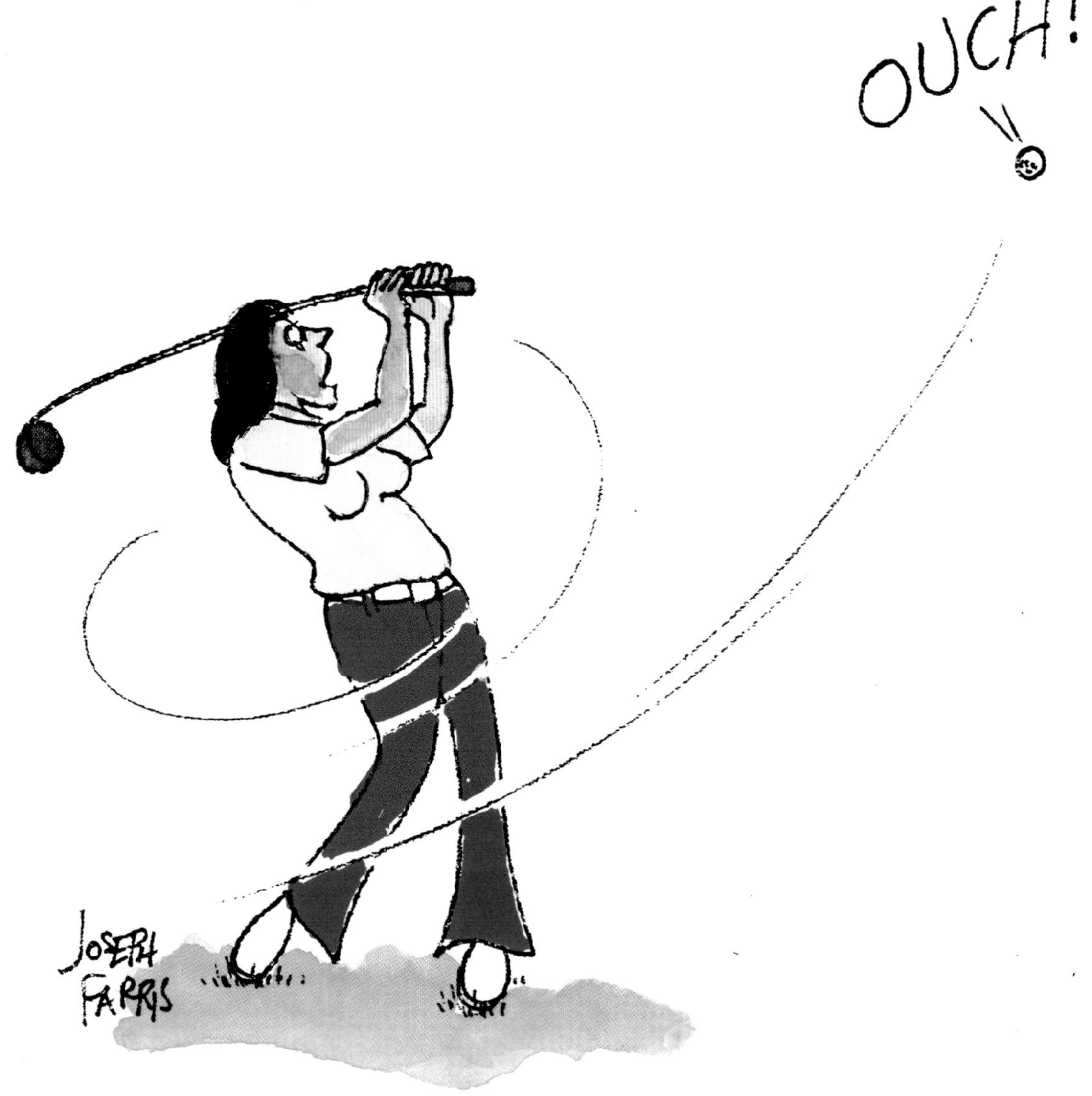
OUCH!
JOSEPH FARRIS

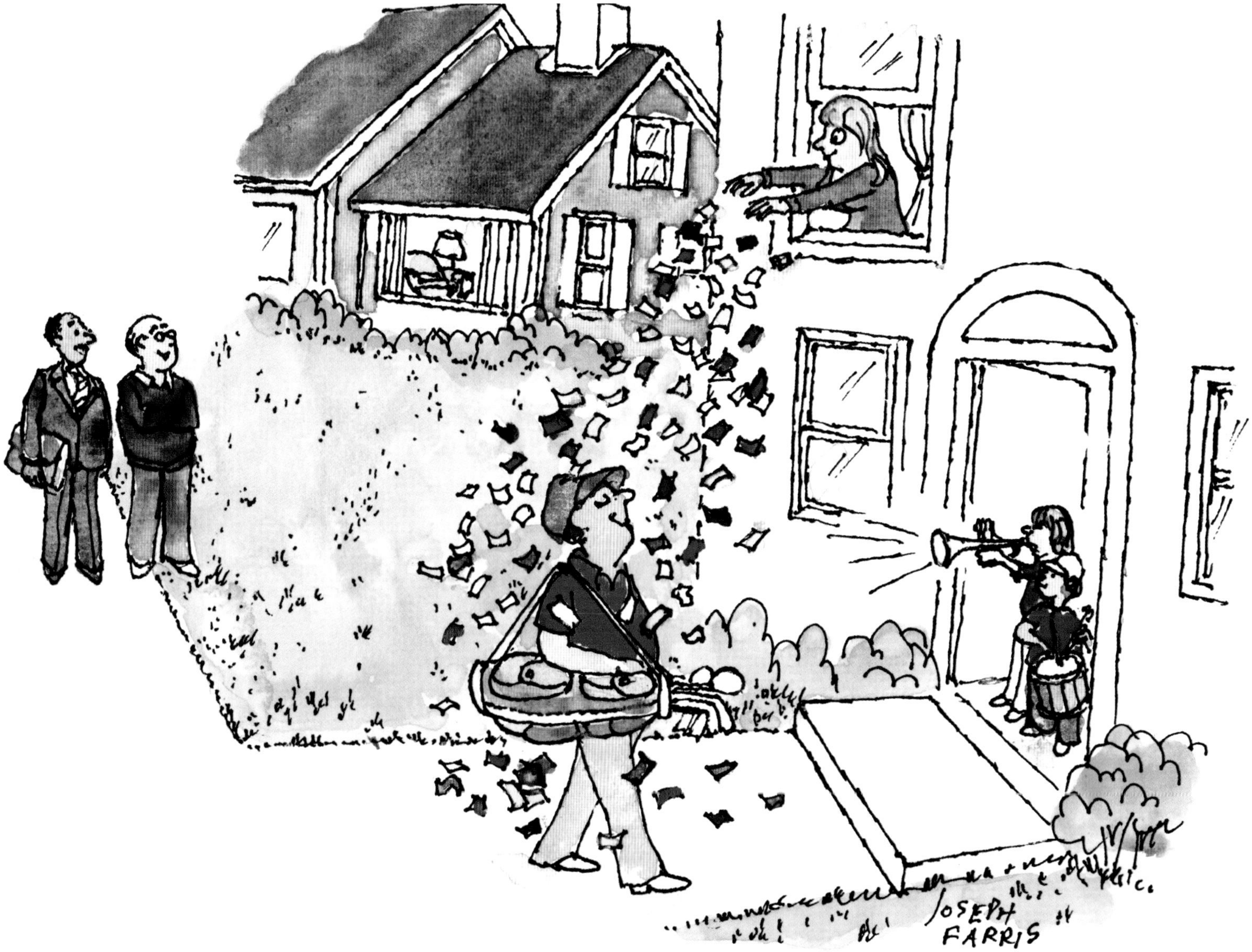
JOSEPH
FARRIS

“He broke a hundred!”

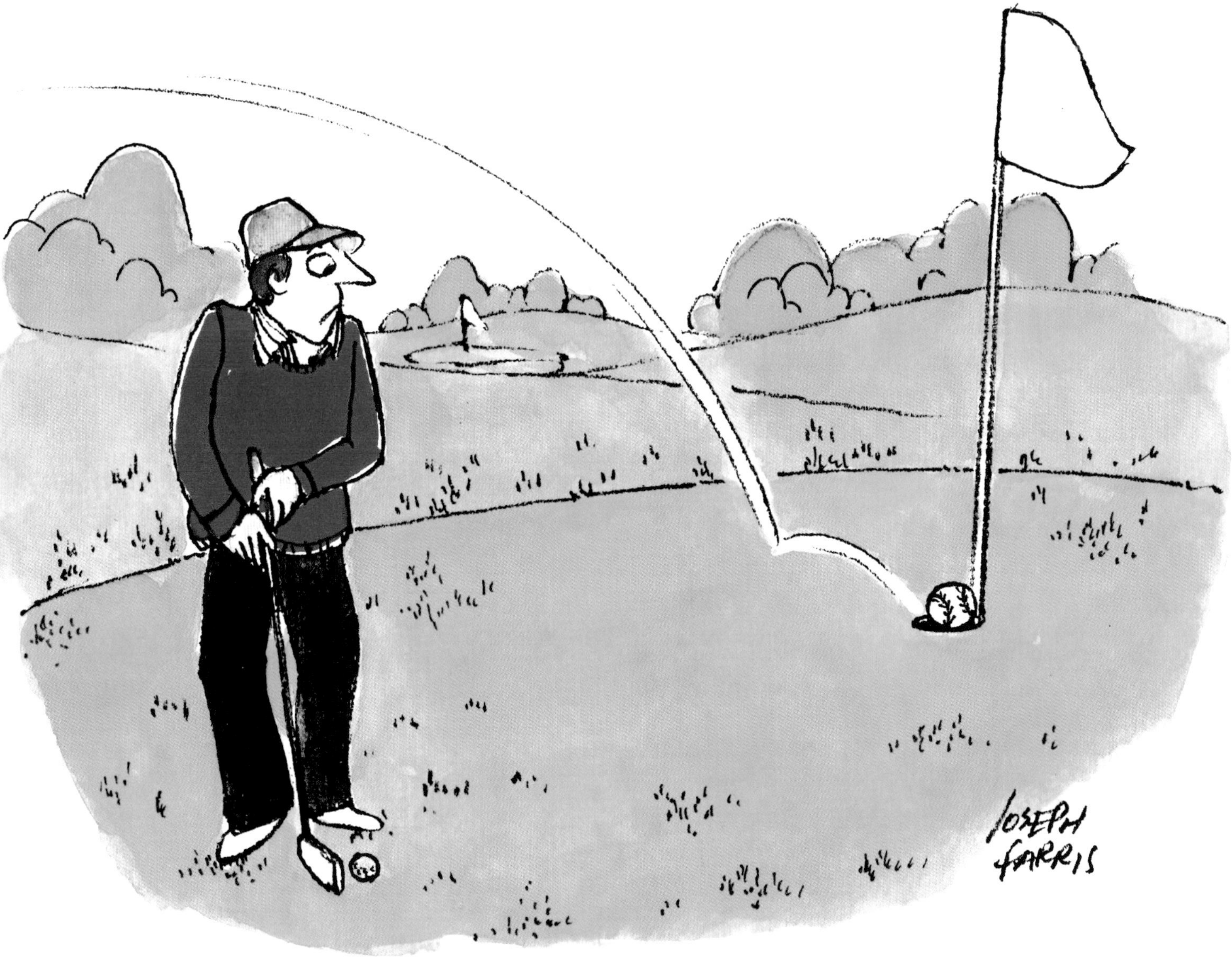
JOSEPH FARRIS

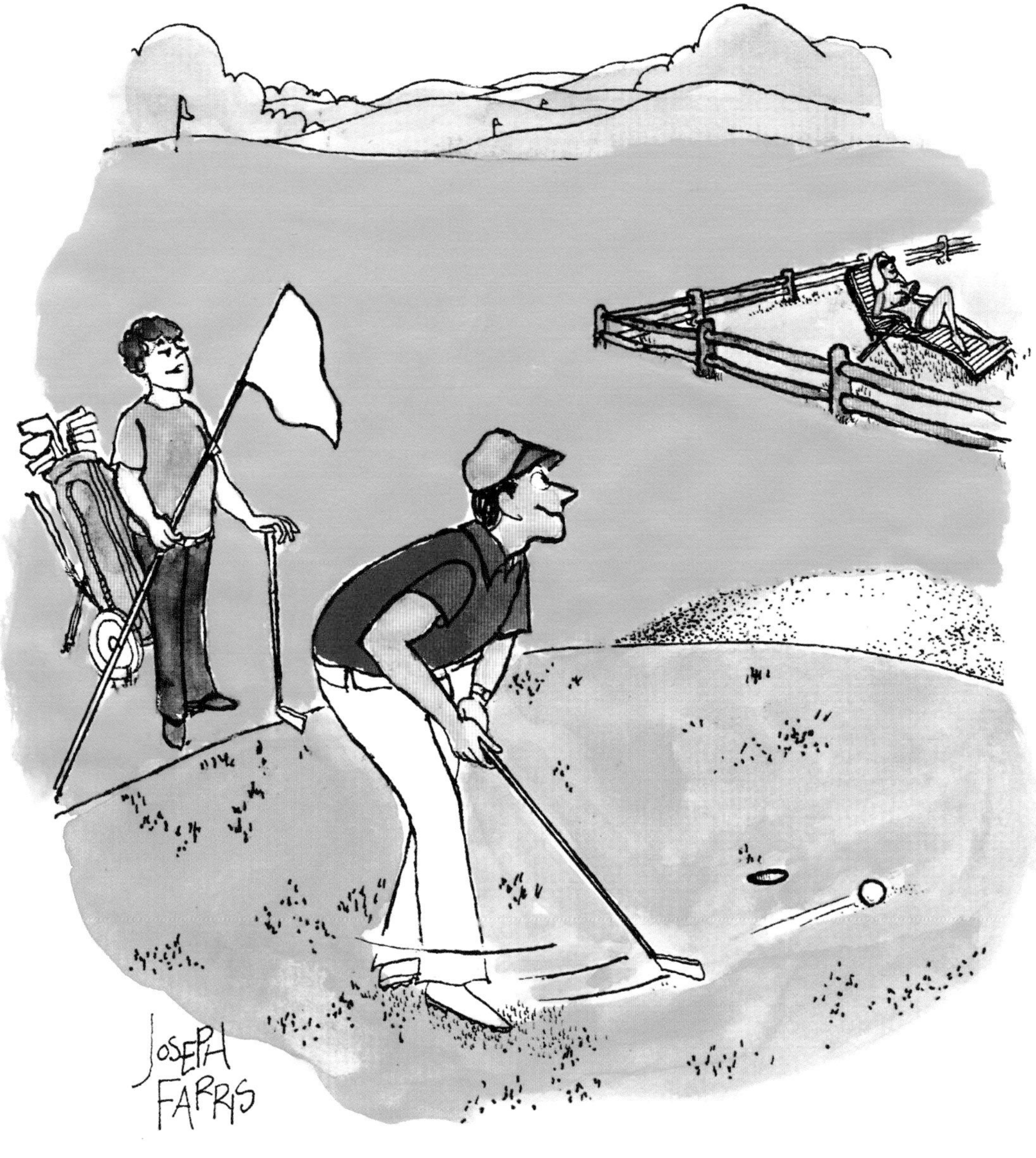
JOSEPH FARRIS

“You’re not alone. No one makes par on this hole.”

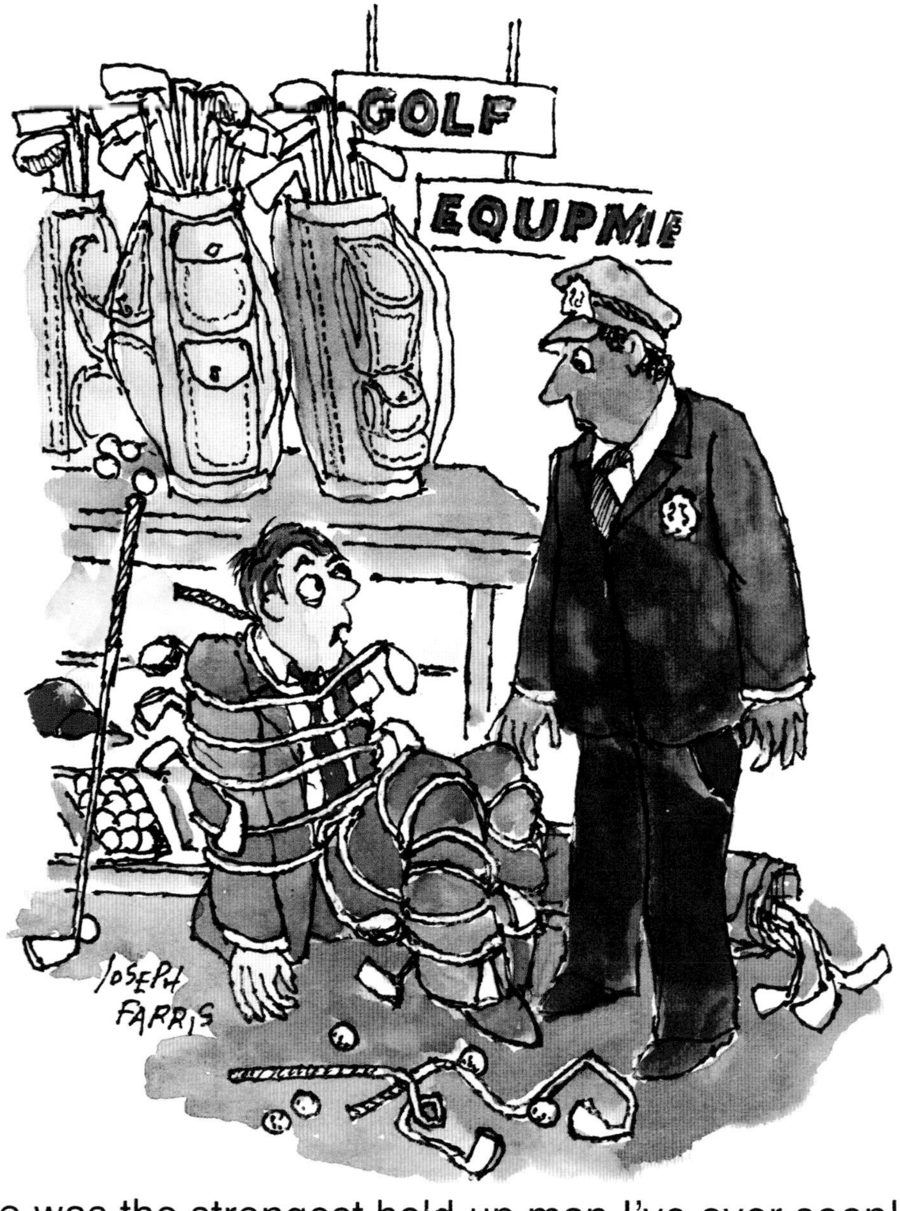
GOLF
EQUPM
JOSEPH FARRIS

"He was the strongest hold-up man I've ever seen!"

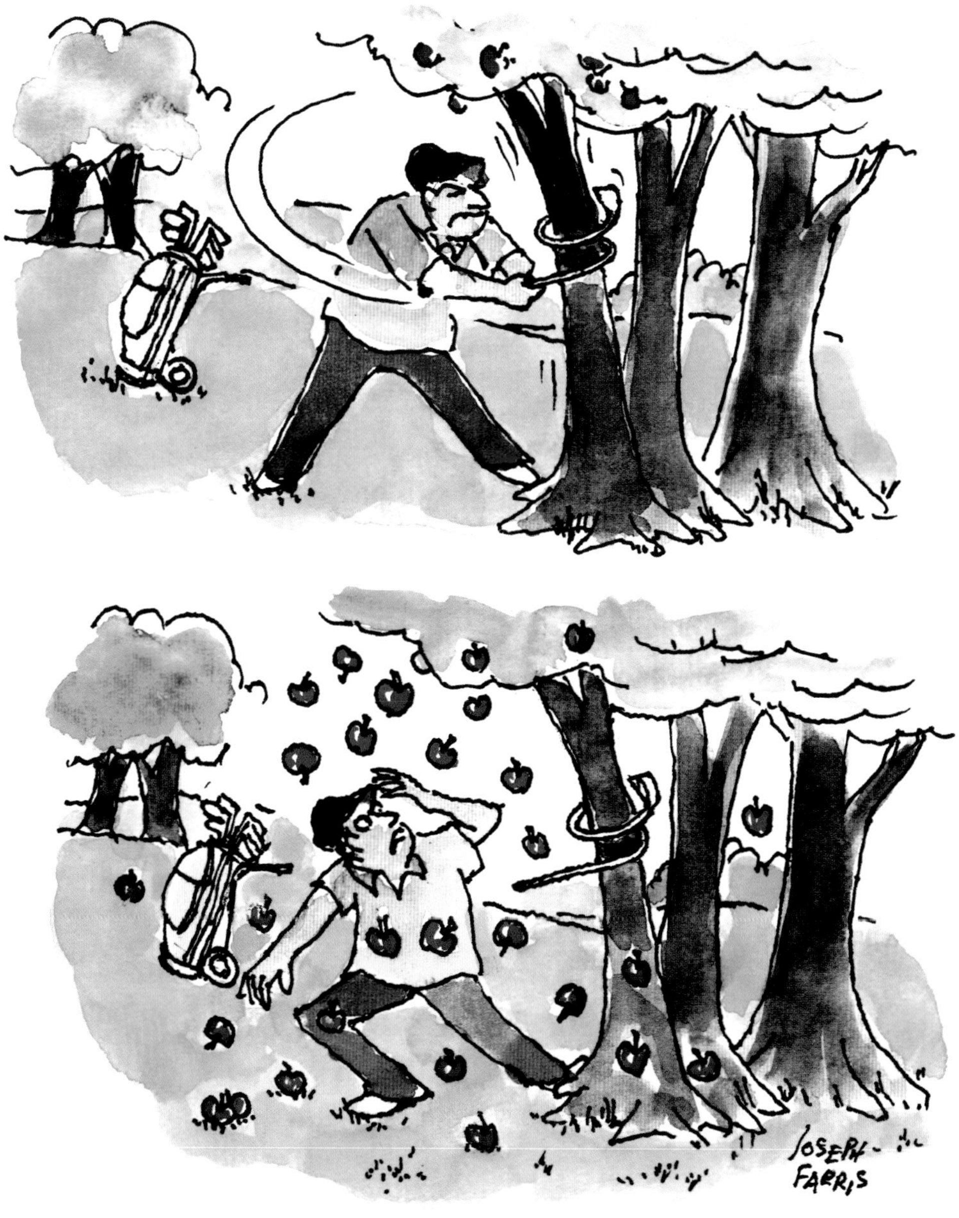
JOSEPH FARRIS

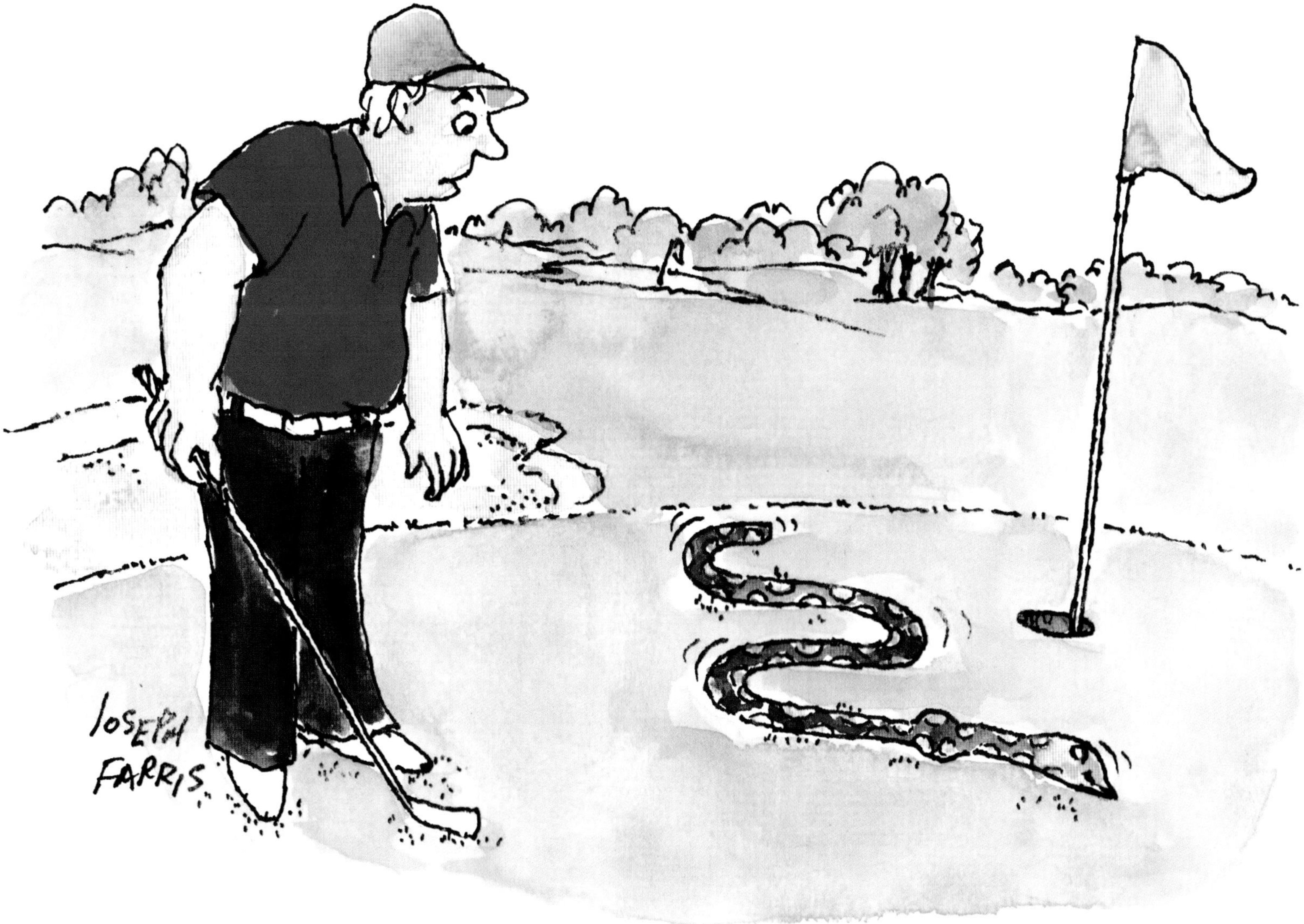
JOSEPH
FARRIS

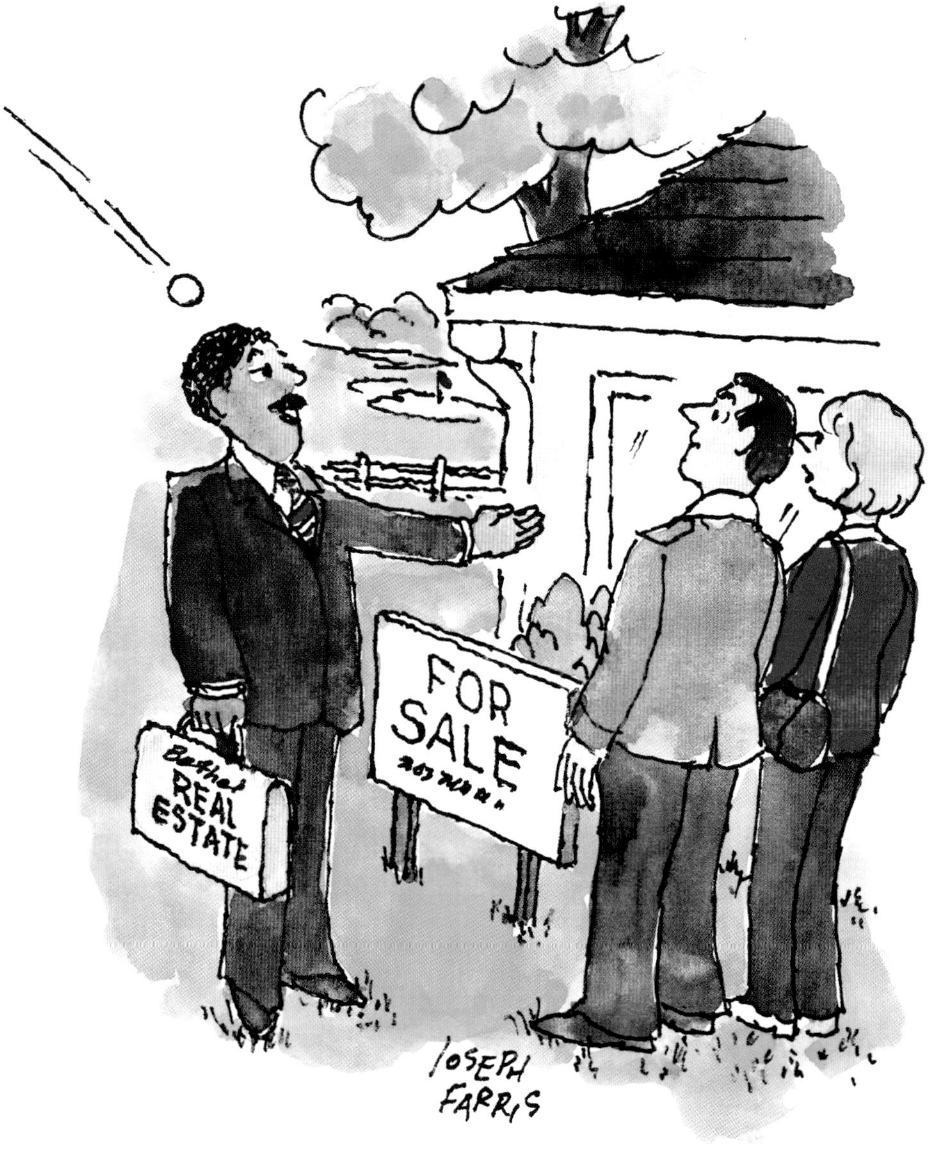
FOR SALE
REAL ESTATE
JOSEPH FARRIS

"And it's only a nine iron away from the golf course."

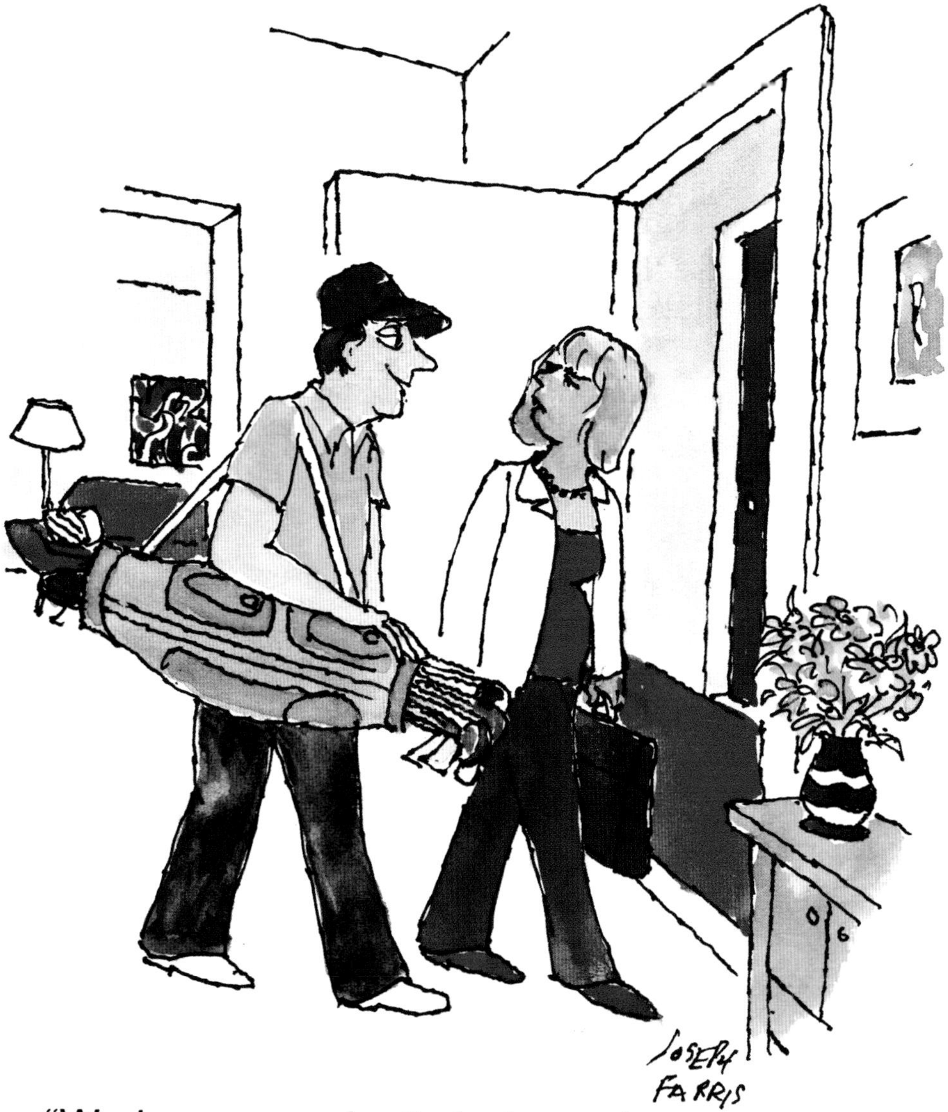
JOSEPH
FARRIS

"We have a perfectly balanced marriage. You're all work and no play and I'm all play and no work."

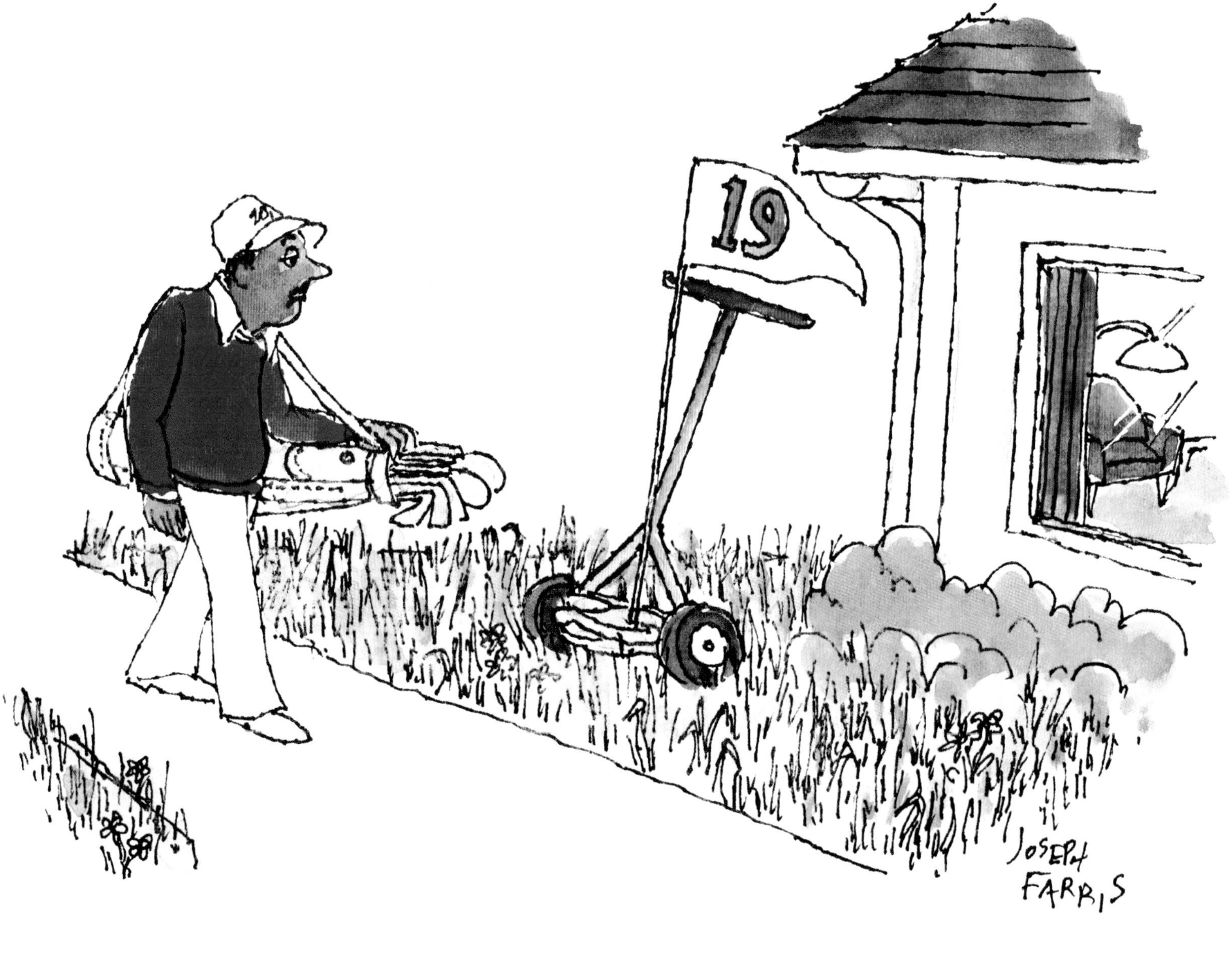
19
JOSEPH FARRIS

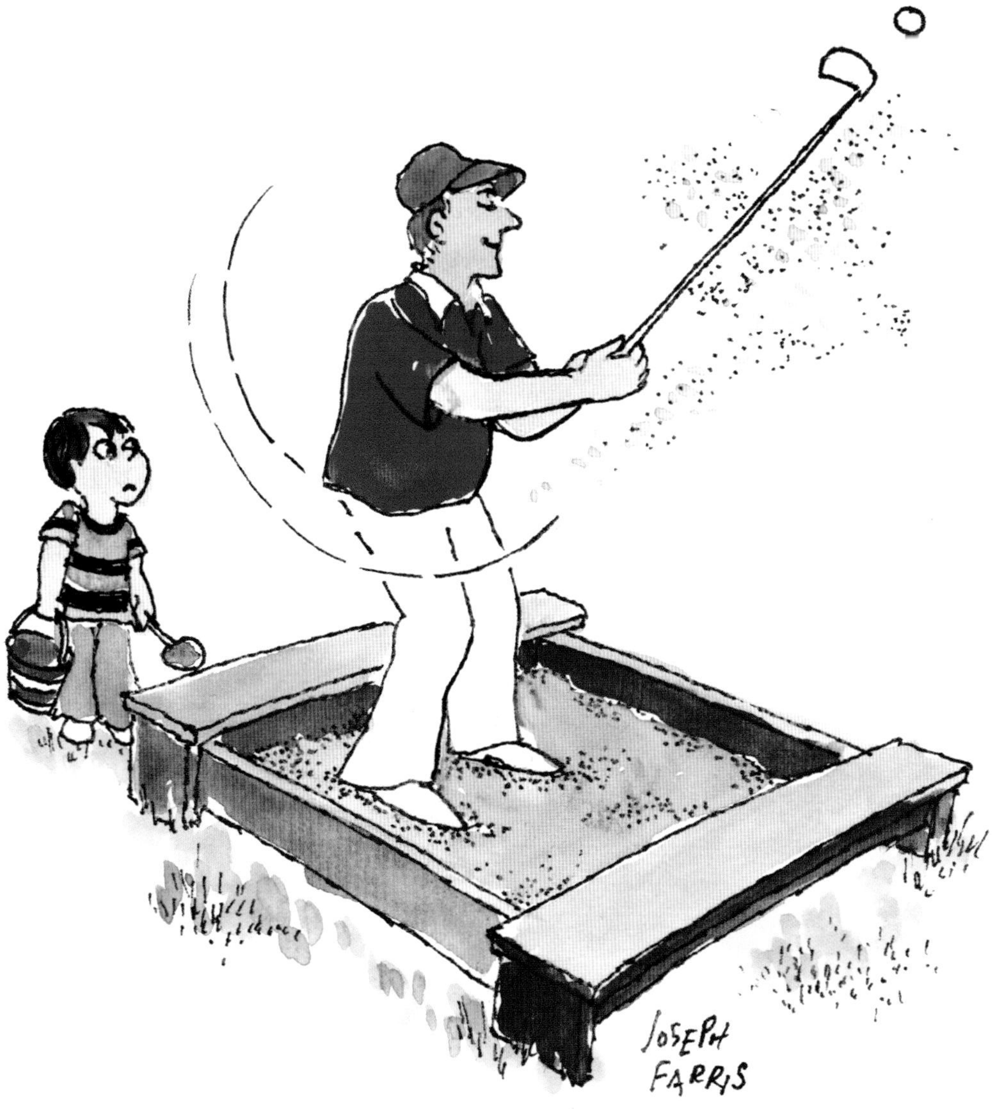
JOSEPH FARRIS

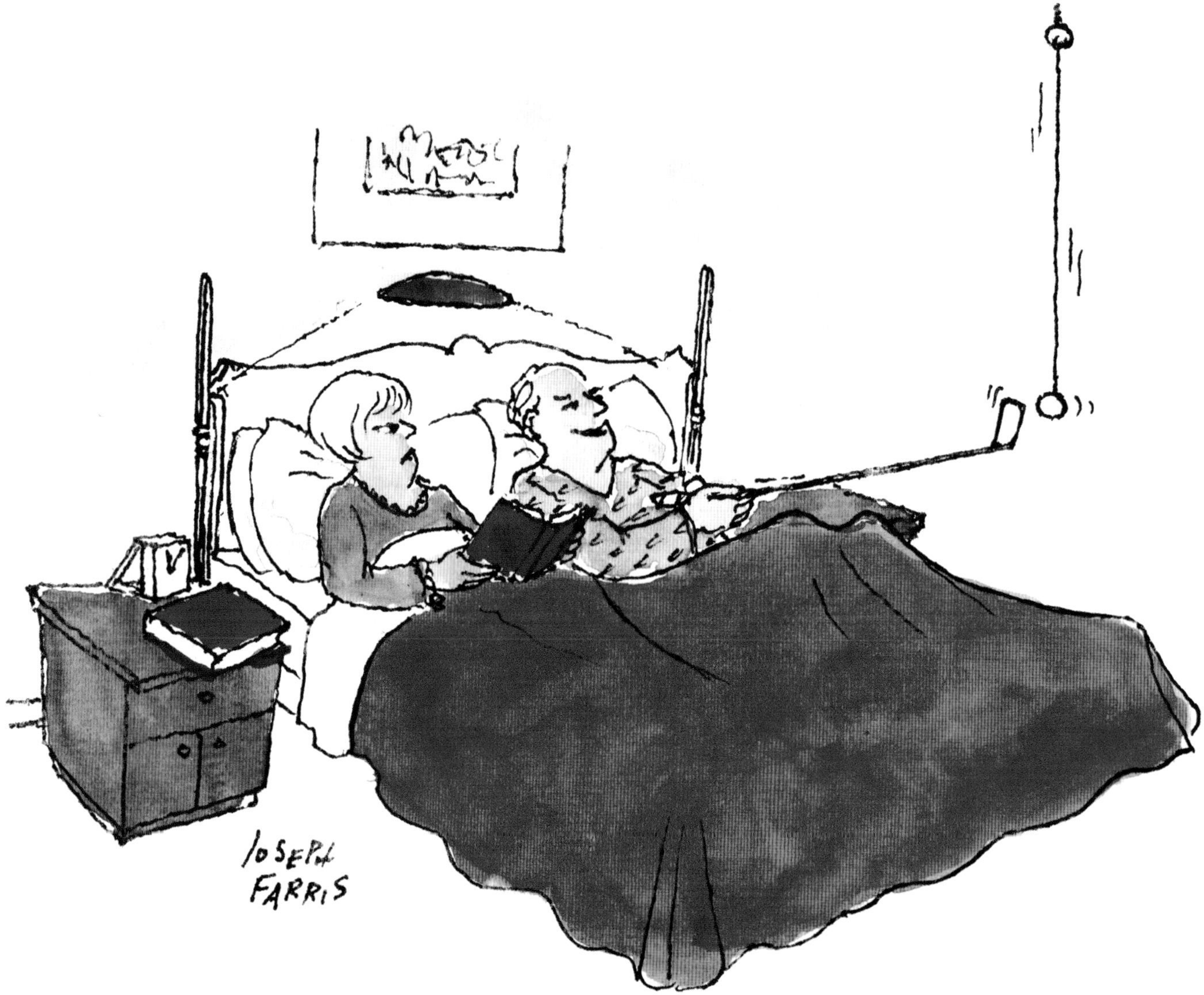
JOSEPH
FARRIS

"You like to read in bed, I like to golf in bed."

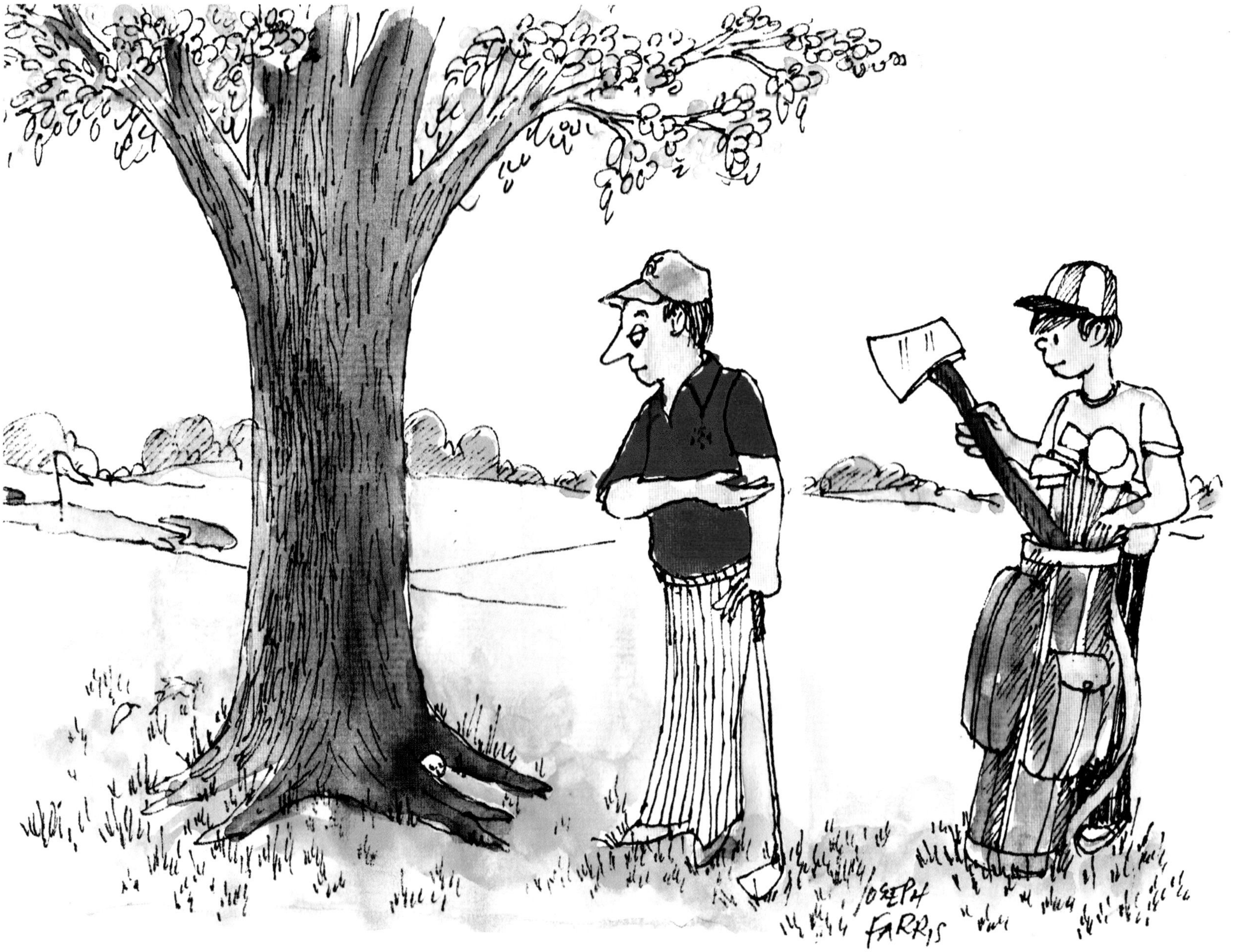

JOSEPH
FARRIS

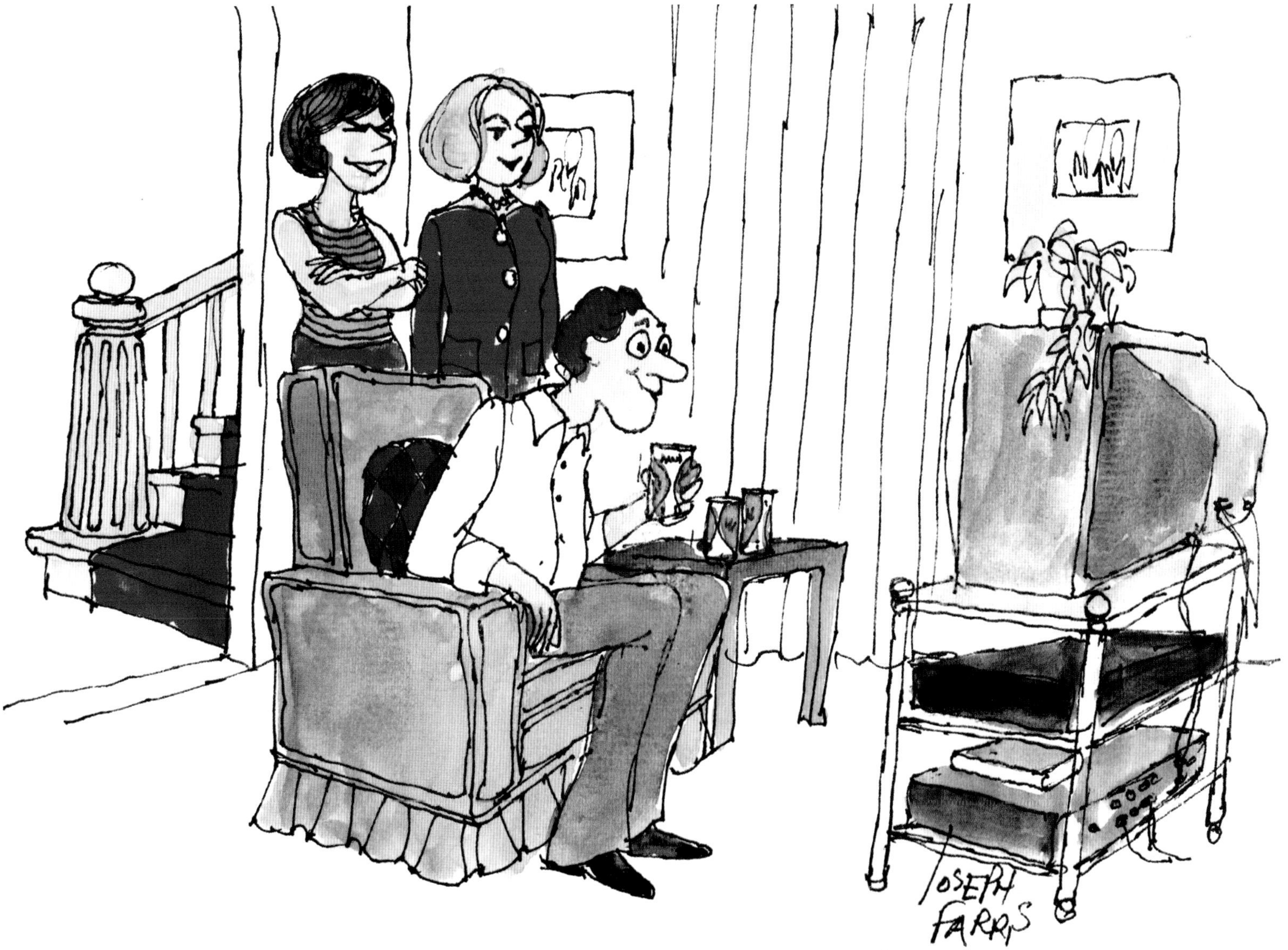
JOSEPH FARRIS

"It's his claim to fame. He hasn't missed a Master's tournament since he was seven."

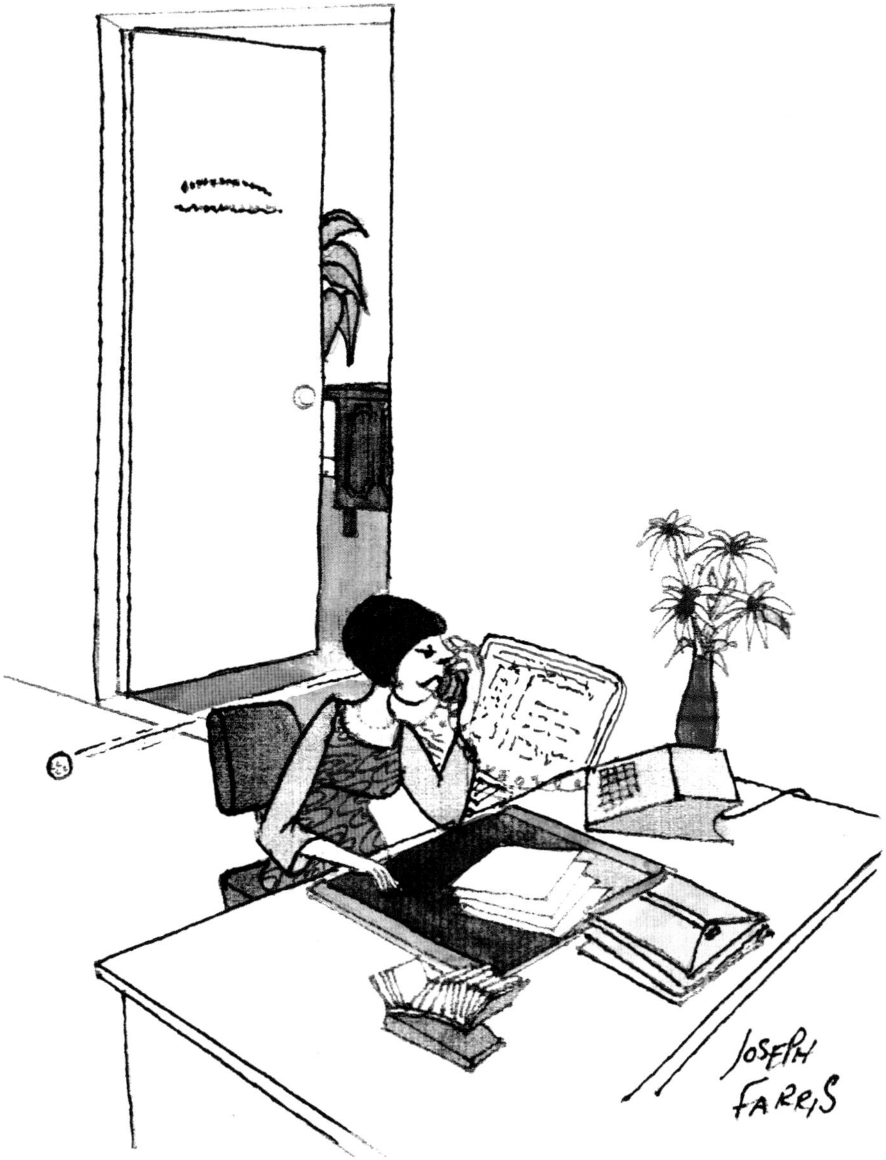
JOSEPH
FARRIS

"I'm sorry but she's in a meeting."

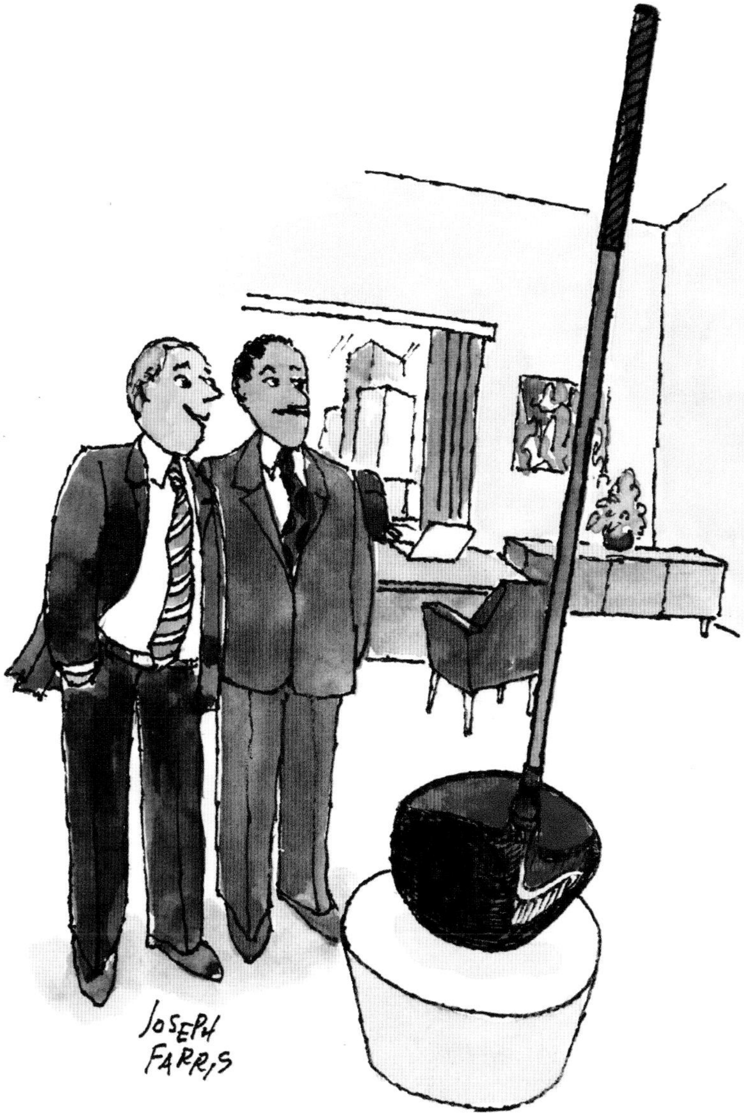
JOSEPH FARRIS

"I don't know much about art but
I know what I like."

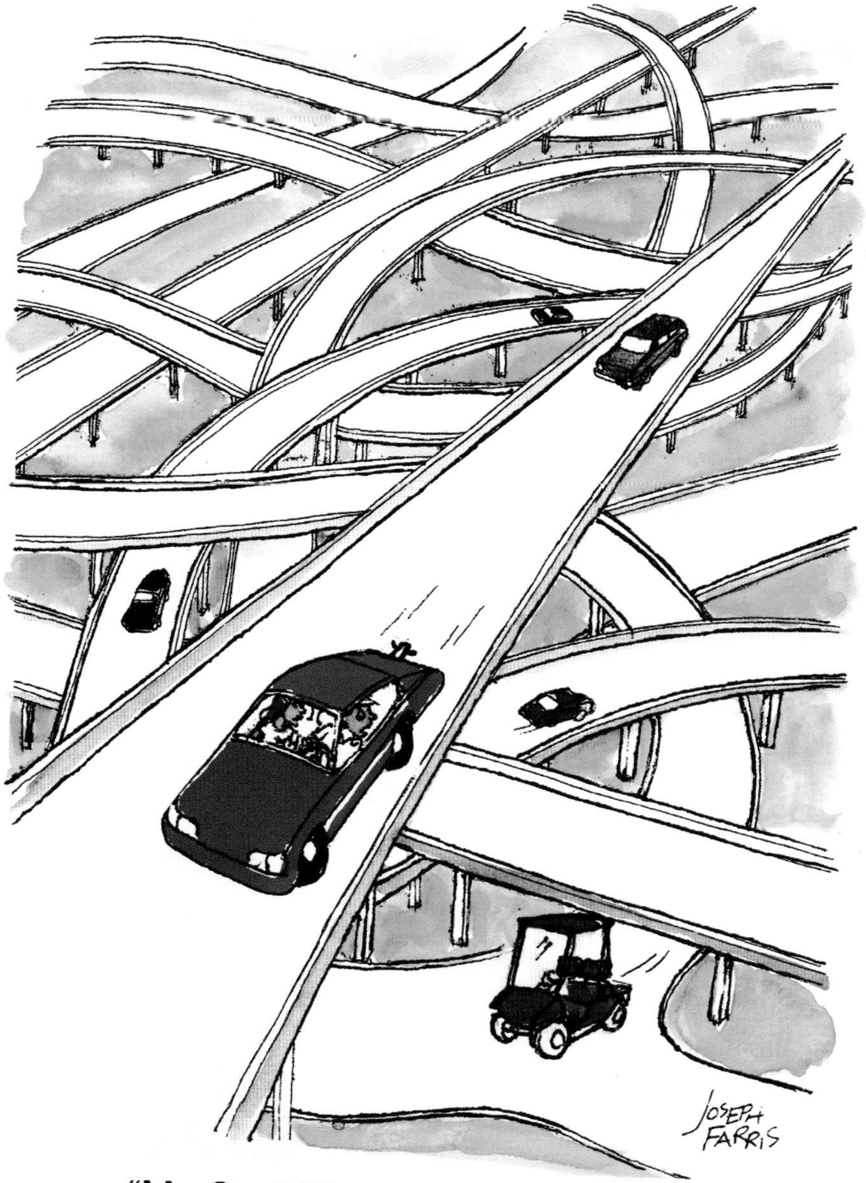
JOSEPH
FARRIS

“My God! There goes our golf cart!”

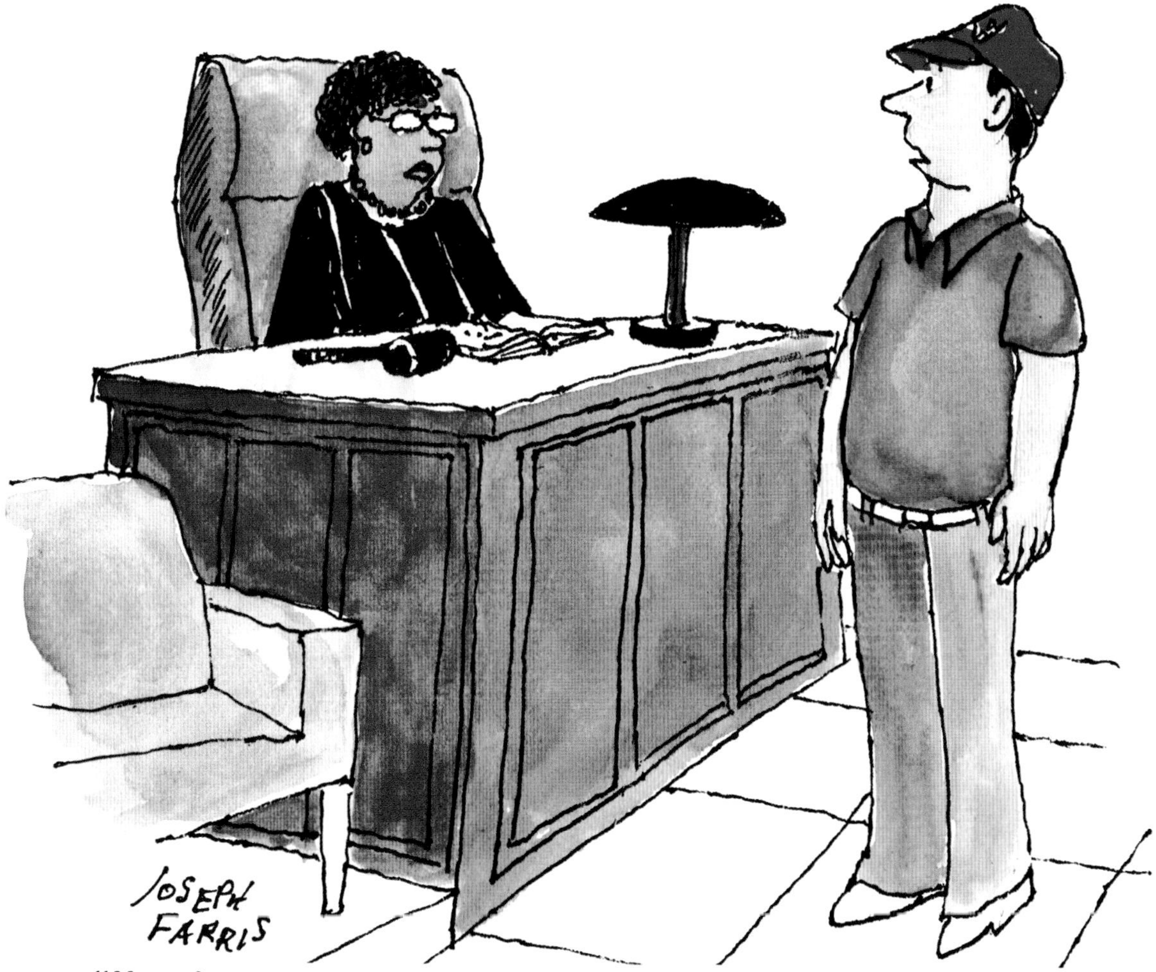
JOSEPH
FARRIS

“I’m here on extenuating circumstances.I bogeyed the first hole, hit into a bunker the third, triple bogeyed the fourth hole, hooked the sixth, landed in the water in the seventh...”

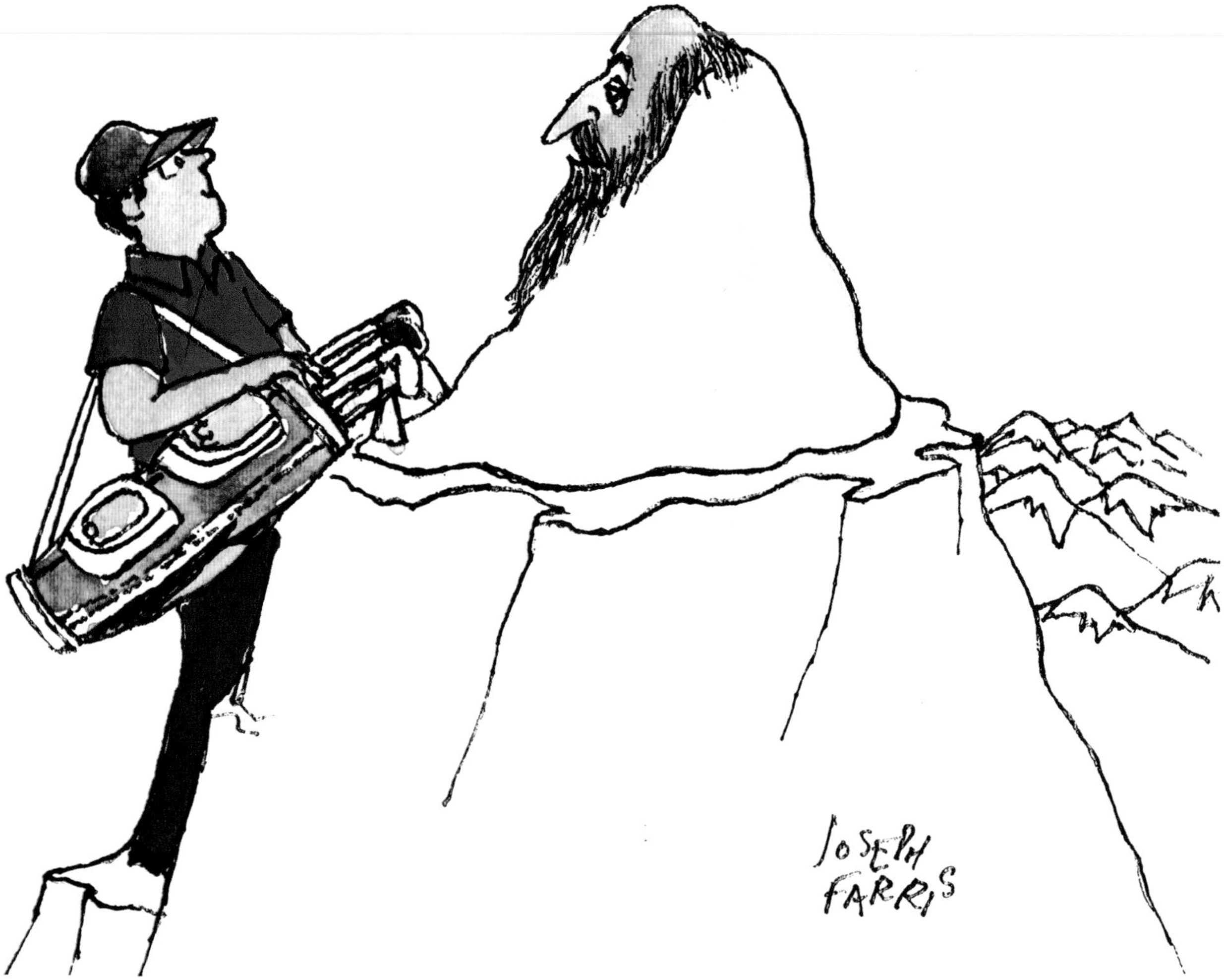
JOSEPH FARRIS

“Golf is mostly mental. Go to Amazon and order my book, *A Sure Way to Conquer the Mental in Golf*.”

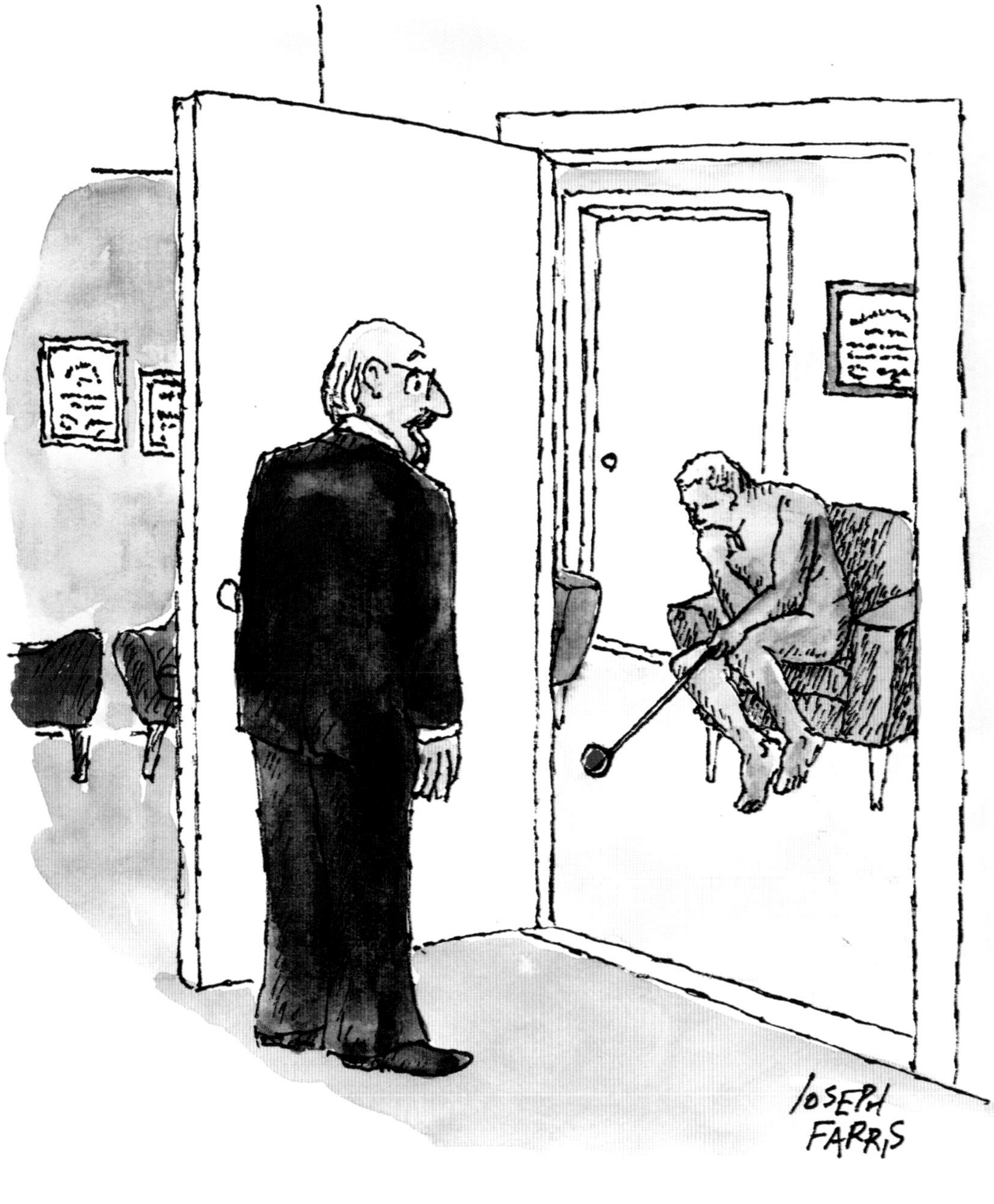
JOSEPH
FARRIS

1

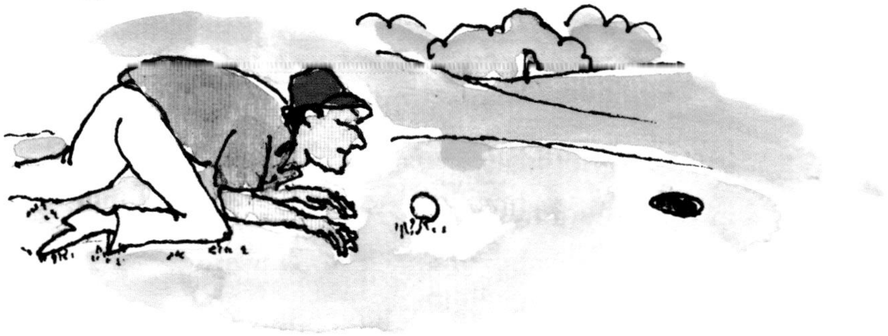

2

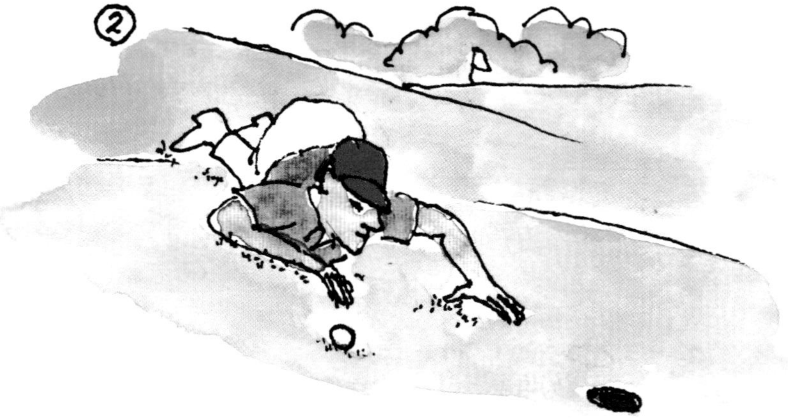

3

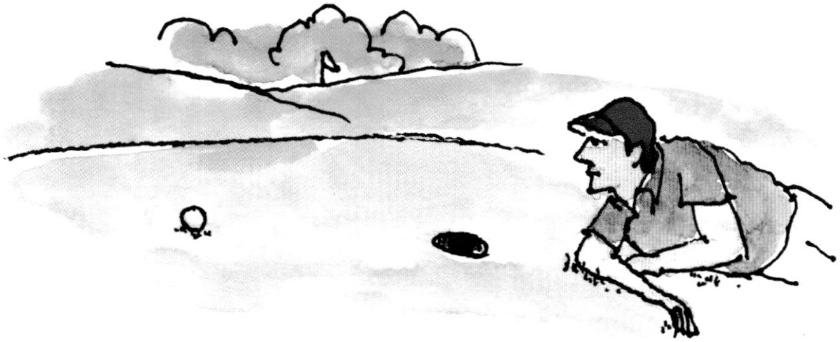

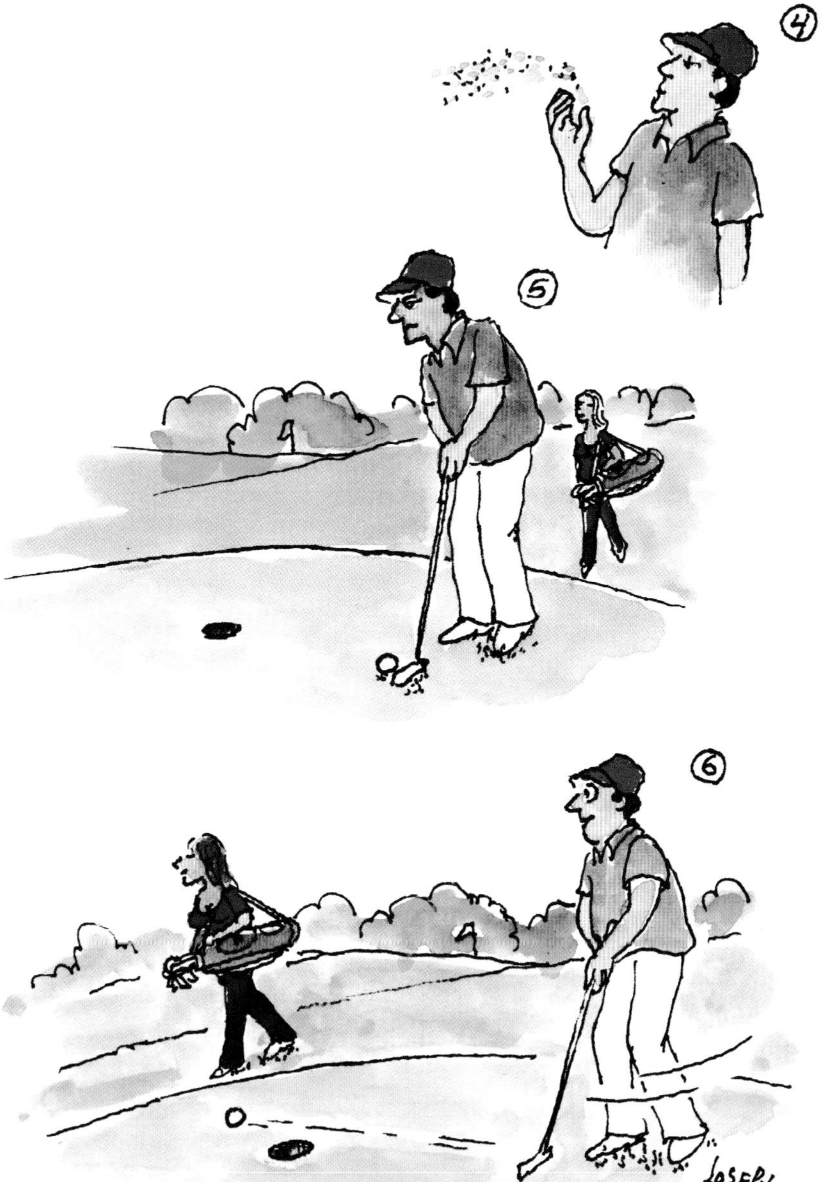
4
5
6
JOSEPH FARRIS

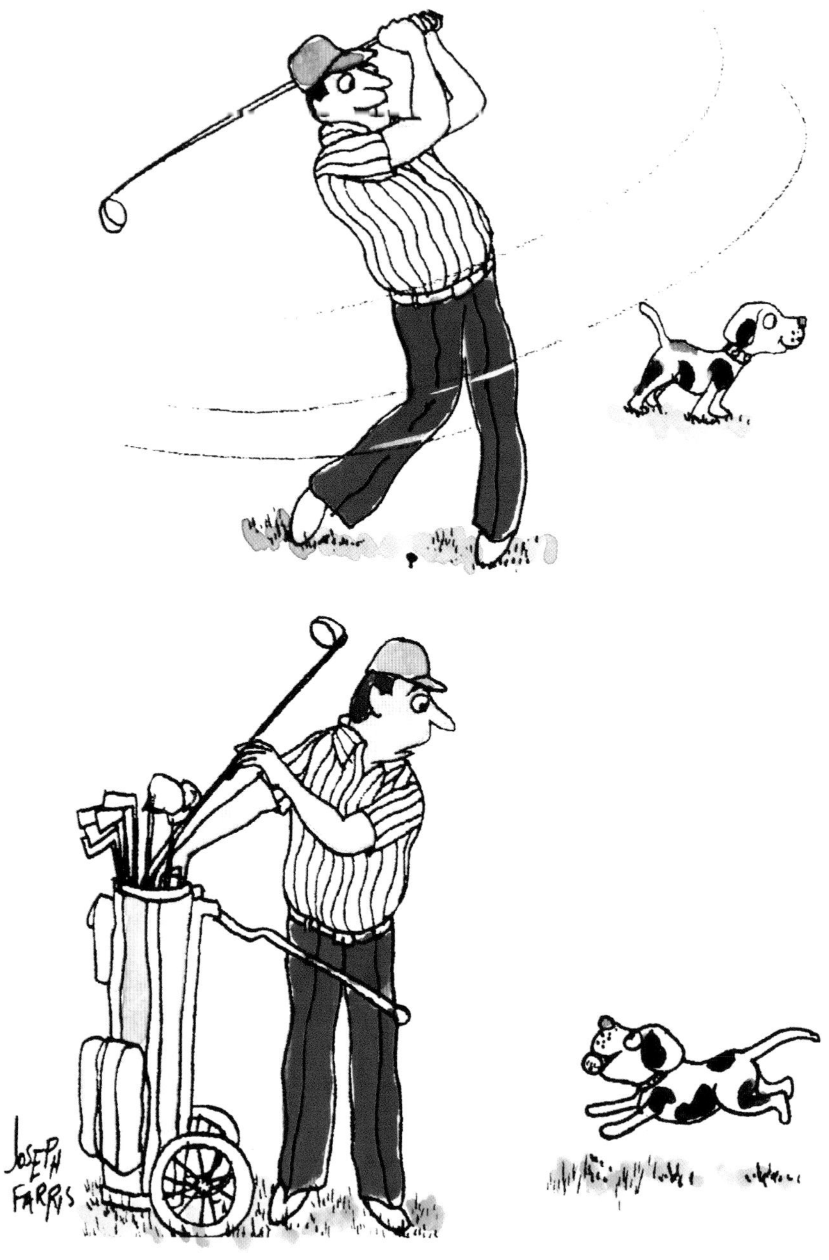
JOSEPH FARRIS